# TECHNOMOBILITY IN CHINA

# Technomobility in China

*Young Migrant Women and Mobile Phones*

*Cara Wallis*

NEW YORK UNIVERSITY PRESS

*New York and London*

NEW YORK UNIVERSITY PRESS
New York and London
www.nyupress.org

References to Internet Websites (URLs) were accurate at the time of writing.
Neither the author nor New York University Press is responsible for URLs that
may have expired or changed since the manuscript was prepared.

LIBRARY OF CONGRESS CATALOGING-IN-PUBLICATION DATA
Wallis, Cara.
Technomobility in China : young migrant women and mobile phones / Cara Wallis.
p. cm. — (Critical cultural communication)
Includes bibliographical references and index.
ISBN 978-0-8147-9526-2 (cloth : alk. paper)
ISBN 978-0-8147-8481-5 (ebook)
ISBN 978-0-8147-9527-9 (ebook)
1. Women—China—Social conditions—21st century. 2. Women—Social networks—China.
3. Migration, Internal—China—History—21st century. 4. Technology and women—
China. I. Title.
HQ1767.W3295 2012
305.40951—dc23
2012027892

New York University Press books are printed on acid-free paper,
and their binding materials are chosen for strength and durability.
We strive to use environmentally responsible suppliers and materials
to the greatest extent possible in publishing our books.

Manufactured in the United States of America
10 9 8 7 6 5 4 3 2 1

*For John*

CONTENTS

ILLUSTRATIONS

ACKNOWLEDGMENTS

This book could not have been possible without the generosity, insights, and friendship of many people or without the support of numerous organizations, both in the United States and in China. I am thankful to the Annenberg School for Communication for generous funding while I was conducting fieldwork and writing this book. The initial fieldwork would not have been possible without a year-long National Resource Center Foreign Language and Area Studies grant, administered by the East Asian Studies Center at the University of Southern California (USC). The Center for Feminist Research at USC provided travel and research support as well. Funding for follow-up research trips in 2010 and 2011 was given by the Department of Communication at Texas A&M University. I would also like to acknowledge the Melbern G. Glasscock Center for Humanities Research at Texas A&M University for a publication support grant.

Throughout the years since I began this research, I have been extremely fortunate to have worked with several amazing friends and colleagues who have not only shared their knowledge and experience, but have also provided crucial emotional support. Sarah Banet-Weiser has been a mentor, friend, and constant source of encouragement. Sandra Ball-Rokeach has taught me much about the field of communication. Manuel Castells added analytical and intellectual rigor to this project. Stanley Rosen helped me to sharpen my arguments and analysis. Anne Balsamo's passion for questions regarding culture and technology has inspired me, and her infectious smile has often lifted my spirits. I am thankful as well for many other friends and colleagues I met while at USC who helped me think through this project at different stages, including François Bar, Melissa Brough, Sasha Constanza-Chock, Carmen Gonzalez, Larry Gross, Charlotte Lapsansky, Jingfang Liu, Travers Scott, Araba Sey, and Cindy Shen.

This book crosses disciplines, and I am indebted to many whose work provided early inspiration and who subsequently offered their insights and support, including Scott Campbell, Stephanie Hemelryk Donald, Jonathan Donner, C. Cindy Fan, Guo Liang, Mimi Ito, Cecelia Milwertz, Lisa Naka-mura, Sun Wanning, Tan Shen, and Zhao Yuezhi. I am especially thankful to Heather Horst for her friendship and encouragement and to Rich Ling for his warmth and willingness to share his knowledge of all things mobile. This project also benefited from the friendship and insights of Jenny Chio, Arianne Gaetano, Elisa Oreglia, and Jack Linchuan Qiu.

Many wonderful individuals in China helped facilitate this research as well. Without Bu Wei's friendship and generosity this project could not have been completed. The breadth of her knowledge about rural-to-urban migrants and new media technologies in China is perhaps only rivaled by her willingness to share her time and insights. Sun Wusan is a wonderful friend who also provided personal and professional support, as did Cai Yip-ing, Liu Xiaohong, Liu Yanbin, Xu Yang, Wang Yihong, and Zhang Qi. I am also deeply indebted to Chen Shanshan and Liang Hongyun at the Beijing Cultural Development Center for Rural Women; Han Huimin, Fang Qing-xia, Jiao Fangfeng, and Luo Zhe Liangliang at the Migrant Women's Club; Chen Hu and Luo Zhaohong at the Practical Skills Training Center for Rural Women; and Li Tao, Li Zhen, Qu Ping, and Wang Haiying at the Culture and Communication Center for Facilitators.

At Texas A&M I was fortunate to be part of an amazing writing account-ability group while working on this manuscript. For offering emotional support, feedback on chapter drafts, and, of course, accountability, I am extremely appreciative of Josh Barbour, Jayson Beaster-Jones, Heidi Camp-bell, David Donkor, Tasha Dubriwny, Emily Johansen, Jennifer Jones-Bar-bour, Jennifer Mease, Kristan Poirot, Kirsten Pullen, Srivi Ramasubra-manian, and Molly Warsh. Josh Heuman deserves special recognition for reading every chapter of this book and for helping me to sharpen my theoret-ical arguments. Thanks go as well to Zulema Valdez for reading chapters and talking through different ideas. I also want to thank Kathy Miller and Eric Rothenbuhler for their mentorship as well as other friends and colleagues at Texas A&M's Department of Communication who have offered their guid-ance and support for this project: Jim Aune, Patrick Burkart, Aisha Durham, Rebecca Gill, Randy Kluver, Antonio La Pastina, Jennifer Mercieca, Barbara Sharf, and Richard Street. Xi Cui was a wonderful student and research assis-tant, and his tireless energy helped bring this book to fruition much faster than would have been possible without him.

I am blessed to have many friends in California whose unfailing belief in me and constant encouragement were sustenance throughout this project: Lucienne Aarsen, Gregory Anderson, Reka Clausen, Nancy Currey, Melina Dorian, Janet Goodwin, Linda Jensen, Luo Xinping, Linda Rhine, Molly Smith-Olsson, Gaby Solomon, and Jen Teasdale. Judy Marasco is a great friend, and we have shared so many experiences in and out of China that I feel like her soul is in this project as well.

I also want to thank my parents, Gene and Martha Wallis, and my sisters, Inger Budke and Laura Wallis, for believing in me and cheering me on in all of my endeavors. My husband, John Zollinger, has provided me with unwavering love and support. I am grateful for his dedication to helping me succeed and for his ability to help me keep my work in perspective within the greater meaning of life.

Credit goes to three anonymous readers whose feedback on earlier drafts of the manuscript was invaluable, as well as to Kent Ono, Ciara McLaughlin, Despina Papazoglou Gimbel, and especially Eric Zinner at NYU Press. I also want to thank Edmond Cho and Dave Schlotterback for help with the cover image.

Finally, to all the migrant women who participated in this study I owe heartfelt appreciation for sharing with me and teaching me not only about the role of mobile communication in their lives, but also about hope, dignity, and perseverance. They truly changed my life.

Portions of chapter 3 are based on chapter 4 in Rich Ling and Scott Campbell's (2011) edited volume *Mobile Communication: Bringing Us Together and Tearing Us Apart* by Transaction Publishers and on chapter 4 in Stephanie Hemelryk Donald, Theresa Dirndorfer Anderson, and Damien Spry's (2010) edited volume *Youth, Society, and Mobile Media in Asia* by Routledge. The chapter portions are reprinted here in revised form with permission from the publishers. Portions of chapter 5 appeared in *New Media & Society* 13, no. 3, and are reprinted here with permission from the publisher.

# Introduction

*Mobile Bodies, Mobile Technologies, and Immobile Mobility*

The Harmony Market sits at a busy intersection near one of Beijing's embassy districts, and like many indoor marketplaces erected in the city in the new millennium, it consists of several floors packed with vendors—mostly rural-to-urban migrants—selling everything from souvenirs and crafts to knock-off designer clothing, footwear, and handbags.[1] In the spring of 2007 I met Wu Huiying and Li Xiulan, two young rural women who worked in the basement of Harmony Market selling sports shoes. Li Xiulan was sixteen and from Henan province, and she had been in Beijing for six months working for her uncle. Wu Huiying was seventeen and from Anhui province, and when she had left home at fifteen she had originally joined her older sister, who was selling jeans at another large marketplace in Beijing. She and her sister had lived and worked together for nearly three years, but her sister was expecting a baby and had recently gone home. Wu Huiying had considered returning as well—she didn't particularly care for Beijing or its residents ("They are too proud and look down on outsiders," she said)—but felt like there was nothing for her back home. Now on her own in Beijing, Wu Huiying had sought a job at Harmony Market because she felt she could learn English there due to the large number of foreign visitors. Both Wu Huiying and Li Xiulan worked every day from 9:00 a.m. to 9:00 p.m., with one day off each month, and they ate most meals at the cafeteria on the top floor of the market. Wu Huiying earned a monthly salary of 1,000 yuan (about US $129), and Li Xiulan, because she was still "in training," made 300 yuan (about US $39).[2]

When I first met Wu Huiying and Li Xiulan they were busy writing some Chinese-English translations in a small notebook, and upon discovering I could speak Chinese Li Xiulan asked me how to pronounce some basic English expressions. Once they learned that I was studying mobile phone use, Wu Huiying proudly showed me a bronze-colored Nokia candy-bar phone, upon which she had glued a few rhinestones. It was a basic phone with only voice and texting capabilities, and since it didn't have a model name or number, it was quite possibly a fake. Her older sister had bought it in 2002 for 2,000 yuan (around US $240 at the time, and quite a lot of money for a migrant worker), and she had given Wu Huiying the phone in 2006. The fact that the phone was relatively old, had limited functions, and was a hand-me-down didn't lessen its value in Wu Huiying's eyes. On the contrary, this particular phone was extremely important to her and carried multiple meanings. Without doubt the phone was a significant communication medium. Midway during our conversation Wu Huiying showed me an extra SIM card and said, "This one is for my friends. When I'm working I don't keep it in the phone because I don't want to bother my friends while they are working or to be bothered."[3] The other SIM card, which was placed in the phone during work, was for her family so that they could call her (and vice versa) if something was urgent. Aside from communication, however, this particular phone held other significance. It was Wu Huiying's first phone, and it had become a part of her. She didn't want to upgrade to a new phone because she felt she had no use for other features. With the phone cradled between her two hands, she smiled and told me, "You can't get one like this anymore. It's so precious."

As Wu Huiying and I discussed her phone, Li Xiulan lifted her head up from her notebook and stated that as soon as she could, she was going to buy a brand-name phone with a camera and Internet capability. Although she'd had a used phone passed down from a relative, her aunt had taken it away because she felt Li Xiulan was staying up too late texting with friends and as a result didn't have any energy to work. "She thinks the phone has a bad effect on a young girl like me," she said. We chatted a bit longer, but customers were arriving and browsing the rows of shoes, so I told the two women I should get going. As I was leaving, Wu Huiying asked for my mobile number so she could send me some jokes. Then she said she had to get back to work or her boss (who wasn't present) would get angry, particularly if he saw her using her phone.

My initial exchange with Wu Huiying and Li Xiulan, though in many ways quite ordinary, gives concrete form to numerous abstract forces—globalization, migration, marketization, and "informatization"—that have been constitutive of China's path of "reform and opening" (*gaige kaifang*) over the last three decades. As China has become integrated into the world economy, it has opened itself to global cultural flows, and new identities, life opportunities, modes of consumption, and forms of communication have arisen, yet so, too, have new types of inclusion and exclusion. Though cities like Beijing have reaped the benefits of China's modernization efforts, many rural areas have not. For this reason, like nearly all young rural women in China today, Wu Huiying and Li Xiulan had migrated not only to work, but also to "see the world," learn some skills, and gain some autonomy vis-à-vis parents and other authority figures back home. However, in the city labor migrants face severe constraints due to institutional forces, such as the household registration system, or *hukou*, which confers different and unequal forms of citizenship according to whether one's *hukou* is designated urban or rural (or non-agricultural/agricultural). Even though less stringent than in the past, the discriminatory nature of the *hukou* policy positions rural migrants as second-class citizens in China's towns and cities, where they also must deal with labor exploitation, deep-seated urban prejudices against migrants, and powerful regulatory discourses regarding their inferior "quality" (*suzhi*).

Although Wu Huiying and Li Xiulan were mobile in the sense of migrating from their home villages, like many rural-to-urban migrants in China, their long work hours, rare time off, and confined social world caused them to be relatively immobile in the city. At the same time, this immobility was overcome in certain ways by their use of mobile phones—even basic ones like Wu Huiying's—for navigating various social networks, enjoying forms of entertainment, participating in China's burgeoning consumer culture, and constructing a "modern" self. For them and others like them, however, the phone could also become the locus of various struggles related to gender-, class-, age-, and place-based identities, which are rooted in structures that constrain migrants' social mobility and individual and collective empowerment once they have journeyed to the city.

This book is about such processes of and possibilities for mobility—one physical and one virtual—in the lives of young rural-to-urban migrant women in China like Wu Huiying and Li Xiulan. More specifically, it is an ethnographic exploration of the cultural, social, aesthetic, and economic dimensions of mobile phone use by young female migrants working in the low-level service sector in Beijing. From a nation that, with few exceptions, had severely restricted population mobility prior to the early 1980s, China now has the greatest peacetime internal migration on the planet, with estimates of the number of "peasant workers" (*nongmingong*) or "floating population" (*liudong renkou*) at around 200 million. And though China's teledensity (ratio of telephones to people) was a mere 4 percent in 1980, it now has the largest number of mobile phone subscribers and Internet users worldwide.[4] What are the multiple meanings, habits, investments, and implications of mobile telephony in young migrant women's everyday lives? As a study of the intersections of migration and myriad communication practices and processes, and as an examination of multiple axes of identity and modes of power, this book is about mobility as well as immobility, and it is about mobile technologies as well as "technologies of the self," Foucault's term for the methods of self-fashioning through which subjects are constituted.[5] Drawing on critical/cultural and feminist theories of subjectivity, power, and technology, I theorize mobile communication and migrant women's *becoming* in the city,[6] or how social constructions of gender-, class-, age-, and place-based identities produce particular engagements with mobile technologies, which in turn reproduce and restructure these identities. Though prior research on mobile phones has looked at individual aspects of identity, such as gender, in relation to the mobile phone, none of the researchers have adapted an intersectional framework and very few have examined the co-construction of technology and subjectivity.

This book takes as its starting point the constitutive nature of communication, culture, and technology, or what James Carey has called communication as transmission and ritual. The transmission model—the more common approach—conceives of communication as a process in which messages are sent and delivered across space for purposes of information or control.[7] Communication as ritual, however, is connected to notions of community, belonging, and shared beliefs.[8] To Carey, communication is "a symbolic process whereby reality is produced, maintained, repaired, and transformed."[9] Mobile phones are obviously quite convenient for message transmission— Wu Huiying did in fact send me some jokes within thirty minutes of my departure from the market. Yet equally significant is the way cell phones, as "symbols of" reality, have become key in the constitution of selfhood, friendship, and group solidarity, especially among youth populations. In this sense, the jokes and subsequent messages that Wu Huiying transmitted to me wirelessly had a much deeper meaning than providing some momentary amusement. However, as much as mobile phones can help to maintain community and a sense of belonging, they can also give rise to new disciplines and exclusions, as when Li Xiulan's phone was confiscated. As I will show in this book, mobile phones can thus be implicated in the further marginalization of groups such as migrant workers. Carey's definition of communication provides a basis for my examination of the breadth of practices and depth of feelings articulated to mobile phones. It also offers a way to think more deeply about how communication technology is constitutive of culture and is neither value-neutral nor an autonomous determining force.

Book-length works on the use of mobile telephony by a specific population are rare, and ethnographic inquiries that offer a holistic account of the use of mobile communication by a particular group in a particular place and time are even rarer.[10] China's female migrant population has been the focus of numerous studies by both Chinese and western scholars, and the use of mobile phones by southern factory workers in China has also been studied.[11] However, in both the broader research on migrant workers and the smaller body of literature exploring their use of mobile phones, service workers in the public arena have been underexamined.[12] Yet the contradictory nature of many migrants' service work, where they are paradoxically isolated from others yet integrated within public spaces, has implications for the way they experience the city and use mobile communication. Amid the disjunctures, dislocations, and contradictions that characterize contemporary China, understanding how young rural-to-urban migrant women engage with mobile phones to create meaning and negotiate their lives in the city contextualizes how everyday life is increasingly constituted by and within myriad networks of communication. It also challenges deterministic theories of technology and social change as well as those that posit universal modes of technological appropriation in an apparently flat world. Based on immersive fieldwork over a five-year period, my goal is to offer a broad, though still partial, portrait of the mutually constitutive nature of technology, subjectivity, and power. I also hope to illuminate migrant women's *socio-techno* practices, or the manner in which technology, in this case a mobile phone, is integrated into prior social and cultural practices and at the same time creates new spaces or possibilities for their enactment within the specific social world and material conditions of users.[13] Socio-techno practices are not only about what users *do*, but also the discourses, mental energy, and emotional desires that make up a dynamic mobile phone assemblage.

One could say that mobility—both real and imagined, in the physical and virtual realms—figures as perhaps the defining representation of our globalized world. Inside and outside China, flows of finance, people, media, and ideas (Appadurai's "scapes"), facilitated by communication and transportation technologies, are often impervious to borders and inseparable from the transformation of individual and communal identities.[14] However, cultural values, institutional structures, and material circumstances render experiences of mobility differently. Within the constraints characteristic of migrant workers' lives, I argue that the mobile phone enables "immobile mobility," which I define as a socio-techno means of surpassing spatial, temporal, physical, and structural boundaries.[15] Immobile mobility should not be equated with virtual reality or with those spaces entered into through a computer-simulated environment. Instead, it is grounded in the concrete practices and constraints of the everyday experiences of migrant women, and perhaps other populations that must deal with similar limitations on their control of time, space, and mobility. In using the term "immobile mobility," I also am not emphasizing how low-income households have used cell phones as surrogate landlines that remain in the home.[16] While immobile mobility captures the way that the mobile phone is frequently used from a fixed location (thus negating its mobile element), this is only part of its significance, albeit a very important part given migrants' long work hours. However, as much as immobile mobility is a material socio-techno practice, it is a subjective one as well in that it enables migrant women to enter a new social space that is at once mediated and grounded in the circumstances of their daily lives. Certain socio-techno practices that enable immobile mobility can be understood as enacting resistance, insofar as through such practices migrant women refuse the material conditions that work to limit their sense of themselves and the goals they can achieve. However, other practices may possibly reify migrant women's marginalization. In other words, immobile mobility has a dual logic—it can be liberating and constraining, creating new opportunities for empowerment and disempowerment.

As the term "immobile mobility" implies, the circumstances under which mobile phones are used by young migrant women differ from the "digital natives," or those youth and young adults who have always been surrounded by digital technologies, such as computers and video-game consoles, dial-up and then broadband Internet access, cell phones, digital music players, and, more recently, e-readers, tablet computers, and the like.[17] These young people's various engagements with new media are constitutive of what Henry Jenkins calls "convergence culture," or the numerous social, cultural, economic, and technological transformations that have given rise to the intersection of old and new media, the circulation of content through many media platforms, and a participatory culture that often blurs the boundaries between media producers and consumers.[18]

What socio-techno practices associated with convergence arise among those much less privileged than the "born digital"?[19] In other words, what happens when users aren't surrounded by a plethora of digital devices; that is, when a cell phone is not supplementing a landline (at least during its initial diffusion), when a camera phone is the first camera one has ever owned, when one does not have a personal computer or Internet connection at home, and when the "mobile Internet" is, if not one's first exposure to the Internet, nonetheless the primary means of access? For those who study convergence among more privileged users, there is a tendency to downplay its technological aspect, or the way one device can increasingly handle numerous media functions.[20] However, millions of people in the world must make do with a single delivery technology for most of their digital media use, and almost always it is a mobile phone.[21] Thus, in contrast to what I will term "selective convergence"—such as when a person intentionally chooses to use convergent functions on one device, as in the case of transferring songs from a desktop computer to a phone, or when, for the sake of convenience, a smartphone is used to check email while out of the office or to take a picture because a digital camera was left at home—young migrant women's technology use is often characterized by *necessary convergence*, or the converging of multiple usages on a single device out of necessity because no other device is owned or because the device in one's possession has limited functionality. A young migrant woman taking a picture of a movie star on a television screen, because she either does not have Internet capability on her phone or cannot afford mobile Internet service, is an example of such necessary convergence.

A notion of necessary convergence is not meant to highlight techno-logical convergence while denying culture; rather, it is quite the opposite. Though for more privileged users "the hardware [is] diverging while the content converges,"[22] for marginalized groups like young migrant women both hardware and content must converge on the same device. As this book goes to press, those "born digital" are increasingly utilizing converging func-tions on one device, yet for the opposite reasons that young migrant women engage in necessary convergence. For the former, such a choice is the result of being able to afford superior technology that has recently been developed. For migrant women, necessary convergence is often characterized by both economic constraints and subpar technology. Necessary convergence thus reveals how people evince creativity to fulfill their needs and desires within limited material circumstances.

Both "new media technologies" and "contemporary China" are per-haps two of the most dynamic and rapidly changing formations on the planet. In offering a "living record" of young migrant women's engagement with mobile phones I trace patterns over time and also paint a portrait of a "moment in time" with the broader goal of contributing analytically and theoretically to our understanding of how marginalized groups engage with new media technologies amid myriad constraints.[23] A study of young rural-to-urban migrant women's socio-techno practices addresses a wide range of issues salient within research on contemporary China, migration, mobile telephony, and cultural approaches to technology appropriation. To set the context for the remainder of this book, in the following pages I situate the themes of this study within broader theoretical issues relevant to a cultural study of young migrant women and mobile technology. More specifically, I first consider how diverse modes of power and forms of self-fashioning man-ifest in contemporary China. I then discuss technology as articulation and assemblage as a theoretical framework for this study. These larger theoreti-cal discussions are followed by an overview of mobile telephony studies in a global context in order to show how this book complements such research and charts new terrain. The necessity of attending to gender, class, place, and age is then illuminated through unpacking a commonly used term for young rural-to-urban migrant women, *dagongmei* ("working little sister"). I close with a brief discussion of my location as a feminist ethnographer.

Contemporary China: Subjectivity and Technologies of the Self

China is in the midst of a modernizing project in which the radical socialist utopian vision of Mao Zedong has been replaced by a pragmatic Party leadership that advocates "socialism with Chinese characteristics." Egalitarianism, collectivism, and asceticism have been repudiated in favor of neoliberal market policies that emphasize individual merit, material wealth, and consumption. The ideology of the Communist Party has been nearly completely undermined, and with it its moral authority, yet it maintains legitimacy through delivering economic growth and an improved standard of living for the nation's people. Whereas during the Mao era the pursuit of material wealth was scorned, now "money is god." In the midst of such ruptures, alternative values and lifestyles compete for people's attention, often within a mediated realm of representation. Indeed, certain socialist institutions and ideologies have been decoupled from their prior cultural and political significance, and in many ways the heavy hand of the government has retreated from people's daily lives. However, such new modes of individuality and privatization coexist with an authoritarian state that has exerted tremendous effort toward the social engineering (*shehui gongcheng*) of its citizens, in particular migrant workers.

Understanding the contemporary Chinese milieu can be facilitated through the notion of governmentality, which Michel Foucault defines broadly as the "conduct of conduct," or the underlying rationalities, tactics, and actions of various actors and institutions for the purpose of improving the prosperity, security, and well-being of both the state and the individual, as well as how individuals are integrated into and comply with these rationalities.[24] Governmentality thus encompasses both how to "govern others" and how to "govern oneself."[25] As Elaine Jeffreys and Gary Sigley note, the concept of governmentality focuses not on the exercise of power by the state for the sake of control, but on "the diversity of forces and knowledges involved in efforts to regulate the lives of individuals, and the conditions within particular national territories, in pursuit of various goals."[26] Although it was originally put forth as a means of analyzing the transformations occurring in post-World War II western liberal democratic societies, governmentality's applicability to non-western countries that are undergoing their own economic restructuring and market liberalization in line with global capitalist imperatives has been argued by many.[27] Thus, while "Chinese governmentality" might not emphasize rights and liberty, it nonetheless involves both a "facilitative" dimension—or the "notion of free individuals pursuing their own interest"—and an "authoritarian" dimension—or norms that "become obligatory and enforceable" through state efforts of planning and administration.[28]

Governmentality is not only a way to understand the rationalities of the state or other institutional authorities, but it also illuminates how seemingly personal choices and lifestyles are shaped by these rationalities. Emphasizing this personal domain, Nikolas Rose argues that individuals are encouraged to be "entrepreneurs of themselves" through maximizing their capacities and striving for self-improvement. This "enterprising self" encompasses an ethical dimension as well, where ethics "are understood in a 'practical' way as modes of evaluating and acting upon one's self."[29] A key aspect of governmentality therefore involves what Foucault calls "technologies of the self," which "permit individuals to effect by their own means or with the help of others a certain number of operations on their own bodies and souls, thoughts, conduct, and way of being, so as to transform themselves in order to attain a certain state of happiness, purity, wisdom, perfection, or immortality."[30] Though governmentality accounts for the state's role in guidance of the populace and forming consensus, or "governing from a distance," in focusing on technologies of the self, Foucault stresses that he is most interested in "how an individual acts upon himself."[31] Technologies of the self thus underscore how "freedom" is woven into modes of "self-responsibilization" as the state has retracted from some of its prior obligations to its citizens.

In China, technologies of power and technologies of the self manifest in what Aihwa Ong and Li Zhang call "socialism from afar," where Chinese citizens are encouraged to become "self-animating" subjects within "the political limits set by the socialist state."[32] Clearly, the Chinese government has invested tremendous energy toward "conducting the conduct" of all of its citizens, for example, through encouraging entrepreneurship, on the one hand, and undertaking numerous media campaigns that promote a harmonious, "civilized" society on the other.[33] For example, for several years all over

Fig. 1. A neighborhood sign urges residents to join together in a civilized manner in order to build a beautiful new life.

Beijing and all across China various forms of propaganda have urged citizens to build "civilized" lives, communities, and transportation, to engage in "civilized" behavior or service, and to use "civilized" language (see figure 1). However, as an extremely marginalized population with supposed low "quality" (*suzhi*), rural-to-urban migrants are governed in particular ways, such as through propaganda aimed at making them more "cultured," hygiene and family planning endeavors, vocational training programs, and workplace disciplines. Yan Hairong has argued that recruitment of poor rural women for urban domestic service, which is framed in official discourse as a way for these women to improve their *suzhi* by gaining a "social education" in the city, is a form of neoliberal governmentality.[34] In my conversations with Wu Huiying, Li Xiulan, and dozens of other young migrant women who had left home without a formal intermediary, migration decisions were most often framed as a *personal* choice (though one usually impelled by difficult conditions at home). However, rural-to-urban migration in China is both a result of and requirement for China's development, and thus these women's oft-stated goals of "developing" themselves and learning new skills can be understood as forms of self-entrepreneurship in line with the party-state's modernization imperatives.

As I will show, a recognition of such modes of governmentality that shape subjectivity has important implications for analyzing migrant women's engagement with mobile phones. Just as Sun Wanning in *Maid in China* has argued that China's mass media operate as a "technology of subjectivity" for domestic workers, so, too, I show that mobile phones are literal and figurative "technologies of the self" for young migrant women. As cell phones are articulated to notions of modernity, urbanity, femininity, and sociality, they are constitutive of migrant women's subjectification, or how they recognize themselves as subjects in the city.[35] In both the waged and emotional labor expended in buying and using the phone, they are also part of what Foucault calls the "care of the self" as well.[36] As a "mobile technology" in multiple senses of the term, mobile phones are also implicated in powerful contemporary Chinese discourses of self-improvement through acquisition of skills—technological, linguistic, "civilizing"—that migrant women internalize, enact, and reproduce via the mobile phone. In certain cases, when migrant women use mobile phones to resist employers' attempts at control, the phone also becomes entangled in vectors of disciplinary power.

While the ascendance of "governmental" power is sometimes thought to sweep away the notion of a "disciplinary society," as I will argue, depending on the context, disciplinary power can still operate with force in the lives of young migrant women.[37] Women's bodies have been shown to be the site of numerous configurations of power, and this is even truer for female migrants, who are disciplined through multifarious regulatory regimes and discourses.[38] Though migrant women, like all Chinese citizens, are compelled to self-manage and optimize their capacities, in the workplace they are also often subject to managerial techniques aimed at molding them into "docile" bodies through instilling a self-regulatory gaze. Thus, rather than seeing governmentality and disciplinary power as two distinct forms of power separated by time and space, I will show that they both still function to produce subjects, with one having more force than the other under certain conditions. As mobile phones are articulated to diverse forms of power, they can be emancipatory but they can also be enslaving. In the lives of young migrant women, for communicative and symbolic purposes and in consistent and contradictory ways, the phone can often become the nexus for various practices and techniques of power.

Theorizing Mobile Technologies: Technology
as Articulation and Assemblage

How does one capture the multiple logics, discourses, and power relations
within which contingent uses and understandings of mobile technologies by
young migrant women emerge and take flight? From its inception, the inter-
disciplinary and international nature of mobile phone research has meant
that scholars have approached this matter from a number of different angles
and theoretical perspectives. For example, some have drawn upon general
notions of the mutual shaping of society and technology.[39] Others have used
domestication theory, originally conceived as a way to understand the stages
through which domestic technologies such as personal computers are introduced into the "moral economy" of the household. When this theory has
been applied to studies of mobile telephony, however, quite often it must
be supplemented by other theoretical frameworks to be able to account for
the diverse locations in which mobile phones are used, the vast array of user
practices, and the multiple meanings ascribed to mobile phones across space
and time.[40]

As useful as these approaches are, very few mobile phone studies are
grounded in critical or cultural studies of technology. Noting this gap,
Gerard Goggin applies the "circuit of culture" in his comprehensive analysis
of the rise of "cell phone culture."[41] Originally devised by du Gay and colleagues to understand the Sony Walkman, the circuit of culture posits five
processes—production, consumption, representation, regulation, and identity—that must be considered to fully understand a cultural artifact.[42] Like
domestication theory, however, the circuit of culture is inadequate to fully
account for the cell phone as a networked technology. Goggin therefore also
uses actor-network theory (ANT), which refuses binary oppositions between
technology and society, and considers the agency of both human and non-
human actors in how a technology is shaped.[43] A significant critique of ANT,
which Goggin acknowledges, is its inattention to gender and power.[44]

Mobile communication scholarship thus far has generated knowledge
about the deep and extensive manner in which mobile phones have been
incorporated into social and cultural life. Because my concern is with the
mutual constitution of technology, power, and subjectivity, to theorize mobile
phone practices I utilize the concepts of articulation and assemblage, which
have most often been associated with Stuart Hall and the work of Gilles

Deleuze and Félix Guattari, respectively, but have been taken up by numerous critical and cultural scholars as a framework for theorizing, among other things, the social world, neoliberalism in primarily non-western contexts, feminist theories of the body, and the dynamic and interwoven relationship between culture and technology.[45] In my use of articulation and assemblage, I draw on this diverse scholarship, in particular that of Jennifer Daryl Slack and J. Macgregor Wise, who, in their individual and collaborative work, have employed articulation and assemblage to capture the fact of technology as not just a bounded "thing" but as existing within and interdependent with a number of "energies, activities, interpenetrations, and investments."[46]

An articulation, as defined by Stuart Hall, can best be understood as a connection of different components that become unified under particular conditions. In other words, it "is a linkage which is not necessary, determined, absolute and essential for all time."[47] The theory of articulation draws attention to myriad connections among distinct elements—ideologies, social groups, practices—that appear to create a unified discourse. However, articulations are always contingent on a range of factors in a specific historical conjuncture. The elements articulated can never be assumed to have a necessary correspondence (they could be quite different), yet their unity is also not completely random.[48] For example, when mobile phones first became popular in the United States in the early 1980s, they were primarily viewed as a tool for elite businessmen and were articulated to notions of wealth, convenience, productivity, and upper-class and upper-middle-class white-collar labor, among other things. During the 1990s when youth in Western Europe and Japan began acquiring mobile phones, new articulations emerged, especially as text messaging became a distinct youth practice.

Investigating such diverse articulations means "mapping the context," not only to locate a phenomenon—technological or otherwise—within a certain context at a certain time, but also to understand what distinct phenomena make this context what it is.[49] This context, or "web" of articulations, is then what makes up an assemblage, which can be viewed as a dynamic network in which heterogeneous elements—bodies, technologies, desires, discourses, disciplines, signs—are articulated, or joined together.[50] In other words, they are not separate and distinct but function within and through one another.[51] Moreover, assemblages create territories that have particular qualities, claims, and potentialities.[52] As Wise notes, while an assemblage is "not a set of predetermined parts," it also is not a "random collection of things" because "there is a sense that an assemblage is a whole of some sort that expresses some identity and claims a territory."[53] However, assemblages are not stable; they become deterritorialized, or shift and change, only to be reterritorialized, or reassembled into a different shape with different elements.[54] In the case of a mobile phone, there is the actual physical object as well as its articulated elements, including ideas, practices, and emotions; how these take a particular dynamic form, or constellation, constitutes the phone's assemblage. This assemblage will thus include human and non-human bodies, actions, feelings, and statements, which are not static but are involved in processes of assembly and disassembly, which then lead to new articulations emerging within a revised assemblage.[55]

My purpose in viewing technology as articulation and assemblage is not to get lost in theoretical abstraction. Rather, in the spirit of Deleuze and Guattari and echoing the words of Elizabeth Grosz, I take articulation and assemblage as *tools* to be utilized, shaped, developed, and experimented with.[56] These tools should help illuminate the mutually constitutive nature of technology and culture and the multiple practices, values, meanings, and emotions that make up young rural-to-urban migrant women's engagement with mobile phones. As Ong notes in her study of neoliberalism in non-western contexts, using articulation and assemblage places the emphasis not on predetermined grand narratives of global societal transformation but rather allows "conceptual openness to unexpected possibilities and resolutions" in the way in which terms, discourses, and practices emerge and are negotiated within a specific conjuncture.[57] In a similar manner, I wish to avoid taken-for-granted understandings of mobile phone use that have emerged among populations quite distinct from young rural-to-urban migrant women. Mapping the territory of migrant women's mobile phone assemblage means looking not only at the mobile phone itself, but also to the flow of relationships within which it is given meaning as well as its power to "assemble specific bodies, passions, and representations in particular ways."[58] Such a perspective in its very formulation considers issues of subjectivity, agency, and, crucially, power.

Mobile Communication in a Global Context

My interest in this project began during a return visit to China in 2002, the same year Wu Huiying's sister purchased her bronze-colored Nokia phone.

After living, studying, and working in China in much of the early to mid-1990s, I had been away for a while and was on a long-anticipated return visit. The changes in Beijing's physical infrastructure—new ring roads packed with cars and a formerly unimaginable array of shopping malls, restaurants, and bars—were dramatic. However, what left the most indelible mark on me was the ubiquity of mobile phones in a nation where until rather recently having a personal landline was the reserve of a privileged minority.

Right around this time, some of the first mobile phone studies had been published by Mizuko Ito, Rich Ling, James Katz, and others who were examining how this "personal, portable" technology was becoming a central artifact for identity construction and social networking, especially among youth populations.[59] With few exceptions, however, the subjects of these studies were usually educated, comparatively well-off, urban teenagers and college students in developed countries.[60] It thus raised the question—what about mobile phone use by more economically or socially marginalized young people, like China's young adult rural-to-urban migrants, who face extreme limits on their agency and autonomy? How do they use mobile phones in their everyday lives, which are characterized by numerous structural and material constraints?

Since I first began asking these questions, the field of mobile phone studies has developed quickly, as scholars from multiple disciplines and in diverse geographic locations have contributed to a growing body of research on the various social and personal dimensions of mobile telephony.[61] Outside of China, such work has focused on how mobile phones lend themselves to the dislodging of space, the blurring of time, and more flexibility and fluidity in coordinating schedules.[62] In emotionally close relationships mobile phones are said to enable "ambient virtual co-presence" or the "tethered self,"[63] and teens and young adults especially use mobile phones for forms of "digital gift giving."[64] At a more individual level, the mobile phone has been shown to be connected to fashion, personal identity, and modes of self-presentation.[65] Gendered discourses, differences in display, and types of usage of mobile phones have also been found.[66] Larissa Hjorth, in particular, has focused on gender performativity via mobile phones through mapping "cartographies of personalization" of gendered mobile media in Asia.[67]

While many of the studies cited above have investigated mobile phone use of middle-class users, in particular high school and college students, with few exceptions the focus in China has been primarily on rural-to-urban migrant workers, especially those laboring in the nation's southern factories.[68] Just as migrants in transnational contexts keep in touch with friends and family via mobile phones, China's rural-to-urban migrants maintain translocal networks via cell phones[69] and use them to establish new friendships and romantic relationships.[70] Moreover, there seems to be a consensus that migrant workers use mobiles as key signifiers of status (which I will question in chapter 2),[71] yet there is less agreement on how effective mobile phones are for job seeking and helping migrants to raise their incomes.[72] In his analysis of the "information have-less," which includes rural-to-urban migrant workers, Jack Linchuan Qiu has examined their use of "working-class ICTs," such as inexpensive mobile phones, prepaid phone cards, text messaging, and Internet cafés.[73] In his mapping of the interconnection between social differentiation and informational stratification, Qiu is one of the few who puts class at the forefront of his analysis of institutions, discourses, and practices in order to reveal how a "working-class network society" is emerging in China.

## Technology Use and Social Differentiation

As a whole, this body of research in and outside of China has significantly deepened our understanding of how the mobile phone has become part of everyday life in a variety of contexts. However, within the fields of mobile phone studies and migration scholarship more generally and as they intersect in China more specifically, there are still important questions that remain unanswered. For example, how is social differentiation and subjectivity constitutive of disparate access to, understandings of, and meaning-making practices around technology? Feminist studies of technology—often focused on white western women—have shown the reciprocal, fluid, and contingent manner in which gender and technology shape one another, be it through sexual divisions in the workforce, gendered uses of technology, or technology's role in forming gendered bodies.[74] However, as Leopoldina Fortunati notes about mobile communication studies, although gendered dimensions of mobile phone use have been described, rarely has such work problematized how gender and technology are co-constructed, nor has it examined how particular material conditions produce distinct uses of technology.[75] An exception is Hjorth's work on how the mobile phone has been domesticated in line with gendered and local identities in the Asia-Pacific region, yet a gap remains in research on this area in the People's Republic of China.[76] More-over, while in both academic and popular accounts, the trope of the young Asian female has emerged as an urban, sexy, tech-savvy consumer of new media, this construction inadvertently creates a false totality, leaving out a large segment of young women, including rural-to-urban migrants, whose limited material circumstances and use of "have-less" technology confines them to the margins of imaginations of "Asia."[77]

My goal, therefore, is to build on and extend such work by shifting the focus from primarily urban, western, or Asian middle-class and upper-mid-dle-class girls and women in school or in the workforce to a group of young Chinese women considered to be at the margins of society and thus in pos-session of less social, cultural, and economic capital. In so doing, I illuminate fine nuances in the ways that gendered uses of, and discourses about, tech-nology are produced and circulated within contemporary China. Not only gender, however, but also race and class are central to discursive construc-tions and appropriations of media technologies, as numerous cultural stud-ies of technology have shown.[78] Yet, in the Chinese context, as I will discuss in more detail below, "place" is often a more salient category than race or ethnicity.

While research on rural-to-urban migrant workers' uses of mobile phones has emphasized the urban-rural divide in China, in general the same cri-tique leveled by Fortunati regarding research on gender and the mobile phone could also be applied to issues of class; that is, in researchers' descrip-tive focus (except in Qiu's work mentioned above), they take class as a given rather than analyzing how technology and class are co-produced.[79] Although I will show in this book that gender is indeed a salient force, I also argue for the necessity of looking at how the intersections of gender as well as class, place (e.g., the rural "Other"), and age produce migrant women's subjectivity and engagement with technology.

*Who Are the "Global Youth"?*

The young Asian female and the western, urban, middle-class youth who have figured so prominently in mobile phone scholarship were the ones who were most likely early on to have access to mobile telephony once it diffused and even now to have the financial means to keep up with the latest tech-nological advances. Researching their technology use is important, yet the inordinate focus upon them ignores a vast swath of youth and young adults around the world and intentionally or not perpetuates a view of "global youth culture" that corresponds with the objectives of transnational corporations and marketers.[80] Clearly "youth" is a slippery term that takes on divergent meanings in different places, as many have noted.[81] In terms of age, various definitions of youth coexist. Some define youth as the teenage years, while the United Nations designates youth as those aged between fifteen and twenty-four. In China, youth is defined as those aged fifteen to twenty-nine.[82] Aside from age, however, there seems to be a broad consensus that rather than view youth as a distinct stage, it should instead be seen as a context-dependent process, or "social achievement," that is produced by numerous actors, institutions, and discourses and is "bound up with questions of power and materiality."[83]

It is certainly true that the young women in my study do not fit neatly into the dominant notion of global youth culture, which currently means tech-savvy, brand-conscious youth with loosely shared experiences of schooling and negotiating parental authority, and with a degree of leisure time, disposable income, and interest in certain forms of popular culture. Such youth prevail in media representations and in much of the literature on "digital natives."[84] They also figure prominently in the imaginations of global corporations eager to capture a young, lucrative market in China. For example, in her study of advertising in China, Jing Wang has detailed how feminine products are marketed to the "new modern girl" as well as how Motorola erroneously assumed that western signifiers of cool "global youth," such as indie music, could be utilized in the marketing of mobile music to Chinese youth.[85] Though migrant youth might not be the trendsetters that global marketers lust after, they nonetheless are often attracted to the allures of consumption, because one's consumption level in China is supposed to denote not only one's economic capital, but also one's cultural capital and "quality." Young migrant women may not have much time to "mess around" and "geek out" with new media technologies like their more privileged peers in the West; nonetheless, their engagement with mobile phones is central to their experience in the city.[86]

If we acknowledge that youth is marked by a range of concerns of young people in diverse contexts, then we must also allow that it is not only media and marketers, or parents and teachers—the authority figures so central to dominant constructions of youth—that produce people as "youth." Surrogate forms of power operate with similar effects in places like China, where patri-archal familial norms, disciplines, and notions of female docility infiltrate the workplace, thereby placing migrant workers within "parent-child" relation-ships. In most mobile phone research, however, power has been remarkably undertheorized.[87] In the few studies that have explicitly analyzed power rela-tions, power is viewed as something repressive and resting in the hands of authority figures such as parents or teachers; the phone is then constructed as an emancipatory device.[88] One of my central concerns, however, is to the-orize how modes of power and discourse are articulated to and constitute mobile technologies and mobile bodies. It is to one particular mobile body that I now turn.

## China's *Dagongmei*: Gender, Age, Class, and Place

In contemporary China, the cultural shifts in goals, values, possibilities, and opportunities discussed earlier have not only given rise to diverse forms of power, but also affect the way in which citizens are encouraged to be "self-animating subjects." On the one hand, in leaving the land, young rural-to-urban migrant women have greater opportunities for personal agency and autonomy than previous generations of rural women. On the other hand, they are simultaneously positioned within numerous cultural and structural constraints, such as the rigid *hukou* (or household registration system), sal-ary differentials, status- and gender-stratified labor realms, and complex and contradictory discourses that are mapped onto their bodies. Theorizing their mobile phone assemblage thus necessitates considering how all of these forces intersect. In transnational contexts, feminist scholars have long recog-nized the importance of the intersections of multiple axes of identity, such as gender, class, and race, as constitutive of shaping migration experience.[89] An intersectional framework thus offers a means of breaking away from the privileging of one aspect of identity over another in order to avoid distortions and exclusions.[90] Such a lens considers more than just how discrete, static categories of identity are interconnected; it also shows how they are always in play, even if at different moments one might be more important in shaping experience than another. The significance of the intersections of gender, age, class, and place in this study can be demonstrated through unpacking a com-monly used Chinese term for migrant women—*dagongmei*.[91]

A highly gendered term, *dagongmei* combines the words "work" (*dagong*) and little sister (*mei*), and it means "working little sister" or "maiden worker." *Dagongmei* connotes a young, unmarried woman, who, as a younger "sister," has low status and few rights. Pun Ngai notes that *dagongmei* "implies an inferior working identity inscribed with capitalist labor relations and sexual relations."[92] The gendered nature of the term becomes pronounced when one notes that its counterpart, *dagongzai*, a word sometimes used for male migrant workers, means young men "laboring for the boss."[93] *Dagongmei* has more powerful gendered connotations in the context of Chinese familial patriarchy—young migrant women are "working little sisters"—while young migrant men are simply laborers, but not "little brothers." This distinction has implications for the jobs into which migrant women are funneled: domestic, service, and sex work as well as industrial work that perpetuates the "myth of nimble fingers."[94] According to Ching Kwan Lee, managers and bosses in southern Chinese factories who employ *dagongmei* often view them as "like lambs, very pure and compliant" and merely girls who work "while waiting to be married off."[95]

The construction of *dagongmei* as little working sisters waiting for marriage highlights how their age is also central to their subjectification in the city. As Tamara Jacka notes, especially for women, marriage "marks the entry into the social order . . . whatever position migrant women occupy in the city, it is seen as only temporary—their 'real' adult status begins when they return to the countryside, 'settle down,' and become wives and mothers."[96] Their position as young women thus contributes to their liminality in the city. Though they are seen as neither children nor full-fledged adults, some employers nevertheless feel justified in treating them as children, paying them less, and in some cases, subjecting them to rigorous workplace disciplines. Moreover, their journey to the city is nearly a rite of passage, constitutive of their age, their desire to broaden their horizons, and, for those from the poorest regions, their view that the countryside offers them nothing. In Yan Hairong's words, "'youth' is therefore a strategic site of action" and migration is a "troubled process of subject formation for rural youth" because the city is the only place where they can gain a modern subjectivity.[97] To call them "youth," then, "foregrounds age not as a trajectory, but as identity" and emphasizes "the here-and-now of young people's experience, the social and cultural practices through which they shape their worlds."[98]

Beyond gender and youth, the term *dagongmei* also evokes a low-status labor category. This "inferior working identity" noted by Pun above is clearly evident when contrasting the term *dagongmei* (and *dagongzai*) with *gongren*, the Mao-era term for worker. Prior to the economic reforms, the *gongren* were the highly privileged class of urban workers, the "masters" of the nation employed in state or collective enterprises and as such entitled to numerous lifelong social welfare benefits. In contrast, the *dagongmei* and *dagongzai* have minimal rights and virtually no job security. Like the low-skilled "precariat" around the globe,[99] they thus represent a class of workers indicative of a capitalist market that extracts surplus labor.[100] As China has joined the global market, migrant workers, as always temporary workers, provide the "flexibility" demanded by late capitalism. In the context of China's marketization and globalization, the term *dagongmei* has emerged as a classificatory strategy that enables the exploitation of workers in the name of "*socialism with Chinese characteristics*" (my emphasis added). Such restructuring of labor relations is, according to Pun, "the subsumption of class analysis in order to hide class positions and social privileges," and as such it is part of a political strategy designed to support a neoliberal discourse of open markets and individualism.[101]

Finally, a *dagongmei* is not only young, gendered, and classed; she is also "placed." She is an unskilled, low-paid female worker, and she is also, and must be, from rural China. For this reason, her location in the urban environment greatly differs from a woman who is a city resident. Even if they happen to hold the same job, which is extremely rare, their positions in asymmetrical networks of power and opportunity mean that they will experience the city and their employment very differently. I will explore the origins and consequences of this urban-rural divide more fully in chapter 1. Here I only wish to point out that in contemporary China, because development policies since the mid-1980s have focused on the eastern coastal regions and large urban centers, the countryside, particularly in less well-off provinces, has increasingly been positioned as "left behind" or, in Yan's words, as "a wasteland of 'backwardness' and 'tradition.' "[102] This teleological view of the city as the vanguard of progress and development is not unique to China, nor is the urban-rural dichotomy a recent result of post-Mao reforms. However, as China has set itself on a course to "catch up" and "develop," the "quality" (*suzhi*) of the people has been seen as central to improving the quality of the nation. The countryside and peasants, then, become objectified as lacking quality, and peasants are seen as the backward, traditional Other against which progress and development can be measured. Such a blanket assessment places the origin and perpetuation of this "social reality" onto the geographic domain of the countryside and the mental and physical bodies of its inhabitants rather than structural and institutional factors that discursively produce these conditions.

In sum, *dagongmei* is a subject position produced by structural, cultural, and social factors that rely on dominant discourses of gender, age, class, and place. It thus operates as a form of power to normalize the exploitative conditions faced by migrant women and their low position in the gender and societal hierarchy. However, like all identity categories, the term *dagongmei* is a social construction and a false totality and one that can never be completely fixed. Nonetheless, it illuminates the necessity of employing an intersectional framework to understand the socio-techno practices of young migrant women, how these practices are characterized by immobile mobility, and how they are constitutive of migrant women's subjectification in the city.

## Feminist Ethnography

To map migrant women's mobile phone assemblage, this study used immersive, ethnographic methods. The goal was to generate what Clifford Geertz calls a "thick description" through a logic of discovery.[103] My research began in the summer of 2005, and the bulk of the fieldwork was conducted for ten months during 2006 and 2007. This initial fieldwork was supplemented by follow-up trips of varying lengths from 2008 to 2011, as well as email, online chat, and phone calls with key informants. The participants in the study were primarily young migrant women, as well as a small number of migrant men, from rural villages and a few towns in various provinces in China. They had usually migrated to Beijing after finishing at least some junior middle school and were employed as low-wage workers mainly in marketplaces, restaurants, and beauty salons though a few worked as service staff in government-owned companies. In addition to participant observation at worksites and residences, I conducted numerous semistructured interviews and gathered a small number of mobile phone diaries from key informants. I also analyzed Chinese internal migration and telecommunications policy, media representations of rural-to-urban migrants, and advertising discourses of mobile phone companies (see the appendix for more details on the research methods).

This research is based in ethnography, but by now it goes without saying that using the term "ethnography" raises questions about the problematic nature of cultural representation and a reliance on experience to generate truth. The critiques of ethnography are multiple, valid, and by now well known.[104] James Clifford notes that in ethnography there are always exclusions, unintentional distortions, the inevitable speaking for the other, and the imposition of meaning.[105] As a feminist ethnographer, I sought constant self-reflexivity and to let my participants speak of their own lives and experiences.[106] At the same time, I am not positing a self-knowing, authentic subject that can speak the truth of her real situation through language. Years ago Joan Scott addressed the problem with relying on experience as "uncontestable evidence," particularly to illuminate the lives of marginalized groups.[107] As Scott argues, experience cannot simply be taken at face value; instead, an investigation of a group's experience must always include an analysis of how difference is socially constructed and constituted by discourse, and how discourses function to produce experience in specific, historical conjunctures. Rather than looking at the products of difference, we must analyze the way power operates to produce subjects through discourse. Such an assertion does not deny human agency, yet this agency is never fully free. Acknowledging the socially constructed nature of experience means we can still maintain it as a mode for understanding because it is the primary way we know our own and others' ways of being in the world.[108] It is a means of tapping into people's understanding of their place in the world, the practices that anchor (or disrupt) this position, and the feelings and emotions attached to such practices and positions.

Perhaps the biggest problems that remain with ethnography are power differentials between researcher and "subjects" as well as the potential for othering and essentializing of these subjects. My own background as a white, middle-class, American scholar perhaps could not be further removed from that of the women in this study, many of whom came from extremely poor families and often did not have more than a middle-school education (many had less). At the same time, they were experts on the topic I was studying. I can also only hope that my own instances of being "othered" in China— in particular while living in China in the late 1980s and early 1990s, and being heckled, cheated, pointed at, and occasionally touched, depending on where I was—gave me greater empathy to the situation of migrant women in Beijing. I do not mean to downplay my position of privilege compared to migrant women, who in the city are treated as outsiders, though in their own country. And certainly our relationships were framed by issues of class, race, nationality, and unequal access to social and cultural capital. Yet, for all of these reasons I was also somewhat of an object of curiosity for them. Reflecting on such situations, Wendy Weiss notes, "There is objectification on both sides, which is part of the process of understanding begun by defining ourselves first through the opposition of 'the other.'"[109] This process of understanding proceeds through dialogue, exploration, and what the Chinese call *huxiang bangzhu*, or "mutual help." As much as the women in this study gave to me—of their time, knowledge, friendship, and even handmade gifts—I hope I also gave back to them, through helping them with their limited English, occasionally serving as a translator with customers, taking them out to a special meal, and, most important, showing them respect and that their lives mattered.

Julie Bettie notes in the introduction to her study of Mexican American and white girls in an American high school that to perform reflexive ethnography means recognizing that the text "is not simply the result of an even negotiation between ethnographer and subject, because in the end authority literally remains with the ethnographer, as *author* of the text."[110] In other words, regardless of my desire to let women's voices speak in this study, and for them to articulate their own understanding of what mobile phones mean in their lives, ultimately the final interpretation is mine. Nonetheless, I hope the end result is what Donna Haraway calls a "joining of partial views."[111]

Feminist ethnography is not "feminist" because it is conducted by women who, as women, have certain inherent traits. Instead, it is based on an acknowledgment of power relations, a desire to let silenced voices speak, intersubjectivity between researcher and participants, and, perhaps most crucially, reflexivity.[112] Thus, the politics of ethnography cannot be erased, nor should they be. For it is ethnography's politics that forces recognition and negotiation of issues of power and difference, and by extension potential realizations of social change.

Overview of the Book

In this book I explore young rural-to-urban migrant women's uses of mobile phones as these are constitutive of these women's urban subjectivity. The research is situated within the processes of China's marketization and entry into the global economy, and the concomitant forces of modernization, migration, and informatization. It examines how the intersections of gender, class, place, and age produce particular socio-techno practices characterized by immobile mobility. After a chapter that provides background for the non-China expert, the remaining chapters illuminate the cultural, social, aesthetic, and economic dimensions that map the territory of migrant women's engagement with mobile phones.

Chapter 1 outlines the specific socio-cultural context of contemporary China at the beginning of the 21st century. To set the stage for the rest of the book, this chapter discusses the reforms of the post-Mao period, the history of the urban-rural divide perpetuated by the *hukou* (household registration system), and the phenomenon of rural-to-urban migration. I examine China's discourse of development and modernity and how it configures rural women ideologically as an "Other" to be reformed and improved, as shown most explicitly through a discussion of the *suzhi* discourse. I also discuss two "revolutions" in China: the "consumer revolution" that began in the 1980s and the rapid development of China's telecommunications infrastructure, which led to the diffusion of new media technologies in everyday urban life. Throughout the discussion I emphasize how shifting ideologies related to gender, class, and place have played a pivotal role in shaping rural women's experience, during both the Mao-era planned economy and China's reform-era embrace of markets and global capitalism.

In chapter 2 I situate the mobile phone specifically within China's quest for development and modernity. After a discussion of "alternative" modernities, I show how in 2006-2007 a mobile phone was an important signifier of urban modernity for rural women. I also argue that the mobile phone is a technology of the self that is articulated to self-shaping as well as disciplines and exclusions. In addition, I illustrate how cell phones allow women to participate in a form of consumer citizenship (or the "comfortable life" promised by the government) in contrast to the legal and social citizenship they are denied in the city. Another key point in this chapter is that discourses surrounding mobile phone use align with notions of gender essentialism that have become prominent in the post-Mao era. In the final section of the chapter, I explore more deeply the constitutive nature of gender and technology by presenting an in-depth case study of a beauty salon.

In chapter 3 I examine young rural-to-urban migrant women's use of mobile phones for expanding and enriching various types of social relationships. I situate this discussion within Chinese concepts of selfhood and *guanxi* (relationship) and relate these to Pierre Bourdieu's notion of social capital. A key question thus explored throughout the chapter is whether migrant women's mobile-enabled networked sociality enables them to build their social capital in ways that will improve their life conditions. In discussing how more and more migrant women access the Internet via their mobile phones, I also introduce the concept of "necessary convergence." A final theme explored is the way that mobile phones allow for greater autonomy in dating. A key point of this chapter is that while immobile mobility allows migrant women inclusion in expanded and enriched social networks, these tend to reinforce their identity as migrants, or "not Beijing people."

Chapter 4 builds on the notions of immobile mobility and necessary convergence through examining migrant women's uses of camera phones. For nearly all of the informants in this study, a camera phone was the first camera they had ever owned. Though many women involved in the initial fieldwork did not have cameras in their phones due to financial reasons, those who did manifested creativity in asserting a personal digital aesthetic. In this chapter, I engage with theories of imaging and photography in order to discuss how migrant women use camera phones to represent the world, construct the self, transcend limited circumstances, envisage new possibilities, and plan for the future. I argue that such imaging practices are ultimately about self-making and actively deploying the imagination. The chapter concludes that in using camera phones to both represent and construct reality, migrant women exercise individual agency and engage in efforts at personal transformation, which is a first step toward societal change.

As with chapter 4, chapter 5 continues to elaborate the notions of immobile mobility and necessary convergence through analyzing mobile phones and labor politics. I first examine whether mobile phones can enhance migrant women's economic opportunities, such as by helping them to find a better job or increase their income. I also show how employers utilize mobile phones for purposes of surveillance and how migrant women use mobile phones as tools of resistance. This chapter argues that despite their use of mobile phones, migrant women remain relatively immobile in the labor sphere.

In the conclusion I tie together the various themes and provide a final analysis of the diverse practices, understandings, and investments that make up young migrant women's mobile phone assemblage. I avoid an "either/or" empowerment versus subjugation argument and instead summarize how a focus on the articulation of various socio-techno practices provides a more nuanced account of the co-construction of technology and subjectivity.

1

Market Reforms, Global Linkages, and (Dis)
continuity in Post-Socialist China

In October 2008, a graphic appeared in an online KDS forum populated mostly by Shanghai residents. Utilizing the international symbol for "prohibited," it featured several words and abbreviations in both English and Chinese enclosed in a red circle with a red slash across it (see figure 2). In the center of the circle were the letters WDR. Above WDR a phoenix hovered over Chinese characters that read "Phoenix Man" (*fenghuangnan*), and inside the circle were also the phrases "New Shanghai Man" and "Western Digital Man." For those familiar with China's online realm, "no WDR" was easily understood as "no *waidiren*," or "no outsiders," and referred more specifically to rural-to-urban migrant workers in China's cities. "Phoenix Man" and "New Shanghai Man" were variations on the same implied meaning.[1]

This graphic—expressing the common prejudice against migrant workers not only in Shanghai, but also in urban areas across China—could have

Fig. 2. No *waidiren* (no outsiders).

gone the way of much Internet content; that is, it might have generated a few comments and then quickly been forgotten. As is so often the case in Chinese cyberspace, however, it went viral after it was reposted on Tianya.cn, one of the most popular online forums in China, with a message criticizing the xenophobia of Shanghainese.[2] And again as is so often the case, once it caught the attention of the larger body of China's "netizens," it set off a firestorm of opinions and discussion. Some posters chastised the "arrogant" and prejudiced Shanghainese and ridiculed the perceived deficiencies in the city's men and women. Several were critical more generally of anyone who viewed outsiders (i.e., migrant workers) as stealing urban jobs while draining city resources. Many others, however, agreed with the sentiments expressed in the graphic and blamed migrant workers for crowded cities and high crime rates.

In that this online debate directly and indirectly raised numerous contentious issues—the importance in China of place/locality for notions of belonging and exclusion; the gaps between urban and rural residents; the discriminatory nature of China's *hukou* (household registration system); and related notions of culture/education (*wenhua*), class, gender, and wealth— it presents a microcosm of the larger socio-cultural context of contemporary China. With forum participants referring to issues of development and modernization along with social ills like prostitution and corruption, their comments also allude to the achievements and challenges of a society that is still in the midst of a profound transformation. The fact that this debate— and many others like it[3]—took place online is also significant, for it is representative of China's remarkable growth in telecommunications in the last few decades: the nation's numbers of Internet users and mobile phone subscribers are the largest in the world and continue to grow. Finally, just as this online discussion reveals ruptures along a local/outsider, or urban-rural demarcation, it is indicative of the way such divides have been exacerbated by China's reform policies of the last three decades.

This chapter highlights key disjunctures and continuities that constitute the assemblage of post-socialist China in order to provide a backdrop for understanding young rural-to-urban migrant women's engagement with mobile technologies. Over thirty years ago the Chinese government embarked on a course of development that unleashed processes of change, the consequences of which nobody, either inside China or "China watchers" outside the country, could have predicted. To jumpstart a stagnant economy and make a clear break with the Maoist past, in 1978 the Chinese leadership, under the direction of Deng Xiaoping, boldly embarked on a program of "reform and opening" (*gaige kaifang*). Through advancing the "four modernizations" (in industry, agriculture, science and technology, and defense), eliminating class labels and class struggle, and integrating China into the global economy, the government sought to bring stability and prosperity to a nation still recovering from the economic, political, and social upheaval wrought by the Cultural Revolution (1966-1976).[4]

The last few decades have thus seen a shift from a planned economy emphasizing heavy industry to a market economy—or "socialism with Chinese characteristics"—based on export processing (primarily centered in "Special Economic Zones" [SEZs] around China's eastern coastal areas), the growth of the domestic service sector, and consumerism as a way of life. The marketization of China's economy and its overall course of development have followed a teleology—where "some must get rich first and then others will follow"—that has emphasized "catching up" with other industrialized nations and reclaiming China's rightful place on the world stage. It has also necessitated a profound ideological reconfiguration and repudiation of Maoist frugality and austerity, perhaps summed up most succinctly in the famous statement attributed to Deng Xiaoping, "To get rich is glorious" (*zhi fu guang rong*).[5] Certainly many Chinese have benefited materially from the changes brought about by the reforms and China's entry into the global market economy. The nation's growing urban middle class now has access to new housing with modern amenities, automobiles, myriad forms of leisure and entertainment, and the latest technological devices. However, development has been extremely uneven, and not everyone has benefited equally from these economic, societal, and technological transformations.

To explore the differential manner in which China's citizens have experienced the reforms, in the following discussion I begin with an overview of the origins and outcomes of China's *hukou*. I show how current economic policies favoring the cities and coastal areas as China has sought to "link tracks with the rest of the world" (*yu shijie jiegui*) have worked in tandem with the *hukou* policy effectively to produce a society divided between the urban and rural areas. Next, I explore the phenomenon of rural-to-urban migration in China with an emphasis on the characteristics, material circumstances, and desires of young female migrants, or *dagongmei*, as well as the way China's *suzhi*, or "quality," discourse positions female migrants and rural areas as backward while upholding China's urban centers as the source of modernity and progress. I then examine two "revolutions" in China: the urban consumer revolution, which has been strongly articulated to essentialist notions of gender and distinct social strata, and the explosive growth of telecommunications, in particular of mobile phones. Though I separate all of these phenomena for analytical purposes, they have emerged from interwoven processes, and as they intersect with notions of gender, class, and place, they are constitutive of the mobile phone assemblage of young rural-to-urban migrant women.

## Hukou and the Urban-Rural Divide

China's *hukou* has been likened to a "caste-like" system that has created severe social stratification in the People's Republic of China.[6] Though the *hukou* policy has roots in Imperial China's *baojia* system—which was designed as a method of social control and taxation—its particular manifestation during the Mao era created an extremely modern and powerful mechanism of population management and organization.[7] Today, despite economic liberalization and social transformations that have substantially weakened the *hukou* as a method for regulating people's mobility, the household registration system still has profound effects in determining one's life possibilities.

*Hukou Policy under Mao*

In the early years of the People's Republic, as urban overcrowding, unemployment, and food shortages prompted fears of social instability, in 1955 the government issued a directive that categorized people as belonging to either "agricultural" (farmer/peasant) or "non-agricultural" (worker) households, according to whether they lived in a rural or urban area and regardless of whether some designated as "peasants" were not actually engaged in agricultural work. In the countryside the government also hastened collectivization in order to increase agricultural productivity, while Mao's development strategy emphasized urban industrialization.[8] In 1958, with the "Regulations on *Hukou* Registration in the People's Republic of China," migration policies were further restricted, and control was centralized in the urban Public Security Bureau (PSB). These regulations solidified the *hukou* policy and dictated that all citizens were for the most part destined to live their lives in their designated *hukou* location. Household registration was subsequently established at birth, and changes in residence were strictly controlled. Institutionalized separation between rural and urban areas was thus solidified and with few exceptions would remain intact for the next two decades.[9]

During the Mao era, enforcement of the *hukou* system was possible due to a centrally planned economy and what Dorothy Solinger has referred to as the "urban public goods regime" whereby urban residents—the vaunted "workers"—were entitled to a range of social welfare benefits such as education, healthcare, employment, and housing allocated through their state work unit (*danwei*).[10] They also received food ration tickets based on their possession of an urban *hukou*. In contrast, rural residents—"peasant farmers"—were denied this "iron rice bowl" and were supposed to be self-sufficient through the rural agricultural cooperatives. In addition to providing grain for themselves, rural residents also had to produce food for people living in cities. Because an urban household registration guaranteed such a wide range of state-provided benefits, it was associated with a better material standard of living and an exclusive, privileged status. Thus, Zhang Li argues that the *hukou* should not be seen only "as a system of population management and material redistribution but rather a badge of citizenship with profound social, cultural, and political implications for the lives of Chinese people."[11]

Though Mao's revolution was predicated on peasant support, and in official rhetoric Mao himself exalted "poor" and "middle" peasants as the vanguard of China's Communist revolution, the profound irony of Mao's *hukou* system was that it did not just divide China spatially; it also created a hierarchical distinction between the city and the countryside and between urban and rural residents.[12] It is important to point out, however, that stigmatization of China's rural inhabitants has roots far preceding Mao. China's reformist intellectuals of the early 20th century, in their attempts to explain the nation's defeats at the hands of foreign powers and the decline of imperial society, targeted peasants and China's countryside as symbolic of what they perceived as China's "backwardness" and "weakness." In their thinking, which was greatly influenced by western notions of modernity, building a modern nation entailed repudiating traditional Chinese culture with its "feudalism" and "superstition" that were most deeply rooted in the countryside.[13] As Myron Cohen observes, China's farmer peasants—the vast majority of the population—were thus configured by most reformers as passive, pitiful, and in need of education and guidance by an enlightened, urban elite.[14] It was also during this time that the word "peasant" (*nongmin*) entered into the Chinese vocabulary, a result of Japanese influence. As an abstract "modern" word, it could take on a powerful discursive function as one of the "basic negative criteria designating a new status group, one held *by definition* to be incapable of creative and autonomous participation in China's reconstruction."[15] Hence, the urban-centered *hukou* policy was one area where Mao's revolution ideologically paralleled the past it was supposedly burying.

The *hukou* policy also demonstrated continuity with China's patriarchal, institutionalized gender discrimination. Though lineage in China is traditionally derived through the male line, and Mao's class labels were also inherited through the father, until 1998 a child's household registration was passed on through the mother. This policy, which obviously contradicted Chinese custom, was meant to limit mobility as much as possible.[16] The ways in which one's *hukou* status could potentially be changed—joining the army and possibly being discharged to an urban area; gaining admission to an urban university; and becoming a Communist Party member and moving up the Party ranks—all also unfairly advantaged men. By designating that *hukou* pass through the mother, the state effectively limited its economic obligations should a male with urban *hukou* have dependents with rural *hukou*.[17] On the other hand, the most common way for rural women to change their *hukou* was through marriage migration. However, this usually meant a change from one village to another—in other words a change in *hukou* location, not status—because marriages between urban and rural people were (and are) extremely rare. Even if such marriages took place, these unions would not result in transference of a rural *hukou* to an urban one. Thus, rural women's geographic (rural-to-urban) and social mobility were severely restricted by the *hukou* policy.

*Economic Reforms and Inequality*

When the Chinese government instituted market reforms in the late 1970s it first focused on rural areas. Agricultural collectives were dismantled and the "household responsibility system" was instituted, which enabled rural households to hold long-term land leases and gain more decision-making power in agricultural production. Greater agricultural efficiency created more surplus labor, which at first was absorbed by township and village enterprises (TVEs) that were developed in rural areas under a policy of "leave the land but not the village, enter the factory but not the city" (*li tu bu li xiang, jin chang bu jin cheng*).[18] Limited markets were also permitted, and as a result of such policies peasant farmers benefited tremendously. From the late 1970s to the mid-1980s, the ratio of urban to rural per capita personal income dropped from 2.37:1 to 1.70:1.[19] Market mechanisms also meant that access to food and other goods in urban areas were not necessarily linked to urban household registration, and peasant farmers could sell their surplus grain and produce and offer menial services in market towns. All of these conditions enabled the beginnings of China's rural-to-urban migration.

In the mid-1980s, however, the state changed its reform focus from agriculture to export processing and integration with the global economy. One result was that the TVEs shifted to a capital-intensive rather than a labor-intensive approach and thus were less able to accommodate rural surplus labor.[20] At the same time, although a small number of SEZs had been created at the beginning of the reforms to attract foreign direct investment (FDI), beginning in the mid-1980s and especially in the 1990s, central government policies favored the SEZs and eastern coastal cities as targets for development. For example, before the mid-1980s there was very little foreign capital in China, yet in 1995 China received US $35.9 billion of FDI, nearly 40 percent of all of the FDI that the world's low- and middle-income countries received that year.[21] Shenzhen near the Hong Kong border, China's first SEZ, was established in 1980 and since then it has gone from a rural backwater to a city of over 12 million with an average annual growth rate of 28 percent.[22]

Although poverty had sharply declined during the first years of the reforms, inequality in income distribution, especially between urban and rural areas, started to rise after the mid-1980s. According to Azizur Rahman Khan and Carl Riskin, the designers of China's policies thought that just about everyone would benefit from the reforms and that increases in inequality would be mitigated by reduced poverty and be outweighed by greater growth.[23] However, though China through its reforms had managed to greatly enhance its economic efficiency, this was at the cost of economic equity. Huang Yasheng argues that in contrast to the "rural entrepreneurial decade" of the 1980s, China's urban-centered state-led capitalism since the 1990s has led to rural decline.[24] For example, the urban-to-rural per capita personal income ratio rose to 2.6 by 1994.[25] Such an urban-rural divide intersects with regional disparities, as development—much of it fueled by foreign capital and intentionally concentrated in eastern coastal provinces—has generated much greater wealth in these areas, including in some towns and villages, than in China's central and western regions. Urban workers have also been affected as a result of massive layoffs at inefficient state-owned enterprises. For all of these reasons, by the mid-1990s China had become one of developing Asia's more unequal countries.[26]

In 2000, after a Party secretary from a rural township in Hubei province wrote a letter to then Chinese Premier Zhu Rongji about the difficult conditions, poverty, and dire state of agriculture in the countryside, renewed attention was given to what has been called the "three-rural crisis" (sannong wenti).[27] Nonetheless, by 2002, although overall income disparity had declined in China compared to the preceding decade, there was a rising gap between average urban and rural incomes.[28] In 2004, urban residents' income was 3.21 times that of rural residents; in 2005 it was 3.22, and in 2006 it was 3.48.[29] In 2007, China's Gini coefficient was 0.48.[30] Policies that had indeed linked China with the world (i.e., global capitalism) while favoring urban areas and eastern coastal regions thus set the course for what would come to be known across the country as a "tide of migrants" (*mingongchao*).

## The Floating Population and *Hukou* Erosion

Though in the mid-1980s rural peasants had engaged in non-farm work, particularly in the TVEs mentioned earlier, as the urban-, eastern-centered economic reforms progressed and as the old apparatuses of state control were broken down, more and more rural residents were compelled to "leave the land." China's construction boom of the late 1980s drew male migrants to the thriving eastern cities while domestic service, or *baomu*, became one of the most common jobs for migrant women. Because a person's *hukou* was increasingly less tied to food and housing subsidies in urban areas, by the early 1990s more and more rural migrants began to enter China's larger cities. Between 1985 and 1990 there were 35.3 million rural-to-urban migrant workers.[31] By 2000 this number had increased to about 90 million.[32] Currently, the "floating population" (*liudong renkou*) is estimated to be around 200 million.[33] In 2007, Beijing had over 5.4 million migrant workers out of a total population of approximately 17.4 million.[34] It should be noted, however, that accurate numbers of migrants are notoriously hard to obtain, both because the word "migrant" can have several meanings and because of the large number of migrant workers who often do not register in their new location and thus are difficult to track in surveys and census counts.[35]

Although rural migrants have substantially contributed to China's economic development, this does not mean that they have been welcomed or smoothly incorporated into urban areas. In China's cities, migrants have troubled many of the taken-for-granted social and cultural assumptions that have characterized the People's Republic since its founding, including the separation of urban and rural residents as well as who has access to certain jobs and a range of benefits. Furthermore, because until recently the work unit was the only proper location for employment and containment within the socialist system, and because migrants are considered "temporary" workers and as such are not entitled to most of the benefits or subject to the mechanisms of surveillance that were once a function of work-unit affiliation, many urbanites view them with a mixture of suspicion and fear. Migrants are often blamed for overcrowding and crime in cities as well as for taking coveted jobs in the downsized industrial sector, as evidenced in the debates surrounding the "no

WDR" graphic discussed earlier. Migrants are also frequently characterized as "uncouth" (*tu*), "backward" (*luohou*), and "disorderly" (*wuxu*).[36]

In addition to such discursive constructions, migrants face significant material and institutionalized constraints in China's cities. They are segregated into low-paying, low-status jobs, and they tend to make half of what urban residents make.[37] They also are forced to lead what has been called "isolated lives" because they work such long hours, do not have the time or money to enjoy leisure spaces, live in segregated areas, and have little meaningful social contact with urban residents.[38] Forms of exploitation faced by migrants in the workplace include a lack of labor contracts, forced overtime, unpaid wages, unsafe working conditions, and little or no health insurance benefits.[39] These problems tend to be exacerbated in large cities like Beijing and Guangzhou.[40] Migrant workers are also subject to police and government mistreatment. In one of the more infamous cases of such harassment in Beijing, an entire migrant village housing thousands of migrants from the Wenzhou area of Zhejiang province was demolished by authorities on the premise that it was illegal and had undermined state authority.[41]

Still, due to the phenomenal growth in the number of rural peasants in China's cities, over the years the government has been forced to make concessions regarding the rigid *hukou* system, though these policies have often lacked coherence. In the mid-1990s, in place of restrictions on temporary residence in cities, the Ministry of Labor required all migrants to obtain three certificates—an identification card (*shenfen zheng*), a temporary residence card (*zanzhu zheng*), and an employment card (*wugong zheng*)—so that they could legally live and work in cities. These cards were supposed to cost approximately 20 yuan total, but a survey conducted in 1996 among migrants in four cities revealed that most were paying ten or twelve times this much, meaning these cards had become another means of exploiting migrant workers.[42] For this reason, some migrants avoid obtaining these cards altogether, earning them the label of *sanwu* or the "three withouts."

In March 2003, a migrant named Sun Zhigang was stopped in Guangzhou, and when he was not able to produce any of his cards, he was put in a detention center in accordance with state regulations. While in confinement he was beaten to death, and his case generated such a public outcry that afterward the laws on forcible detentions and deportations of migrants without permits were changed.[43] Sun Zhigang was a college graduate with an urban (although non-local) *hukou*, which is the likely reason his case generated such outrage. However, after the rules were relaxed and more homeless and beggars were seen on the streets of many urban areas, repatriation and detention were quietly reinstituted, as were random ID checks.[44]

Other policies have also been implemented, but without the hoped-for results. As mentioned earlier, in 1998 *hukou* rules were amended so that children could inherit either the mother or father's *hukou* location. However, the wording of this law gave great latitude to individual provinces and municipalities, and it specifically stated that large cities like Beijing and Shanghai should strictly control the number of local *hukou*.[45] As a result, this policy was not formally written into law in Beijing until 2006.[46] Furthermore, while migrant children had previously been banned from attending urban schools, these restrictions were also gradually relaxed, although the prohibitive fees still keep many migrant children from enrolling. Instead, they attend poorly funded and substandard migrant schools, which in many cases are formally illegal and subject to periodic government closures.[47]

In line with neoliberal market polices, *hukou* has also been commodified in different regions. In 1993 *hukou* reforms carried out in a number of small towns and cities enabled migrants who had a stable residence and employment (of more than two years) to obtain an urban *hukou*.[48] Further measures in 2001—the so-called deep reform—eventually abolished migrant quotas in small towns and cities in order to absorb some of the millions of surplus rural workers who could not make a living by farming.[49] Policies in large cities have been more restrictive, such as the "blue-seal" *hukou*, which allows certain "talented"—meaning educated and/or wealthy—people to buy an urban *hukou*. When Beijing introduced such a scheme in 2001, it was explicitly for those who had invested heavily in private enterprises in the city.[50]

In 2005, a "fourth reform" of the *hukou* system (which was really a continuance of previous initiatives) had the goal of abolishing the agricultural/non-agricultural distinction and replacing it with a "nationally uniform *hukou* system" that would only distinguish between permanent versus temporary *hukou* (or local versus non-local). While this was hailed as a radical and progressive change in the *hukou* system by the Chinese and foreign media, critics have observed that the changes are merely "cosmetic" and in fact do not help China's peasant farmers or rural-to-urban migrants and in some cases may disadvantage them.[51] Moreover, changing the name of the type of *hukou* will not diminish the deep prejudices against migrant workers without other institutional reforms. In general, particularly in large and more prestigious cities, *hukou* reform has mainly privileged the wealthy and educated, while the vast majority of migrant workers in low-wage, unskilled jobs remain excluded.

Despite the lack of substantial *hukou* reform, in recent years the government has taken a somewhat more compassionate, though still contradictory, view of migrant laborers, in recognition of the fact that China's economy depends on them and that the countryside cannot support the large amount of rural surplus labor. Since 2003 the central government has promulgated a series of new regulations and laws that have focused on labor protection and limited social welfare benefits, such as medical insurance, for rural-to-urban migrants.[52] However, these have been unequally implemented and difficult to enforce. In 2007 there were further announcements about impending major *hukou* reforms. In May and June of 2010, the State Council issued pronouncements that once again included *hukou* reform.[53]

John Knight and Lina Song have called the *hukou* system an "institutionally imposed invisible Great Wall which divides rural and urban people and generates substantial differences in their levels of economic welfare."[54] This has recently become a *visible* wall in cities like Beijing. Under a "sealed management" policy ostensibly to reduce crime, the government has built walls around "villages" in outlying districts that are primarily home to migrants.[55] These walled enclaves, which are locked from 11:00 p.m. to 6:00 a.m., and are as much about control as they are about fighting crime, present a striking contrast to the gated communities that have arisen in recent years to house China's new rich. Although during the Mao era and the early years of the reforms, the *hukou* created institutionalized exclusion based on whether one was in a rural or urban area, its current effect has been to produce exclusion based on economic haves and have-nots.[56] The fact is that elites in urban areas have a vested interest in maintaining the *hukou*, as does a state that relies on the cheap labor of migrant workers. The vast gap that exists between the urban and rural population means that even if the *hukou* were actually abolished, the entrenched discrimination against rural residents would not quickly dissipate. Thus, China's *hukou* policy has profound implications for the experience of young rural-to-urban migrant women.

## China's *Dagongmei*

Although there are significant differences among those who "go out to labor" (*waichu dagong*) in China's urban areas in terms of demographic characteristics and reasons for migration, discursive constructions of age, gender, and rurality intersect with structural impediments such as the *hukou* to produce somewhat similar experiences of migration for young rural women.[57] Such an assertion is not meant to imply that young migrant women are a unified mass, yet a brief examination of migration patterns, discriminatory and exploitative labor conditions, and motivations for leaving home reveals how migration and multiple axes of identity are mutually constitutive.

*Migration Patterns and Employment*

In the early stage of the reforms the majority of migrants were male, yet recent years have seen greater gender parity.[58] Nearly 70 percent of female migrants are aged fifteen to twenty-nine, and slightly more female than male migrants make up the fifteen-to-nineteen and twenty-to-twenty-four age ranges.[59] The majority of these young women are single and unskilled, and they have usually completed at least some junior middle school. Most have not had formal jobs before, so they generally find employment that falls within the "three Ds:" dirty, dangerous, and demeaning. Young rural women's employment options are particularly circumscribed due to "notions of gender-appropriate labor" and multiple forms of discrimination that intersect with the *hukou* policy.[60] Like women involved in transnational migration around the globe, most find jobs as household maids (the *baomu* mentioned earlier), as unskilled industrial or low-level service workers, or as sex workers.[61] Those who are poorer or less educated tend to take lower-status jobs, which then combine with ethnic and regional differences to create further stratification within the migrant community.[62]

Female migrants are said to have lower job expectations than their male counterparts and, again like migrant women in other global contexts, are thought to be "docile" and less likely to protest unfair work conditions, though this is not necessarily true.[63] They do work that urban women are unwilling to do—work that is monotonous, low paying, and often arduous—and they are also excluded from many employment options reserved for urbanites. If they do have the same jobs as urban women, they receive less pay and have less job security. They also often make much less than their rural male counterparts even when age, education, and type of occupation are considered.[64] They are subject to various forms of exploitation

and harassment as they are often placed in situations where employers supervise them in both the workplace and their place of residence in
"parent-child" relationships. Those who work as domestics or in cottage
industries encounter a reduced access to social space due to long hours and
isolated working conditions while those in China's southern factories are
relegated to what has been called a "dormitory labor regime."[65] Even young
women employed in service work in the public arena tend to stay within
migrant social networks and find housing with employers or in cramped
rooms with relatives or other migrant women. Their relatively restricted
mobility within the city contrasts with male migrants' more unrestrained
movement.

*Motivations*

Despite the well-known hardships of the city, young rural women have
numerous motivations for migrating. In earlier research, the most common reasons given were to escape poverty or to improve the overall financial
status of the family; thus, several scholars have understood migration as a
household strategy, where a young woman's labor in an outside town or city
is designed to improve the economic standing of the entire family.[66] While
some scholars have found that money sent back home by female migrants
was important in improving the family's livelihood, others have disputed
the significance of remittances.[67] In general, rural women are less likely to
migrate for economic reasons compared to men.[68] In my fieldwork, only
those young women from the poorest families sent money home, and only a
handful did this on a regular basis.

   An emphasis on their own growth and fulfillment is indicative of the "second generation" or "new generation" of migrant workers, or those born in
the 1980s and 1990s, who, unlike their parents, have never known extreme
hunger and quite often have never engaged in farm work.[69] These young
women often decide to leave the village on their own for personal reasons,
in some cases against their parents' wishes. Some young women may migrate
in order to postpone marriage or to evade an unwelcome arranged marriage.
Because young women's production is considered surplus labor except in the
most impoverished rural households, others feel bored or useless at home
after dropping out or being forced to quit school (often so that another sibling, usually a male, can go to school). Migration thus offers a chance to "see

the world," "broaden one's horizons," and "seek opportunities for development" through learning new skills.

All of the above reasons indicate that, for many young rural women, labor migration is a way at least temporarily to gain some autonomy by escaping the restrictive patriarchal conditions of their villages, where they tend to occupy the bottom of the family hierarchy. Thus, several studies conducted during the 1990s found that more female than male migrant workers were likely to indicate that they were satisfied with their experience.[70] In her study of migrants in Chengdu, Louise Beynon found that more important than the women's wages or changes in their actual autonomy was "the *perception* of autonomy and independence," achieved through their making a "space of their own" in the city and escaping "rural drudgery."[71] Arianne Gaetano also asserts the importance of the symbolic value of migrating, but as secondary to the actual agency migrant women are able to exercise through their migration experience.[72] More recent surveys have found that few migrants, both male and female, are satisfied with their life in the city.[73] Nonetheless, for most it is still better than the lives they face back home.

Finally, the opportunity to save some money to be used for various purposes in the future cannot be underestimated. For example, a woman's earnings may improve her marital choices or her ability to start her own business some day.[74] Cindy Fan found that, for a significant number of women, their income from working in a city clearly helped to raise their status back home even though upon return they still had to contend with institutional and cultural forces that constrained their potential agency.[75] Rachel Murphy also noted that the experience of working in a city allows some rural women to gain enough income and skills to become entrepreneurs upon returning home. However, their success is hindered by smaller social networks, limited access to resources, and gender norms that emphasize a woman's role in tending to domestic concerns. Still, their urban experience gives them a certain amount of status and autonomy vis-à-vis their husbands and other relatives, and it often leads to their exercising forms of agency absent among non-migrant rural women.[76]

The above discussion shows that young women's migration must be viewed as a multifaceted phenomenon in which gender, class, age, and place intersect and are constitutive of flows of power at the level of the family, workplace, and larger institutions of contemporary China, most notably the *hukou* system and the structural and cultural barriers it has produced.

Such "gendered geographies of power" operate in transnational migration flows as well.[77] As with young Mexican men and women who go to work in the United States or in the *maquiladoras* along the U.S.-Mexican border, migration is now a "rite of passage" for China's rural youth.[78] The fact that so many young people (and able-bodied men) are engaged in labor migration while children, middle-aged women, and the elderly remain in the villages is expressed in a colloquial term for the countryside that has emerged in recent years: the "38-61-99 army" (*sanba liuyi jiujiu budui*), where "38" refers to International Women's Day (March 8th), "61" refers to International Children's Day (June 1st), and "99" is the "Double Ninth Festival" (September 9th), a Chinese holiday honoring the elderly.[79] At the same time, young people's rural-to-urban migration in China is distinct from transnational contexts due to China's particular modernization path, the legacy of the *hukou* system, and the state's embrace of certain neoliberal modes of governmentality, in particular the *suzhi* discourse, to which I now turn.

## Female Migrants and *Suzhi*

Certainly for many young women the allure of migration stems from how urban cosmopolitanism and modernity have been configured in China. For decades the nation's project of modernization has privileged the city, positioning it as the origin and source of a revitalized and proud Chinese economy, culture, and nation, and by extension, the desired location, or rather the *only* location for constructing a modern self. The countryside, by contrast, has been framed as an economic and spiritual wasteland, where remnants of "feudal" tradition and conservative and outmoded "peasant" values operate to lock people in perpetual stagnation. In Yan Hairong's words, "embedded in the post-Mao culture of modernity is an epistemic violence against the countryside that spectralizes the rural in both material and symbolic practices."[80] The discursive construction of the countryside as inherently wanting often ignores both Maoist and reform-era policies and institutions as well as global structural forces that have created this "social fact." It also neglects consideration of the diversity of China's countryside. Nonetheless, the chance to broaden one's horizons through exposure to an urban, globalized environment is a performance of modernity not available to those in China's small villages despite recent efforts to build a "new socialist countryside."

Constitutive of this "spectralization of the rural" is the notion of *suzhi*, or quality, which has become predominant in China in official as well as popular discourse in the past couple of decades. The English translation of "quality" does not really completely convey the Chinese meaning, which encompasses quality as a whole, as well as qualities, in particular one's bodily, moral, and educational *suzhi*.[81] The *suzhi* discourse first gained widespread prominence in China through propaganda campaigns designed to promote the one-child policy initiated in 1979, when limiting the number of China's people was seen as a way to improve the quality of China's population as a whole.[82] *Suzhi* was also invoked when China embarked on educational reforms in the late 1980s, where "education for quality" (*suzhi jiaoyu*) stressed "education for the purpose of improving the quality of the people."[83] *Suzhi* is now so widely used to evaluate so many domains that Yan calls it a "catch-all discursive basket" that denotes a new mode of value that necessitates a "structural adjustment in the sphere of human subjectivity."[84] *Suzhi* can thus be understood as a form of neoliberal governmentality, where self-development and self-management are key qualities of what Nikolas Rose calls the "enterprising self."[85]

In China, cultivating one's physical, moral, and psychological *suzhi* can take many forms. It generally entails developing skills, manners, self-discipline, and refinement, and this can be accomplished especially through work discipline and through education of all kinds, including learning a foreign language and gaining technical skills.[86] In current usage, *suzhi* implies qualities that are internalized at a deep level and that are based on one's upbringing. In order to avoid negative connotations, however, emphasis is placed on possibilities for improving *suzhi*.

All Chinese citizens are meant to shape themselves in accordance with the *suzhi* discourse, yet because understandings of *suzhi* produce distinct rankings of groups of people, both those in the countryside and migrants in the city are especially subject to critiques of their *suzhi*. One's internal *suzhi* is supposed to manifest in one's outward appearance, so migrants' lack of education and their supposed poor upbringing—a result of substandard educational facilities and poverty—are mapped onto their rustic appearance and behaviors, especially newly arrived migrants. The Chinese government at numerous levels has issued plans for raising migrants' *suzhi*, and training centers and labor recruitment organizations deploy the language of *suzhi* in their enlistment efforts.[87] It is no surprise, then, that popular discourse in China is frequently quite open about the perceived "backwardness" of

China's countryside. The media (and some scholars) especially deride the "low quality" of rural women,[88] and sensationalized news stories about the sexual depravity of rural women reinforce these stereotypes.[89]

For young migrant women, then, the city is often viewed as the *only* place where they can improve their *suzhi* through "gaining some skills" and becoming "modern." Compared to men, more female migrants place a high value on city life and more of them migrate to cities as opposed to townships or other villages.[90] Thus, as mentioned above, for many, more significant than the economic rewards or improvement in social status is the symbolic importance of migrating. Second-generation migrant workers, both male and female, are more likely than the generation before them to embrace city life and to strive to improve their *suzhi*. In the city, these migrants tend to compare themselves and their standard of living to their urban peers rather than their counterparts back home in their villages.[91] They are more likely to enroll in education and training courses in the city and are more inclined to participate in China's burgeoning consumer culture, as will be discussed below, through spending most of their salaries on consumer goods like clothing and mobile phones rather than sending remittances home.

## China's Consumer Revolution: From a "Society of Relative Comfort" to a "Harmonious Society"

When the Chinese government embarked on its economic reforms in the late 1970s, one of the key aims was raising the standard of living for China's citizens. As part of the modernization drive, Deng Xiaoping set a goal that ordinary people would be able to achieve "a '*xiaokang*' or a relatively comfortable life by the end of the century."[92] Between 1978 and 1990, per capita income doubled (after adjusting for inflation),[93] and it has continued to grow at an average annual rate of 8 percent.[94] Such processes, along with increases in inequality, have had a profound impact on how Chinese citizens from all backgrounds live their everyday lives.

During the planned economy, consumption in China was characterized by few choices and similar patterns among nearly the entire population; it also lingered at a basic subsistence level for thirty years.[95] Socialist asceticism was enforced through exhortations for "hard work and plain living" and through attacks on any pursuit of material comforts or luxury as evidence of "corrupt bourgeois culture."[96] The Deng-era leaders sought to repudiate this mode of

thinking and did so not only through policy reforms but also through ideological work that encouraged citizens to make and spend money. As mentioned earlier, the countryside first benefited from these reversals, and in the
early years of the reforms rural residents were quick to build new houses,
buy machinery, and enjoy better food. Urban consumers quickly followed
suit, starting in the mid-1980s.

China's booming economy and spending on domestic consumption were
temporarily slowed as a result of the government crackdown on Tiananmen
Square on June 4, 1989. However, after Deng Xiaoping's "Southern Tour" in
1992—in which he promoted further marketization and globalization, or a
"socialist market economy"—economic development, consumer spending,
and making money as a central goal became prominent features of Chinese
society. Deng's tour and the escalated economic reforms that followed were
as much about economic as political pragmatism. Since 1992 consumerism
has emerged as a dominant ideology and one way for the Communist Party
to preserve its legitimacy.[97]

This decades-long "consumer revolution," along with a neoliberal discourse that emphasizes entrepreneurialism and the enterprising self, has had
several consequences, especially since the mid-1990s. After the Third Ple-
num of the Fourteenth Party Congress in 1993, the regional disparities discussed earlier were exacerbated, yet urban inequality also grew as thousands
were laid off from state-owned enterprises. As work units began focusing on
productivity and efficiency, they in turn reduced many of the social welfare
benefits formerly guaranteed to their employees. The work unit also became
less and less associated with state-controlled consumption.[98] Deborah Davis
has argued that this separation of urban production and consumption—particularly as housing, food, and other resources were increasingly commodified—meant greater autonomy in daily life for urban residents as well as for
rural peasants, who were able to enter towns and cities to engage in business
and labor.[99]

The decreased importance of the work unit in urban residents' lives and
the gradual erosion of the power of the *hukou* system occurred simultaneously with the creation and marketization of new forms of leisure, entertainment, and self-fashioning. Prior to the 1990s, aside from outdoor parks there
were very few public areas for socializing, which meant that socializing usually took place in friends' homes, where an invitation to "dinner" could mean
spending the whole day as food was prepared, cooked, and leisurely eaten.

By the mid-1990s in cities like Beijing all kinds of western fast-food outlets and chain restaurants, bowling alleys, bars, and karaoke venues had cropped up.[100] Such places were not just indicative of increased foreign investment in China or the compromise legitimacy of the Party. They enabled new opportunities for sociality and personal networking as well as greater individual autonomy because socializing outside the home or work unit could take place away from the purview of employers and sometimes meddlesome colleagues.[101] The flood of foreign media—films, music, and magazines—as well as designer clothes and other luxury goods further influenced everyday values and desires for new lifestyles.

These new modes of consuming in turn created new modes of status differentiation, identity construction, and social polarization. When consumption was severely constrained during the Mao era, one's social status was primarily determined by one's class status and political correctness. Consumption was not completely severed from status connotations, however, as revealed in definitions of the "three big items" (*da sanjian*) that delineated the most desirable consumer items in different eras: bicycles, wristwatches, and sewing machines in the 1960s and 1970s; washing machines, color TVs, and refrigerators in the 1980s; and telephones, air conditioners, and VCRs in the 1990s.[102] Now there are so many goods and so much wealth in China that the *da sanjian* has become a notion of the past.

In a nation where the exchange of political rights for material comforts has been solidified as state policy, consumer citizenship—the expression of agency and identity through consumption practices[103]—has become for many the primary means of signifying their place and worth in the Chinese nation.[104] The influx into China of designer clothing boutiques and upscale household-furnishing stores attests to this fact, as they are meant to cater to a rising class of educated, private entrepreneurs and young white-collar workers who define themselves through following local and global trends in clothing fashions, personal style, and consumer electronics. Some have thus noted that commercial freedoms have created a space for greater civil liberties and political autonomy in China.[105] As Ong and Zhang argue, however, consumption as part of broadened notions of individual expression exists within a social domain that is constituted by its interrelationship with an authoritarian Chinese state, or what they deem "socialism from afar."[106] Furthermore, the neoliberal principles that the state has adopted favor the elite and rising middle class as long as they do not cross certain discursive boundaries set by the state. In other words, those with "high *suzhi*," whose personal consumption and entrepreneurial activities drive China's economic growth, enjoy a form of citizenship that "low *suzhi*" groups are incited to desire but are denied. Rural residents, rural-to-urban migrants, and laid-off urban workers have been severely constrained or left out altogether from participating in the modes of consumption that have come to define belonging, success, and one's "quality" in contemporary China.

These disparities are by no means accidental. When Deng Xiaoping set forth the goal of enabling ordinary people to achieve a "relatively comfortable life," he was explicitly referencing a classical-era text—*The Record of Rites* (*Liji*). As Lu Hanlong notes, "This society of 'relative comfort,' where people pursued private interests and gave priority to advancing family interests, was … considered morally inferior to the society of 'great equality' " that had preceded it.[107] For Deng and the other reformers it was therefore seen as a middle ground, on the way toward equality for all, and it was acknowledged that inequality would occur—"some must get rich first and then others will follow"—and state-imposed laws would be necessary to regulate people's actions.[108]

Many did in fact get rich, but many others did not follow, as indicated by the urban-to-rural income disparities discussed earlier. As certain policies have engendered a rising middle class, in recent years China has become increasingly socially stratified, not only in terms of rural-urban but also intra-urban inequality.[109] However, in popular discourse and official rhetoric, because "class" has deep connotations with the "class struggle" and antagonism perpetuated under Mao, the language of class (*jieji*) has been erased and replaced by that of "social strata" (*shehui jieceng*).[110] The irony is that while "strata" is supposed to displace "a class-based conflict model," class polarization has all the while dramatically intensified.[111]

After increasing unrest in rural areas and concerns about overall social stability in the wake of rapid marketization and development, in 2004 President Hu Jintao put forth a vision of constructing a "harmonious society" (*hexie shehui*) rather than focusing solely on economic growth.[112] In 2006 the Hu Jintao–Wen Jiabao leadership began efforts to build a "new socialist countryside," in particular by enacting policies to ease the economic burden on China's peasants—such as building rural infrastructure, lifting a centuries-old agricultural tax, and eliminating tuition fees for rural schools—and to raise their incomes in order to spur domestic consumption in the countryside.[113] The government's $586-billion stimulus package in November 2008 in the midst of the global economic downturn was also partially aimed at achieving similar goals, yet given the rampant corruption in China, especially at the local level, it is unclear if the desired outcomes will be achieved.

## The Construction/Consumption of Femininity in the Post-Mao Era

New forms of distinction and discrimination based on social strata or spatial separation are only one result of China's consumer revolution. In line with China's market reforms as a whole, it has also had profound implications for men and women's status and for hegemonic notions of gender. At the earliest stages of the reforms, women's position in society and the discursive construction of gender quickly seemed to take "two steps forward, one step back."[114] As Maoist notions of "equality" gave way to an emphasis on "quality" (*suzhi*), starting in the early 1980s due to the downsizing of unprofitable state-owned enterprises, many middle-aged urban women were the first to be laid off, forced into early retirement (*xiagang*), or urged to "return home" in order to leave jobs for men.[115] The discarding of "old" female workers along with the stagnant, centrally planned economy has been paralleled by the rise of an urban-based service economy. As a result, new gender-segregated occupations have emerged, affecting both urban and rural women. As Zhang Zhen notes, in post-socialist China, the rusted "iron rice bowl" has been replaced by the "rice bowl of youth" (*qingchunfan*), a term referring to the trend in urban areas in which "a range of new, highly paid positions have opened almost exclusively to young women" as long as they are attractive and demure.[116] Images of "vivacious, young female eaters of the rice bowl of youth" thus signify "a fresh labor force, a model of social mobility, and the rise of a consumer culture endorsed by current official ideology."[117]

This "rice bowl of youth" has emerged in tandem with the relatively new urban spaces for commodity consumption mentioned earlier. In high-end restaurants, bars, and clubs, and in shopping malls filled with designer boutiques, young women trade their looks for material comfort. Female university graduates as well are required not only to have brains but also beauty, and they are at a disadvantage when competing with their male counterparts because they are often expected to have higher skills and to meet certain height and weight standards.[118] In numerous service agencies that have emerged in the reform era, young, educated, attractive urban women have become—along with the establishments in which they are employed—signifiers of Chinese cosmopolitan modernity. In post-socialist China's teleology, they represent progress and the future, in contrast to the anachronistic, "worn-out," laid-off middle-aged female workers.

While such consumption and commodification of female bodies in the workplace represents a mode of sexual politics far removed from the Mao era, it has ties with both China's patriarchal traditions and with what L. H. M. Ling has termed contemporary "global hypermasculinity," or the way in which the state's "manly" pursuit of economic development renders its citizens as "hyperfeminized": subordinate and self-sacrificing yet lacking a political voice.[119] Of course, it is not only young urban women that are commodified in contemporary China but also migrant women whose labor power is necessary for China's development. As mentioned earlier, young migrant women are funneled into gender-specific occupations where their labor is desired and consumed precisely because it is feminized and sexualized. While currently nearly 38 percent of urban women are engaged in so-called female jobs, nearly 56 percent of female migrants are employed in the lower strata of such jobs that entail long hours and minimal pay.[120]

The rise of a gender-segregated labor market to fill the consumer demands of a primarily urban populace has occurred hand-in-hand with essentialized notions of gender in popular and official discourse in contemporary China.[121] Like so many arenas that have undergone substantial reorganizing since 1978, current gender ideologies have evolved through the invocation of deeply engrained patriarchal cultural values and a simultaneous concerted effort by the Chinese state and many of its citizenry to reject and bury its Maoist past. Mao famously declared that women "hold up half the sky," and during the Mao era women's participation in the labor force was assumed to ensure their emancipation. Though there is still debate about to what degree Chinese women were truly liberated under Mao and to what extent their liberation was "postponed," most agree that women's equality hinged on their adherence to male norms.[122] Such state-regulated gender "equality" was extremely visible during the Cultural Revolution, when large numbers of women participated in the public realms of labor and politics. As molding the collective and expunging individuality became paramount, femininity or any assertion of a feminine identity was virtually eliminated and there arose what Mayfair Yang has called an " 'erasure of gender and sexuality' (xingbie muosha) in public space."[123] This "gender erasure" was manifested in androgynous styles for women, including baggy clothing, cropped or braided hair, and makeup-free faces, as well as women's maintenance of a bodily comportment, speaking style, and mannerisms that adhered to dominant masculine standards.[124] The most iconic image of women from this time is that of the fabled "Iron Girls," a group of young female workers who were industrious, brave, technically skilled, and symbolic of the boundless energy and unswerving enthusiasm necessary to build socialist China. They represented the Maoist slogan that "the times have changed, whatever a man can do, a woman can do too."[125]

In contemporary China, the rise of a consumer culture has been paralleled by heightened notions of essentialized gender, where women's "natural" qualities and abilities (or lack thereof) relegate them to certain segments of society and the economy.[126] With the reforms of the late 1970s and the lifting of state-imposed androgyny, many women were eager to assert a "female consciousness"[127]—a selfhood they felt had been subsumed by Maoist rhetoric and one that was easily commodified in the form of feminine fashions, cosmetics, permed hair, and other outward manifestations of dominant modes of femininity. As a way to repudiate Mao and in particular the Cultural Revolution, the gender politics of that era were said to be an embarrassment and, like much of the Maoist past, out of line with human nature. A public discourse emphasizing "natural" gender distinctions based on biological traits thus became prominent, with women constructed as having special charms, grace, and gentleness.[128] Since then, such constructions of essentialized gender can be found in both popular and official discourse in everything from tracts on youth sex and dating to medical advice.[129]

However, the most noticeable forms of these essentialized gender distinctions appear in the mediated images of women in the advertisements, beauty magazines, and television shows and films that have proliferated as a result of marketization and globalization.[130] While Chinese women in media representations of the 1980s were often cute, coy, or delicate, now they are just as likely to be provocative and highly sexualized. As in the West, these images are both highly alluring and vastly out of reach for many women. Still, they serve a pedagogical role about the meaning of gender in contemporary China. In Harriet Evans's words, they are "important indicators of the ways in which state and market, often indistinguishable in the way they operate, make use of—and exclude—women's bodies for commercial and political purposes."[131] Moreover, the commodification of women's bodies in both the workplace and the realm of representations is indicative of local and global intersections and understandings of gender and labor. Just as the labor force presents limited options for certain women, mainstream construction of gender "collapse the possibilities of femininity and femaleness into a composite image that is urban, educated, content, materially successful and beautiful."[132] It is no wonder, then, that the majority of media in China are targeted at this urban, educated elite.[133]

Thus, certain notions of what it means to be a modern woman in China today negate others, and certain women, especially female rural-to-urban migrants, are erased from constructions of ideal femininity. Women's bodies then become both objects to be consumed and projects to be improved. As will be further explored in chapter 2, consumer practices and associated notions of essentialized gender—and increasingly those linked to the consumption of technology—have become a crucial means for migrant women to claim a "modern," female identity.

## Telecommunications Development in the Reform Era

To lay the foundation for this study of rural-to-urban migrant women's mobile phone assemblage, one final realm that must be explored is the extremely rapid growth in telecommunications that has taken place during the reform era. Of particular importance are not only the growth of China's fixed-line and mobile phones, but also how transformations in technology diffusion and access—the result of state policies and priorities as part of China's modernization and integration into global capitalism—have created new modes of inclusion and exclusion.

### Early Growth

Maoist modernity—with its unswerving faith in a teleological drive toward a Communist utopia—recognized the importance of technological development. For Mao, however, technology was mostly associated with industrialization that would be achieved through mass mobilization of the productive forces. Under Mao, the state-owned telecommunications system was relatively underdeveloped, highly centralized, and focused only on the needs of the party elite.[134] In 1975, China's teledensity (the number of telephones per one hundred persons) was only 0.33 (a rate achieved in the United States by the late 19th century).[135]

When Deng Xiaoping and his fellow reformers came to power, they prioritized investment in telecommunications and transportation in order to spur economic growth, attract foreign capital, and raise people's standard of living.[136] From 1985 to 1990, telecommunications services grew at an annual rate double that of China's soaring gross domestic product, which averaged 10 to 12 percent annually.[137] From 1990 to the beginning of 1993, the growth rate was four times that of GDP.[138]

Despite the government's stated goal that ordinary citizens would be able to enjoy telecommunications, during the 1980s telephones continued to be configured as devices for the elite. Although installation rates previously had been very low, in 1980 China's Posts and Telecommunications Bureau began to charge an exorbitant 2,000 yuan (about US $297)[139] per installation, and by the end of the decade this fee had increased to 6,000 yuan and in some places was even as much as 20,000. Despite the outrageous cost, many people were willing to pay and to wait up to two years to get a phone installed in their homes.[140] Of course, millions could not afford such fees, and in the early 1990s it was not uncommon for two or even three families to share the same line. Like much of China's development, urban households were favored over rural households in the growth of telephony. In 1990, the urban-to-rural ratio of fixed-line phones in homes was 3.7:1, and only 0.29 percent of the total rural population had landlines in their homes.[141] Eastern coastal regions and SEZs—in line with development priorities—also prevailed: in 1992 the seven most developed eastern cities and SEZs comprised 51 percent of the fixed-line telephones in the nation while the seven poorest and least developed provinces (all inland) accounted for just 5 percent.[142]

Mobile phone use in China at this time was even more limited and stratified. The nation's first analog mobile phone service was established in Guangzhou in 1987, but the growth in mobile phone subscriptions in China, as in much of the rest of the world at this time, was quite slow. By 1992, China had 176,943 mobile phone subscriptions, mostly concentrated in eastern coastal regions, out of a population of 1.17 billion.[143] This small number was due to lack of infrastructure and astronomical fees. In the early and mid-1990s, a cell phone and a registration could cost as much as $4,000, which has been estimated to be the highest in the world at that time relative to per capita income.[144] In the 1990s, the colloquial term for a mobile phone—*dageda,* or "Big Brother Big," a reference to Hong Kong gangsters—reflected its status as a tool reserved for the (usually male) government and business elite, whose work unit picked up the tab for the cost of the phone and the monthly service.[145]

### "Market Socialism" and the "Telecommunications Revolution"

Like China's development in general, the expansion of telecommunications (and the real diffusion of mobile phones) escalated after Deng Xiaoping's Southern Tour and the government's subsequent all-out embrace of the "socialist market economy." As mentioned earlier, starting from the mid-1990s China sought to more rapidly transition from a centrally planned to a market-oriented economy and from an agrarian to an industrialized, urban society. Such transformations not only have had profound implications for urban-rural inequality and rural-to-urban migration, but they also are intricately connected to China's telecommunications growth.[146] In other words, the "diffusion of information technology throughout the country cannot be understood in isolation from China's industrialization. Both processes are in turn closely related to the penetration of the Chinese economy by market forces."[147]

Thus, as China increasingly emphasized marketization, it simultaneously pursued industrialization and "informatization"—or the development of information communication technology (ICT) infrastructure, applications, and services.[148] While the years prior to 1992 are often characterized as the first stage of China's telecommunications development in the reform era, the period after 1992 is distinguished by four subsequent stages that have each greatly contributed to the integration of telephony—both fixed and mobile—as well as the Internet into people's everyday lives. Though China's telecommunications growth during this period has been heralded as a "miracle on top of a miracle," the same policies that simultaneously spurred economic growth while exacerbating urban-rural and regional inequality have also led to the uneven development of China's telecommunications system.[149]

In the second stage of telecom development, liberalization began as the monopoly of the Ministry of Post and Telecommunications (MPT) was challenged by the establishment in 1994 of China Unicom, a joint venture of three different government ministries and thirteen large state-owned companies.[150] When China Unicom formed, the State Council asked the MPT to restructure its organization and to become a regulator that would guard the interests of the state and the public. A separate branch of the MPT then created China Telecom as a means of competing with China Unicom. However, China Telecom's finances and planning were managed by the MPT, which then enjoyed a twin status as both an operator and a regulator. China Unicom could not adequately compete with China Telecom or the MPT, yet it had the support of the central government, and its creation contributed to a viable telecom market, especially in mobile telephony, as will be discussed below.

The third stage of China's telecommunications development began in March 1998 when the Ministry of Information Industry (MII) was created through the merger of the MPT and two other ministries in preparation for China's joining the World Trade Organization (WTO). With this institutional reorganization, for the first time in PRC history, regulation and operation functions were separated from one another.[151] One of the first actions of the newly formed MII was to lower service fees for international calls and Internet usage.[152] The MII also drastically reformed the telecom industry in order to make it more competitive. In February 1999, China Telecom's virtual monopoly of the telecommunications sector ended when it was divided into four separate companies. As a result, the original China Telecom became a fixed-line provider and China Mobile was created for mobile communications.[153] China Unicom focused on cellular telephony, receiving all of China Mobile's Code Division Multiple Access (CDMA) operations and networks, thereby increasing competition.[154]

The fourth stage of China's telecommunications development began in 2001, after China joined the WTO. This stage saw further liberalization of China's market, a reduction in fees for various types of calling and services, and an increase in value-added services.[155] At this juncture, China had six major state-owned telecom companies, with China Telecom and China Netcom responsible for most fixed-line telephony and China Mobile and China Unicom as the two main mobile phone providers. The fifth stage was completed in October 2008 and resulted in three major telecom companies— China Telecom, China Mobile, and China Unicom—all state-owned and all offering fixed-line, mobile, and broadband services. These are all overseen by the Ministry of Industry and Information Technology (MIIT), formed in 2008 to replace the MII. The purported goal of this restructuring was to increase competition and lay the groundwork for the issuance of third-generation (3G) licenses.[156]

As a result of all of these changes, throughout the 1990s and into the new millennium China's fixed-line telephony continued to expand rapidly. By the early 2000s, reflecting China's urban-centered development strategy, most people in cities had private phones in their homes.[157] By 2007 China had roughly 365 million fixed-line telephone subscribers, with a teledensity of 27.8.[158] However, though market liberalization brought competition and expanded service, it also meant that an emphasis on revenues took precedence over equitable access.[159] Thus, the uneven development policies discussed earlier were paralleled in telecom growth, as urban areas had more than double the number of fixed-line phones as the countryside. Still, during this period rural areas also saw tremendous improvements in access to landline telephones, partly through market forces and partly through state policy. For example, the government's *Cuncuntong Dianhua* (Village-to-Village Telephone) project, implemented in the mid-1990s to try to bring universal service (meaning at least one publicly available phone) to remote rural areas, met 80 percent of its goal by 2000, when it was halted.[160] It was brought back a few years later, with the goal that the most remote villages would have at least two telephones, one of which would be publicly accessible.[161] Though all of these accomplishments are significant, they have been dwarfed by China's remarkable growth in mobile telephony over the last decade, which has been constitutive of communications transformations at all levels of society, especially for more marginalized groups like rural-to-urban migrants.

*The Mobile Revolution*

The expansion of mobile telephony in China must be seen within the context of China's distinct economic and telecommunications policies as well as the worldwide growth in mobile telephony—at the end of 2009 there were an estimated 4.6 billion mobile phone subscriptions for a global penetration rate of approximately 67 percent.[162] Particularly in developing countries, the phenomenal expansion of cell phones appears to reflect these countries' "leap-frogging" from minimal fixed-line teledensity to large-scale cellular phone access.

As mentioned above, prior to the Chinese government's protracted efforts at restructuring the telecom industry, cell phone usage in China was very limited. After China Unicom was created in 1994, however, mobile phone subscriptions began to grow exponentially: from 3,629,416 in 1995 to nearly double that by 1996.[163] By the early 2000s, as the cost of handsets and services declined, mobile phones became increasingly ubiquitous in China's cities. In 2000, China had 85.3 million mobile phone subscriptions; by 2002 this number had increased to 206 million, and in 2006 there were 461 million.[164] By November 2011 China had roughly 975 million mobile phone subscribers, the highest number in the world and representing a penetration rate of around 74 percent.[165]

For much of the early 2000s, the bulk of mobile phone subscriptions were located in China's urban centers and in some wealthier rural areas in eastern coastal provinces. For example, in 2001 while the eastern region of the country had a cell phone penetration rate of 19.30 per 100 people, China's central and western regions had rates of 7.75 and 7.20, respectively.[166] As large cities became relatively saturated with mobile phones and the number of new subscriptions declined, China's mobile operators began to look to rural areas as a source of new growth. In 2007, China Mobile added roughly 68 million new subscribers and nearly half of these were in rural areas,[167] yet at this time there were still many parts of rural China with few mobile phones and where some people had never had landlines in their homes. By 2011, however, nearly 90 percent of rural Chinese homes had mobile phones.[168]

### MOBILE USE

The proliferation of mobile phones in China reflects rising demand, expanded service, decreased user costs, and the growth of both the foreign and domestic handset markets. As mobile phones have diffused, in line with the consumption patterns discussed earlier, a highly stratified dual structure of cell phone pricing, service plans, and user practices has emerged. While the elite and rising middle-class use global brand-name smartphones and 3G services, what Cartier, Castells, and Qiu have termed the "information have-less," which includes migrant workers, laid-off employees of state-owned enterprises, and retirees, tend to buy domestic-brand, second-hand, or copy-cat (*shanzhai*) phones.[169] Such stratification is manifest in advertising discourses as well. All over major cities like Beijing, in addition to glitzy shopping malls selling high-end devices, billboards display extremely sexualized images of young women or trendy young men with a mobile phone as the ultimate signifier of urban cool (see figure 3). In contrast, in the countryside, China Mobile's text-only ads—white and red Chinese characters painted atop a bright blue background—are more likely to be found on village walls, sometimes in place of "one-child only" slogans, their commercial messages substituting one form of propaganda for another (see figure 4).

Fig. 3 (top). A Motorola ad in Beijing, November 2006. Fig. 4 (above). A China Mobile ad in a village outside Hefei, Anhui province, October 2009.

### PRICING, PLANS, AND PRESTIGE

China's elite (those with "high *suzhi*") use postpaid cell phone services; however, 87 percent of the nation's mobile subscribers use prepaid phone cards.[170] Vendors selling prepaid cards, often in increments of 50 to 100 yuan (approximately US $6.50 to $13.00), are ubiquitous in supermarkets, outdoor newsstands, and mobile phone stores. Such cards usually offer a variety of pricing plans, including bulk-rate text and instant messaging, a flat fee for mobile Internet use, as well as voice calling where the caller pays but the receiver is not charged. Low-income users like rural-to-urban migrants value such cards for their flexibility;

also, because migrants don't have the income, permanent address, and bank account that postpaid services require, the prepaid cards are more convenient.

Mobile phone usage plans in China are not merely innocuous economic configurations based on rational market forces, however. Like so many other products and services that have arisen in the past decade or so, they bear distinct attributes intended to bestow status and differentiation among users. One of the most noticeable examples of this distinction derives from mobile phone numbers themselves. First, cell phone numbers reveal whether a person is a China Mobile or China Unicom subscriber. China Mobile is the incumbent in the mobile phone market, and as such it tends to offer better coverage and more service options in most areas and thus bestows higher prestige.[171] Second, one's number also reveals the type of service plan one has. For example, China Mobile's "GoTone brand" provides subscribers with a variety of services, including international roaming, mobile Internet, mobile banking,  multimedia messaging service (MMS), global positioning system (GPS), and "mobile secretary." Beyond phone services, GoTone, as the package for "high-end customers," also offers VIP clients "distinguished" airport lounges and a professional-style country club.[172] On China Mobile's website, the company boasts of GoTone's "intangible assets" that are "symbolized in success, self-confidence, and high taste."[173] The blurb for the service even indirectly invokes the language of *suzhi* by comparing GoTone customers' level and quality of "development" to its own.[174] This information is not only available to subscribers or those who have perused China Mobile's promotional materials. Especially in its earlier days, GoTone's prefixes (1340 through 1390) conferred status on their users, especially the 1390 prefix, which signified early adoption of mobile telephony.[175]

Regardless of provider or service plan, one's mobile phone number itself is a mark of prestige. Unlike in the United States where numbers are usually randomly assigned to a cell phone subscriber, in China, SIM cards with mobile numbers must be purchased separately in order to use a phone. Because mobile numbers in China are rather long (eleven digits), numbers that have repeating digits are more expensive because they are easier to remember. Phone numbers are also more costly based on whether they are "lucky" or "unlucky." A phone number with a large amount of eights, for example, will be more expensive, and again confer status, because eight is an auspicious number in Chinese culture. On the other hand, a number ending in four (a homonym for death in Chinese) will be inexpensive and possibly create discomfort for a caller.

### SHORT MESSAGING SERVICE, INSTANT
### MESSAGING, AND SOCIAL NETWORKING

SMS, or short messaging service, also known as text messaging, is an extremely popular form of mobile communication in China. In 2007, 592.1 billion text messages were sent, for an average of 1.6 billion per day and a daily revenue of 160 million yuan (roughly US $21 million).[176] Unlike in Japan, text messaging is not used in China in order to preserve the sanctity of public space. On the contrary, on public transportation, in restaurants, and in stores loud mobile phone conversations are the norm, but these are not necessarily seen as impolite. Instead, one major reason for the popularity of SMS is that it is extremely cheap. One message costs 0.10 yuan or about 1.3 US cents (compared to 0.40 to 0.60 yuan per minute for a local voice call). As mentioned above, bundles of text messages are often offered as part of a service plan, bringing the cost down even more, which is extremely important for low-income users who tend to make far fewer voice calls than wealthier users do.

In China, as elsewhere, recent years have seen a convergence of mobile telephony and the Internet. By the end of 2011, China had 513 million Internet users, and roughly 69 percent had accessed the Internet via mobile phones.[177] Particularly noteworthy is that after 2008 instant messaging and social networking services could be accessed via cell phones relatively inexpensively. Social differentiation has been manifested in these sites as well, as Renren and Kaixin001 cater to university students and white-collar workers, respectively, while QQ is favored by rural-to-urban migrants. Value-added services, such as horoscopes, games, and music by content providers like Kongzhong and Sina, also intentionally target a mostly lower-income youth market.[178] This perpetuation of social differentiation via telecommunications thus reveals the continuity of China's developmental path, where modernization, marketization, and privatization have always resulted in multiple forms of stratification—economic, social, geographical, informational, and, now, digital.

## Conclusion

China has now been in a "post-Mao era" for longer than the Great Helmsman's policies ruled what was at the time a quarter of the world's population. However, the remarkable transformations that have taken place in China since "reform and opening" began in the late 1970s and escalated in the 1990s under the banner of "socialism with Chinese characteristics" have been just as profound as, and for some no less traumatic than, the endless campaigns and societal and political reorganizations characteristic of Mao's revolutionary society. At the same time, the disjunctures of "modernization" undertaken through privatization, marketization, and integration into global capitalism have been accompanied by continuities as well, particularly the enduring cultural and structural legacies that manifest in uneven development and social and informational stratification.

It is important to note that the urban-rural divide discussed throughout this chapter is not uniquely Chinese, as one can find parallels across the globe, especially in places that have had disparate encounters with western modernity. Moreover, China's concentration of development along the eastern coastal regions cannot be separated from the interests of foreign capital and global neoliberal market imperatives. Nonetheless, such global forces find particular localized logics in China as a result of—among other things—specific development strategies, the *hukou* policy, the *suzhi* discourse, patriarchal gender norms, a large rural populace, and a party-state that has foregrounded economic growth and rising consumption as a means of maintaining legitimacy.

As discussed throughout this chapter, China's rural-to-urban migrants are constrained by numerous structural and institutional forces. Amidst the designer boutiques, sports cars, and luxury housing that now dominate large cities like Beijing, and against various forms of discrimination and hardship, migrant workers continue to strive for a better life and to partake in the fruits of China's various "revolutions." The remainder of this book examines how one particular segment of this population—young rural-to-urban migrant women—make meaning, enrich their lives, exercise agency and autonomy, and at times even reinforce their subordination through their engagement with mobile phones.

2

## "My First Big Urban Purchase"

*Mobile Technologies and Modern Subjectivity*

None of my friends from my village are still at home. Everyone has
gone out to work. At home there is nothing. Beijing is developed.
Here I can learn something, but at home there is just farming, and
I'm not good at that.
—Cui Yiping, Beijing, January 20, 2007

In the fall of 2006, I traveled each week to Changping, a suburb in the north-
west of Beijing, to visit a group of thirty-two young women enrolled in a
three-month computer course at the Practical Skills Training Center for
Rural Women. The school is overseen by the Beijing Cultural Development
Center for Rural Women and was designed to provide various types of training—computer literacy, hairstyling, waitressing—for rural women from poor
provinces who were recruited by local Women's Federation cadres.[1] At the
time of my weekly journey to the school—via bike, subway, and bus—Beijing
was in a frantic whirl of preparations for the 2008 Summer Olympics. All
around the city as migrant laborers toiled on construction sites, the *"fuwas"*
(or friendlies), the official mascots of the games, graced everything from billboards to water bottles. While the young women I knew at the school learned
to input Chinese characters and to navigate Microsoft Office, schoolchildren

across the nation studied a special Olympic curriculum, taxi drivers in Beijing struggled to practice rudimentary English, and Beijing residents were instructed—via billboards, neighborhood committees, and public service announcements—on how to conduct themselves properly during the festivities.[2] Marquees strategically placed around the city counted down the days, hours, and minutes until the Games, and in November, when the government hosted forty African heads of state for a trade summit in the midst of blue skies and pristine streets—the result of temporary traffic controls, shuttered factories, and a police sweep of beggars and hawkers—the glitch-free meeting was seen as a successful test run for the main event. In its mission to present a modern, disciplined, "harmonious society" (*hexie shehui*) to the outside world, the government was sparing no effort and no expense.

During my fieldwork, the official reinvention of the nation and the capital was the focus of numerous domestic and international news reports, yet a parallel though much more quotidian quest for personal transformation was manifest in all of the young migrant women I knew. Whether through formal training, such as at the school, or through self-study and on-the-job experience, all expressed a desire to "develop themselves," as they often put it, through working and "studying." For many, their experiences in Beijing made them acutely aware of the differences between their lives at home and the lifestyle and standard of living of many Beijing residents. Those from remote areas were particularly prone to contrasting Beijing with their home villages, which they said were "not developed" and were "very poor."

These young women's framing of their journey to Beijing as an opportunity both for self-development and for an escape from an "undeveloped" rural home reveals how China's internal discourse of development—development of the nation and of individuals—is a powerful force in young rural women's migration decisions. In this context, development is not only associated with economic betterment and the acquisition of new knowledge, but it is also an entry into an imagined modernity—constructed as urban and in opposition to rural "tradition"—that promises personal transformation and access to a new type of life.[3] For rural women, to "develop oneself" means, among other things, gaining skills that enable one to earn a living doing something other than agriculture; participating in consumer practices such as buying cosmetics and fashionable clothes; and enjoying various forms of entertainment and communication. We know from the work of several scholars that these are familiar discourses that migrant women use when discussing their experience in the city,[4] yet we know less about the myriad ways in which such discourses have become articulated to new media technologies. However, as much as access to a technological artifact such as a mobile phone is a spatial manifestation of a nation's technological progress (and equitable diffusion of technology), it also shapes individual desire and subjectivity. As one student, Gu Xia, told me in 2006, "It wasn't until I left my village that I saw a mobile phone. We didn't have them there. My home had a landline. I've seen those, but it wasn't until later when I left that I saw a mobile phone."[5] Her classmate added, "You see other people using a mobile phone and you feel envious. I see it and feel like I want one now. As soon as I earn some money I want to buy a mobile phone."[6] Among other migrant women I knew in Beijing in 2006 and 2007, mobile phones existed in their home villages, but the city offered the opportunity to have the means to afford one. In 2010, this was often still the case even as mobile telephony had increasingly spread to more remote rural areas and more and more rural teens and young adults were owning cell phones.[7]

How do young rural women's understanding and usage of mobile phones intersect with China's discourses of development and modernity? How do gendered practices of self-transformation, which have been documented in earlier accounts of migrant women's lives, coalesce around mobile technologies? What desires and emotions are articulated to mobile phones that are constitutive of diverse expressions of modernity? Can acquisition of a mobile phone be configured as a particular form of citizenship? To return to James Carey's metaphor of communication as transmission and ritual, one could say that as grand symbols *of* and *for* reality, mobile phones are constitutive of a world of technological advancement, of information that flows within "timeless time" and the "space of flows."[8] In this chapter, however, I turn my attention to the ways in which cell phones as ritual have become part of the "symbolic order" and as such are articulated to young migrant women's self-formation in the city, which results in what could be called a hybrid rural-urban subjectivity. This subjectivity is infused with gender, class, age, and place-based meanings that are differentially mapped onto rural and urban bodies, and it is hybrid because it is characterized by a liminality that resists yet does not displace socially constructed binaries of rural-urban (the young women I knew unanimously asserted that they would never be "Beijing people").[9]

My choice of "modernity" as a frame for this discussion is certainly not to reinscribe a binary in which the rural (and its inhabitants) is "primitive" and the urban is "modern," but rather to unpack how these binaries that are continuously reproduced in official and popular discourse in China have become territorialized in and through migrant women's engagement with mobile technologies. My goal is to show how discursive constructions that are constitutive of China's modernization and quest for "development"—including changing conceptions of gender, an emphasis on self-fashioning, particular notions of citizenship and belonging, and a powerful narrative about individual "quality"—are linked to technological consumption and competence.

In the remainder of this chapter, I discuss the mobile phone as it is articulated to and constitutive of modernity. I examine a duality whereby a cell phone plays a key role in producing a modern, urban female subjectivity while at the same time demanding competencies and producing certain disciplines that can lead to exclusion, thus revealing the multiple logics of what I call "immobile mobility," or how a mobile phone offers a means of surpassing, but not erasing, limiting material conditions. I then focus on a particular location—a beauty salon—to explore more deeply the gendered uses and discourses surrounding cell phones. Though part of this chapter presents a historical moment in time—2006 and 2007 in Beijing—and certain aspects of this mobile phone assemblage have transformed since then, my aim is to present a broader theoretical argument about understandings of mobile telephony. That is, a mobile phone should not be read as merely a cool accoutrement of a "global youth culture," as a status symbol, or a social networking tool. Instead, young migrant women's particular understandings of both migration and technology evolve from government discourses of development as well as internalization and translation of these into "technologies of the self." To frame this discussion, I begin with a brief detour through some of the central tenets of modernity as well as feminist and postcolonial interventions in understandings of modernity.

## Modernit(ies)

After I graduated from the middle school in our village, I wanted to go to high school. My older sister was attending the Normal University in Jilin City. Then my parents told me they didn't have the money to send me to high school because of my sister's tuition fees. I was so upset. I felt so betrayed by my mother, and I was so angry I decided to leave and never go back. I had 110 yuan [about US $14] and bought a train ticket to Beijing. It was twenty-two hours and I had a hard seat, but since I had never traveled by train before I didn't know I had a seat and I stood the whole way. When I arrived in Beijing, I took a bus to Dongzhimen, not really even knowing where that was. I had 30 yuan left at that point. I got off the bus and walked around for a while. Everything was strange and I didn't know anyone. Eventually I walked into a restaurant and asked for a job. I told the owner I wouldn't take a job unless housing was also provided, and he agreed. The second day I was in Beijing I called home from a pay phone to tell my parents where I was.... It's hard here, but I've learned a lot and developed myself, and I've never regretted what I did.[10]

The story above was told to me in the fall of 2006 by a young woman I knew named Xiao Luo as we were eating lunch with another Chinese friend in a restaurant specializing in local Beijing cuisine. It was one of Xiao Luo's rare days off from her job waiting tables, and she had graciously agreed to talk with me about her experiences in the city. At the time, she had been in Beijing for about four years, and as far as she knew she was still the only one in her village who had gone to Beijing to work. As we sat in the restaurant with the other customers, who were primarily white-collar workers, we talked about her various jobs, her use of technology, her family back at home, and her boyfriend, whom she had met on her own in Beijing despite her mother's attempts to arrange a marriage for her with a young man in her village.

Xiao Luo's experience encapsulates many of the central tenets of what has been called "modernity"—a mode of being and thinking that embraces change, faith in the future, and a desire for self-transformation as well as personal autonomy, especially vis-à-vis traditional institutions such as the family.[11] Her story also reveals the uncertainty, anxiety, and upheaval caused by such a break with the past, and it is constitutive of the interwoven processes—including industrialization, urbanization, and migration—that are said to be the hallmarks of "modern" life.[12] In contemporary China these coexist with the signifiers of late modernity, including the spread of mass communication and transportation systems and a rhizomatic global capitalism.[13] Though few of the women I met had a story as dramatic and daring as Xiao Luo's, like her, as mentioned above, many framed their journey to Beijing as an opportunity to leave behind a "boring village life," to "see the world," to "study things," and, in essence, to become modern. At the same time, most said that Beijing was an exciting but also different and often alienating place, and one where they didn't always have their bearings.

Modernity is often conceived of through forces—such as globalization or bureaucratization—that seem to defy measures of scope and scale. It is about the increasing disruption and fragmentation of traditional modes of social organization as well as new ways of understanding oneself and one's place in the world. Modernity is associated with freedom and alienation, hope and anxiety, and it is as much a real transformational process as it is a trope for that which is conceived of as the opposite of "tradition." However, the manner in which Xiao Luo and other migrant women experience what Anthony Giddens has called the "consequences of modernity" cannot be separated from the way they are positioned in the particular historical and socio-cultural context of contemporary China.[14]

Master narratives of modernity—such as those of Giddens—seem to assume a universal, singular experience.[15] However, as several feminist scholars have argued, modernity "is not just about men and women, but about *gender*, the cultural, social, political, and economic relations of power between and among men and women."[16] Certainly in China as elsewhere, the processes and formations associated with modernity—including economic reform and rural-to-urban migration—are gendered. Throughout the 20th century and continuing to the present, intellectual debates in China regarding modernity, progress, and national identity have often been intricately linked to gender, in particular to the Chinese "woman," as with the Iron Girls mentioned in the previous chapter. In art and cinema as well, the representation of "woman" has frequently served as a stand-in for the condition of the Chinese nation.[17] At present, conceptions of modernity both reconfigure and instantiate dominant notions of gender, just as they offer both new modes of freedom and new mechanisms of control. Thus, not only is modernity gendered, but it also constructs particular notions of gender. As a result, modernity has distinct implications for men and women because of their different positions in gendered power relations.[18]

Because the experience of modernity is not only gendered, but is also about race, nationality, and other vectors of identity, as well as the intersection of local and global forces, many feminist and postcolonial scholars prefer to use the term "other" or "alternative" modernities. A notion of other modernities challenges a singular version of modernity and forces the recognition that people who are located across geographical, cultural, and social hierarchies will experience modernity differently.[19] Furthermore, the concept of other/alternative modernities emphasizes how notions of the "modern" are fluid and shift in relation to particular historical conjunctures and competing discourses that should not be viewed as merely reactions to western Modernity.[20]

In China, modernity and modernization have been especially powerful and malleable terms used since the early 20th century by intellectuals, government officials, and the common people (*laobaixing*) to understand China's position in the world and to envision and build a strong Chinese nation able to cast off the suffering and humiliation brought about by western and Japanese powers. As Lisa Rofel notes, "What gets called modernity in China is neither a purely localized matter nor a mere instantiation of a universal discourse."[21] Rather, modernity exists "as a repeatedly deferred enactment marked by discrepant desires that continually replace one another."[22] Modernity, therefore, does not only designate certain processes or a particular era. It is also a very compelling trope for a socially constructed way of being and an imagined future.[23]

Clearly, Maoist modernity, which stressed national self-reliance and entailed a quest to mold the collective and build a socialist utopia, meant something quite different from current notions of Chinese modernity marked by forms of neoliberal governmentality that require what Yan Hairong has called structural adjustment of the market and the self.[24] However, they both share a faith in the future, an emphasis on technological progress, and the concerted effort of the state to produce subjects that can most effectively strengthen the Chinese nation. As elaborated in the previous chapter, contemporary Chinese modernity is concerned with building a harmonious society, guaranteeing people a "comfortable life" achieved through wealth and consumer goods, and raising national and individual *suzhi,* or "quality." At the same time, certain people's access to this modernity is severely constrained. Within discourses of modernity, migrant women are viewed as lacking—skills, quality, knowledge—in a manner similar to how colonial discourses positioned non-western peoples.[25] Hence, a young rural woman's understanding of modernity and her engagement with technology in her project of "becoming modern" will differ from an urban woman's as well as both rural and urban men's experiences of these processes. For this reason, modernity is best comprehended through examining the daily lived experiences—the seemingly mundane or quotidian—of ordinary people in specific locales.[26] Dorothy Hodgson thus uses the term "the *production of moderni-ties*" to recognize the various forms modernity takes "as well as the central-ity of people's agency in creatively and actively engaging these processes to produce new and distinct ways of 'being modern,' within shifting structural (such as historical, political, economic, and social) constraints and oppor-tunities."[27] Examining the "everydayness" of the production of modernity entails attending to its multiplicity and to how it is shaped through myriad discourses, knowledges, practices, and power relations.

## Becoming Modern: Urban Life and Technologies of the Self

How then are mobile phones as used and understood by young migrant women articulated to China's discourses of development and modernity, and how are they central in producing a "modern" subjectivity at the level of the everyday? One way to approach this question is first to situate the mobile phone within urban, "feminine" consumer practices that predate its arrival, most notably clothing and makeup. Young rural women's conscious efforts at "self-development" occur through being in a particular place—a city and not a village—and through being engaged in a certain occupation—for example, service work and not agriculture. Another part, however, is achieved through an internalization of powerful regulatory norms that reveal the "direct grip" that culture has on material bodies.[28]

As discussed in the previous chapter, within the social and cultural milieu of contemporary China, the rural has been overwhelmingly con-structed as "lagging behind" and "as a field of death for the modern per-sonhood desired by young women, who imagine the spaces of hope for such personhood to be somewhere else, in the city."[29] However, once in the city, migrant women are subject to stringent regulatory practices regard-ing their appearance, gait, gestures, and speech. Their bodies, like all bod-ies, emit particular signs, in this case signs that signify their rural status, an "abject" status that is essentialized as an otherness in contrast to that which is modern and urban.[30] The normalizing gaze of the urban milieu is thus a powerful force that motivates most young migrant women (though not necessarily older migrant women) to participate in what Sandra Bartky has called the "disciplinary practices of femininity," designed to produce a certain body size; a "repertoire of gestures, postures, and movements"; and an ornamented body.[31] Because these are normalized, they are "part of the process by which the ideal body of femininity—and hence the feminine body-subject—is constructed."[32]

For example, many of the women I knew told me that at home in the countryside they never worried too much about their appearance. They dressed rather simply, they did not use cosmetics, and they kept their hair cut short. In the city, however, they instantly became aware of their "bumpkin" appearance, and part of this awareness resulted from the disapproving stares and verbal scorn of urban residents. In crafting a self that conforms to urban standards of femininity and "quality," they engage in what Rofel, in a slight twist on Foucault, calls "postsocialist technolog(ies) of the self," by which she means the way that consumption and self-fashioning in China are about not only personal happiness and transformation, but also attaining a certain class status and position in the world.[33]

Technologies of the self, postsocialist or otherwise, exist within cultural discourses, structures, and modes of knowledge that produce dominant understandings of how we should conduct ourselves, including, as Theresa de Lauretis has argued, our understandings of gender,[34] and, in the Chinese context, class and place as well. Most young rural-to-urban migrant women certainly cannot attain the middle-class status of many of their urban counterparts, yet for them constructing an urban self means conforming to gender norms that are also in opposition to rurality. Such conscious efforts at molding the self, what Zhu Hong has called "body capital," were quite clearly explained to me by a young woman named Ji Hua.[35] The first time I interviewed her was during one of her rare days off from the restaurant where she worked. When we met, she was wearing a pink fuzzy sweater, tight jeans, high-heeled boots, bright pink lipstick, and a thick layer of eye makeup. Although it was chilly outside, she did not wear a coat presumably because this would have diminished her performance of dominant femininity. At one point in our conversation she told me:

> Clothes and makeup have become really important, especially when I compare myself to a Beijing person. In the countryside, people wear whatever. People aren't that concerned with it because there is nothing to buy. To go shopping for clothes means taking a one-hour bus ride. It's very inconvenient, and anyway we don't have a lot of money.[36]

Several other women also said that they had made a lot of effort at changing their outward appearance once they had moved to Beijing. Such changes were as much a result of the pleasure they took in shopping and wearing clothes they couldn't buy at home as their equally strong desire to avoid the rude stares and remarks of Beijing residents. Still, as has been well documented, migrant women's urban fashion often betrays their rural status, despite their conscious attempt to mask their alterity.[37]

*The Mobile Phone as a Technology of the Self*

Just as clothing and makeup are key factors in most migrant women's self-transformation in the city, during my initial fieldwork period in 2006-2007 it became clear that mobile phones were as well. Nearly every migrant woman (and all the migrant men) with whom I spoke—no matter their salary, occupation, or education—had a mobile phone.[38] In contrast, only two women had computers with Internet connections in their homes.[39] Most of the women I knew earned an average of 800-1,000 yuan/month (approximately US $104 to $130), including overtime, and they usually paid the equivalent of one month's salary and often more for a phone. Some women invested in more costly phones equipped with cameras and music players. Others purchased more expensive foreign brands, such as a Nokia or Motorola. In some cases there appeared to be a trade-off between either buying a Chinese model with a camera and a music player or a more prestigious foreign model without such extra functions. A smaller number of women purchased cheaper phones (between 450 and 600 yuan) or even second-hand and "*shanzhai*" phones that allowed for simple voice calls and texting.[40] Nearly every woman I knew usually spent 50 to 100 yuan per month (about US $6.50 to $13) on prepaid phone cards. By 2008 and 2009, most women had a phone with Internet access, as the cost of the mobile Internet had significantly decreased. They were still paying a large amount of money for their phones relative to their salaries.

The inordinate amount of money that many migrant laborers spend on their cell phones has been noted by other scholars as well as journalists.[41] Most often this phenomenon is interpreted as revealing migrants' desire to affirm symbolically their status through consumption.[42] Such an analysis certainly aligns with numerous theories regarding taste and status, from Bourdieu's notion that one's "aesthetic stances" are a means to "assert one's position in social space, as a rank to be upheld or a distance to be kept," to Baudrillard's rather polemical claims regarding consumption and signification.[43] It seems logical, and even unremarkable perhaps, that migrants would buy expensive phones as showy signifiers of their newly acquired (relative) wealth in the city compared to the poverty they experienced at home. However, it is important to note that there is a range of phones that cost two or three times the "expensive" phones purchased by many migrants. Conversely, discussions of mobile phones as status symbols for migrants rarely point out that the cheaper phones cost less because they are indeed of lower quality and thus do not last very long.

In my fieldwork, I did find that in some contexts mobile phones served as status symbols, yet in a very gendered fashion that I will discuss later in this chapter. For the most part, however, I would like to challenge what I believe is a rather simple conclusion regarding migrants' rationale for buying expensive mobile phones. The phone as a form of symbolic capital may usefully explain *some* migrants' motivation but cannot contain the range of experiences and the deep affect surrounding the purchase and ownership of a mobile phone for the women I knew. In other words, I would like to get beyond what has so aptly been called the "Veblen effect."[44] Consumption practices around mobile phones are not just about meaningless materialism but rather, as others have argued in different contexts, they connect to the everyday formation of subjectivity, the "care of the self" in Foucault's words, and specific social relations and modes of governmentality.[45]

To illustrate my point, let me start by discussing some of the decisions leading up to and involving the actual purchase of the phone. If someone is going to spend a month's to a month-and-a-half's salary on something, clearly buying such an item involves forethought and reflection. In numerous interviews and conversations, it became clear that for every migrant with whom I spoke, the *first big urban purchase* was a cell phone.[46] Although a few items of inexpensive clothing may have been bought before the phone, it was a mobile phone, not a television, computer, music player, or other electronic device, that was the most important and desired item. This was true even with women who had hand-me-down handsets, most often ones that an older relative had given them before they left home. Moreover, purchasing this device entailed serious choices and sacrifices, in some cases even whether to buy a mobile phone or a precious train ticket home after months of being away. When the topic of the actual purchase of the phone was discussed, in every case my informants could tell me the date, time, and place where they bought their phone, the price and how long it had taken them to save up enough money, and usually who had accompanied them. When women recounted this obviously very important event, their tone of voice and smile conveyed deep feelings of personal satisfaction and accomplishment. Prior to these conversations, I had not anticipated such detailed recollections and intense emotions. Chen Jingfei, a young woman who worked at a marketplace, expressed the feelings of many others when she said her phone was "the first, most expensive, important gift to myself, ever."[47] Another woman I knew told me she slept with her phone because it was so important to her.

Donald Slater has argued that "the most trivial objects of consumption both make up the fabric of our meaningful life and connect this intimate and mundane world to great fields of social contestation."[48] He further notes that consumption is about social needs, both in the sense of desiring to live a particular kind of lifestyle with particular types of relationships as well as claiming certain forms of entitlement. Such needs, at once social and political, "are statements which question whether material and symbolic resources, labor, [and] power are being allocated by contemporary social processes and institutions in such a way as to sustain the kinds of lives that people want to live."[49] In China, uneven processes of development have simultaneously compelled rural-to-urban migration and ushered in new modes of consumption while marginalizing the laborers who have made such development possible. In buying an expensive mobile phone, then, young migrant women were claiming a lifestyle they wanted to lead, in addition to the relationships they hoped to sustain, and they were producing themselves in a particular manner, one that contested the dominant discourses surrounding rural women and "backwardness."

Certainly in other studies, in a range of cultural contexts, mobile phones have been found to be important among young people for affective reasons as well as in the presentation of the self or as a form of youth cultural capital.[50] In the Philippines, for example, mobile phones have been articulated to Filipino modernity, which is infused with a mix of sexuality, religiosity, and political agency.[51] In my fieldwork, mobile phones were directly and explicitly associated with identity and modernity as well, but in modes specific to migrant women's subjectification. As Luo Judi, who sold earrings and hair accessories in one of the large marketplaces, told me, "If you live in the city and you don't have a mobile phone—especially someone my age—others look down on you."[52] Other women echoed such sentiments—a phone was clearly part of their urban transformation; along with new clothing and makeup, a phone was often something that set them apart from their peers still at home in the countryside, especially prior to the more widespread diffusion of rural telephony after 2008.

For young migrant women, then, the meaning of mobile phone ownership is polysemic, and this is a result of how the discourses surrounding both China's development and the development of rural women are intertwined. As mentioned in chapter 1, in the Chinese media and in the everyday speech of urbanites, female migrants are often portrayed as passive, backward, naïve, and of general "low quality." They are positioned in such discourses within the context of China's socio-cultural traditions, and they also exemplify the connection made by Chandra Mohanty between gender, capitalism, and globalization, as migrant women are thought to be docile, suited to certain gendered occupations, and easily exploited; hence, they constitute a flexible labor force in the global economy.[53]

Currently, China's modernization is synonymous with the expansion of the market economy; however, the exploitative labor practices this has entailed have often been erased through a discourse in which migration is framed as providing an opportunity for rural women to "become modern" and to benefit, not only financially, but also by "seeing the world," "developing themselves," and "gaining some skills." Through China's structural and ideological transformations, the rural is overwhelmingly positioned as "backward," "uncivilized," and "undeveloped" while the urban has been constructed literally and figuratively as synonymous with modernity, progress, and "quality" (suzhi), as discussed earlier. Suzhi, which encompasses quality as a whole, also "refers to the somewhat ephemeral qualities of civility, self-discipline, and modernity" and is related to how the self is valued as well as a sense of self value in the market economy.[54] Suzhi can thus be understood through Foucault's notion of governmentality, in that the discourse of suzhi emanates from the government but has been internalized by Chinese citizens as something they must cultivate, and indeed want to cultivate, in order to prosper and ensure their own happiness and well-being.[55] In the city, migrant women—because of the intersections of gender, class, and their rural origin—bear a particularly heavy burden to improve their suzhi.

Yet rural women who migrate to the city are not just "duped" into consenting to exploitative work that promises somehow to improve them; they choose this path because they feel they can actually gain something. At the same time, they invariably engage in certain technologies of the self to transform their bodies, mentally and physically, and to consciously, though always partially, shed their "country flavor," as one woman I knew, Zhang Xiumei, termed it. For them, a mobile phone is definitely an important transmission device, as I will discuss in the next chapter, yet it is also articulated not only to youth identity but also to a modern, hybrid rural-urban female subjectivity. Along with dressing more fashionably, reducing their accent, and all of the other disciplines designed to reform their rural bodies, it is part of their process of transforming in the city, or "becoming modern." In this sense, as Louisa Schein argues about the way ethnic Miao in China perform modernity, migrant women similarly "position themselves vis-à-vis modernity through multifarious practices but also struggle to *reposition* themselves, sometimes through deploying the very codes of the modern that have framed them as its others."[56]

In writing on the performativity of identity, Judith Butler argues that self-identity is made "culturally intelligible" through regulatory practices, in particular those that produce "coherent gender norms" and maintain "oppositions between 'feminine' and 'masculine.'"[57] Perhaps it is not surprising, then, that of extreme importance for most women was the phone's appearance, as is quite evident in the following conversation I had with Zhang Xiumei:

CW: May I see your mobile phone?
ZXM: Sure.
CW: It's a Lenovo.
ZXM: Yes.
CW: [*Pointing to the scenery on the screensaver*] Where was this taken?
ZXM: It came with the phone.
CW: It's pretty.
ZXM: No, it's so ugly. I regret buying this phone because it's so ugly.
CW: You regret buying it?
ZXM: Yes, when I first bought it I wanted to choose a good looking one, but this one is so ugly.
CW: It's ugly?
ZXM: It's ugly.
CW: Why do you say that?
ZXM: Because of the color.

CW: What color do you want?

ZXM: White, or pink. I regret buying this. It looks like it has a third eye [*because of the camera lens*].

CW: How much did it cost?

ZXM: 1,200 yuan [about US $156].

CW: 1,200. That's a bit expensive, don't you think?

ZXM: Yes, especially considering how ugly it is. Also, the quality isn't as good as, like, a Nokia or a Motorola. So I regret buying it.

CW: Why did you choose it?

ZXM: I don't know. I was persuaded by a clever salesperson [*laughs*].[58]

Although they rarely displayed their phones, many other women also said their phone had to look "pretty," and like Zhang Xiumei some women expressed embarrassment at having a phone that was too big or old. Many women had decorated their phones with stickers, "jewelry," special covers, or, in a few cases, rhinestones. The stickers were usually photos of themselves alone or with a close friend, emphasizing the phone as a socio-techno representation of the self. Such stress placed on the appearance of the phone coheres with what Mike Featherstone has called the intensifying of "the aestheticization of everyday life" in late modernity and has been noted by others examining the gendering of mobile phones.[59] The concern for the prettiness of the phone, in particular a desire for a pink-colored phone or the application of decorations such as rhinestones, is also clearly an assertion and a reflection of a type of "modern" Chinese female selfhood, which, as discussed in the previous chapter, emphasizes essentialized notions of gender. Zhang Xiumei's regret at having purchased an "ugly" phone reveals the normalization and internalization of these dominant notions of femininity. As a technology of the self articulated to a modern female subjectivity, the phone exemplifies Anne Balsamo's argument that "an apparatus of gender organizes the power relations manifest in the various engagements between bodies and technologies," a point I will explore in more detail later.[60]

As my analysis shows, migrant women craft themselves and engage with technology in accordance with particularly stringent "modes of subjection" in the city. However, unlike some scholars, I disagree that young migrant women merely buy into the false allures of consumption, whereby consumer goods hold an elusive promise of suturing them seamlessly into urban life and masking their alterity.[61] Such a position begs the question: why is it when middle-class or affluent youth purchase and use mobile phones, the cell phone is immediately heralded as a cool artifact of global youth culture, but when economically and socially marginalized young people express the same desires for consumer goods and form identity in relation to such goods, this is called "false consciousness" induced by the evil purveyors of global capitalism? Such a position potentially reifies a marginalized "Other," subaltern subject that these scholars are trying to challenge. I argue instead that owning a mobile phone is an important part of migrant women's construction of identity and the constitution of themselves as ethical subjects in Foucault's sense of the phrase. In purchasing and using a cell phone they gain access to "immobile mobility," or a socio-techno means of overcoming discursive constraints that surround them in the city. With the phone they are engaged in an act of agency through controlling their personal resources, enhancing their own sense of self-worth, and using a device that brings myriad pleasures, including entertainment and social contact. It also allows them access, albeit limited, to the promised "comfortable life." Denied legal citizenship in the city, migrants participate in consumer citizenship in a discursive context in which one's "quality" is intricately linked to one's level of consumption. A mobile phone displays their "quality" as a manifestation of their economic capital gained through labor, and it helps establish their position, however ambiguous, in the city. Still, this device of inclusion does not necessarily convert into other forms of capital. In contrast, it can lead to certain challenges and exclusions, which I address in the next section.

Skills and Disciplines

Just as the mobile phone is articulated to modern subjectivity, it also embodies and necessitates a set of practices and competencies that are constitutive of "self-development" and *suzhi* in contemporary China. Cell phone usage entails particular forms of literacy, technical know-how, and etiquette, which can be understood as forms of embodied cultural capital. Here I discuss each of these aspects of mobile phone use, the challenges they can pose for some migrant women, and certain tactics women use to overcome these same challenges.

Telephony is usually only minimally associated with literacy because even those with almost no reading or writing skills most likely have learned basic numbers and thus can manipulate a telephone keypad to make a voice call with relative ease. However, as opposed to traditional fixed-line phones, cell phones, of course, also have text messaging, and the arrival of smartphones has ushered in all sorts of text-based functions. In China, text messaging is widely used, especially among low-income populations due to the relatively inexpensive cost of a text message. Because of the widespread usage of text messaging, and more recently online chat, mobile phone use in China demands a certain degree of literacy. In fact, because of the design features of basic mobile phones and the way Chinese characters are inputted, text messaging requires two forms of literacy.[62] First, a word must be typed in *pinyin*, or the standardized romanization system of Chinese characters in the People's Republic. For example, for the word *"bao,"* the letters "b-a-o" must be typed. Once inputted, several characters will appear for the pinyin *"bao,"* with common meanings ranging from "hug" to "report" to "full." The user must then select the proper character, and though the most frequently used characters appear first on the screen, sometimes as many as thirty characters might be available as choices because morphemes in Chinese always have several different meanings according to which tone is used. Furthermore, the same combination of letters and tone can have more than one meaning and thus will be represented by a different character. Though predictive text is a feature of Chinese mobile phone interfaces, just as in English this does not always imply ease of use.

Manipulating a cell phone is not just a matter of literacy; however, it also involves certain technical skills. The user of a basic mobile phone must be able to navigate the various functions of the phone, such as the address book, text message inbox and outbox, multimedia messaging service (MMS), and so on. There are also a variety of settings to be controlled, including ringstyles, ringtones, wallpaper images, and the like. Phones with cameras, music players, or games add more technical demands. Additional functionalities, such as video and Internet capabilities, necessitate greater skills. Even users who have grown up with myriad technological devices can experience difficulty learning to manipulate these functions. For individuals who have not been surrounded their whole lives by computers, video-game consoles, digital cameras, and music players, these challenges can be magnified.

In addition to literacy and technical skills, mobile phone use also requires knowledge of conventional telephone etiquette, such as starting phone calls, using minimal responses to indicate one is listening, and being able to tactfully communicate a desire to end a call. Mobile phones have also generated additional rules and norms that a user must learn, and these often demand certain literacy and technical skills. Again, these norms and practices are especially associated with inputting text. For example, consistent with much prior cell phone research among youth, all of the young women I met agreed that text messages must be responded to relatively immediately lest the receiver be thought of as rude.[63] The only exception occurs when the receiver is unable to reply because she is preoccupied or prohibited from using her phone while at work. When I was in Beijing, whenever someone responded to a message more than twenty or thirty minutes after I had sent it, the reply always contained a profuse apology.

I elaborate on these various requirements of literacy, technical ability, and etiquette because among educated users these are often taken-for-granted and are not assumed to pose any difficulty. Many migrant women with whom I have spoken over the years have said that while at first it was difficult for them to learn to text message, or use online chat, or more recently navigate a social networking site, they were in fact able to master all of these functionalities rather quickly. However, for other migrant women, in particular those with limited education and minimal technical skills, the requirements and expectations attached to mobile phone usage can present challenges. Some women I interviewed expressed anxiety about not always knowing which character to choose, and some said they were not always certain how to respond properly to a message, even when they had owned a phone for several months. For example, Hu Lanying worked in the northern part of Beijing in a migrant market where many of those from more impoverished areas were employed.[64] She had only had one year of junior middle school before migrating to the city. When I asked her about text messaging with her friends, she said:

> I like to send and receive messages because it is the only way I stay in contact with my friends. But my friends sometimes send me messages and I don't always have the right words to reply. My friends criticized me for being so slow, and part of it is because of Chinese characters. But it is also because I'm at a loss for what to say. You know my level of education is so low.[65]

Others I knew were also ridiculed by their peers when they didn't understand a message or replied too slowly; in fact, I witnessed such derision and disciplining on more than a few occasions, and this ridicule wasn't necessarily virtual. In one instance, I was sitting in the dormitory of some of the young women who had graduated from the computer training course and who were now working in a company where they inputted financial data and other records from banks and large global companies. One of them was showing me the phone she had just bought. Like so many other women, it was her first big purchase since earning an income, and she was eager for me to see it. As we looked at the phone's wallpaper, one of her co-present peers sent her a message. When she was too slow in typing her reply, all of the other women made fun of her. She was so upset by their teasing—and her loss of face—that she ran out of the room crying as I sat there fairly astonished. I was also the subject of such ribbing when I was too slow to "get" a joke sent in a text—and this teasing came in a follow-up text message.

Cell phones clearly usher in new socio-techno practices, new techniques of power, and internalization of what could be called a regulatory technological gaze. The ridiculing and anxiety about responding to a message described above could be understood as a form of bullying, which is unfortunately a common practice among youth in various countries. However, with migrant women it not only marks in-group/out-group boundaries of peer groups, but it also reifies their marginal status in Chinese society as a whole and functions as a mode of governmentality. Official discourses that position migrant women as "behind" and "in need of development" are internalized and reproduced through migrant women themselves. To avoid such ridicule and discipline, a migrant must work to improve her knowledge and her "quality." In that migrant women seek a means of remedying such shortcomings, we can see how technologies of power thus merge with technologies of the self.

To deal with the challenges posed by inputting text in particular, many migrant women use different tactics to resist marginalization. For some, this might mean making more voice calls even though calling is more costly. Another technique is to rely on gracious friends and colleagues who will discreetly read messages and help type a reply without humiliating the person they are helping. A couple of young women I met who were functionally illiterate substituted complicated characters with simple characters that had the same sound for names in their address books.[66] For others, there is also heavy usage of prewritten messages—of jokes, greetings, and so on—that can be found in inexpensive books available in kiosks throughout the city or downloaded from the Internet, though invariably the women in my study received these messages from friends and then forwarded them.[67] I knew one woman who insisted that about 90 percent of her text messaging content was in the form of prewritten messages. Another informant stated, "The majority of the messages I send are prewritten. Why not? It's easy and convenient, and they can express what I want to say." In essence, with such tactics migrant women are "making do" and creatively engaging in immobile mobility, a means of surpassing, but not fully overcoming, constrained material circumstances.

As I have written elsewhere, however, migrants' reliance on these types of messages can also lead to a reaffirmation of their marginalized status.[68] Take the following message that was sent to me by one of the women I befriended early in my fieldwork:

> In the sea of people, knowing one another is not an easy destiny, and so it is precious. Flowing water will not be blocked by rocks. Our feelings will not be lessened by distance. Wherever you are, my blessing and wish for your happiness will always be by your side.

The flowery language (in the original Chinese) and the sentimentality are emblematic of many messages that my informants exchanged with each other and with me. Somewhat paradoxically, the extreme formality of the language made it especially subject to critique. When I showed such messages to urban residents, there was a near unanimous assessment that the content was too contrived and that the sender was "trying too hard."[69] There was often a very gendered critique as well, in that the migrant women who enjoyed such messages were judged as cultural dupes who indulged in the lowest form of maudlin and melodramatic cultural fare.[70]

Thus, another side of immobile mobility is revealed. As much as mobile phones allow for the transcendence of material constraints and discursive possibilities, they also potentially reinforce these. This idea that prewritten messages are meant to cater to the tastes of "lower social strata" has become widespread.[71] Such an assessment manifests the same reification of urban-rural difference as the disdain expressed in the popular media for rural migrants' tastes and fashions as being "coarse" or "vulgar."[72] Obviously text messages are much more private than fashion choices and not usually subject to public critique. However, with the judgment of such messages, and the general challenges that migrant women can face when using mobile phones, we see how power and discourse operate at the most seemingly mundane level, and that while mobile phones allow for inclusion in an imagined modernity, they can also perpetuate existing exclusions.

The Mobile Phone and the "Gender of Modernity":
A Micro View

Thus far I have looked at how the intersections of gender, class, age, and place, as these are located within the context of government discourses of development and modernity, produce the mobile phone as a technology of the self in the lives of young migrant women.[73] In this section, I explore more deeply the constitutive nature of gender and technology in a context where age, class, and place are subsumed by gender: in beauty salons. In the microcosm of the salon the mobile phone assemblage took on a particular form, and mobile phones, their usage, and language explaining such usage revealed much about the social construction of both gender and technology, and the constitutive nature of both. Although I draw primarily from observations and interviews conducted in beauty salons, several of the practices and discourses that I discuss were prevalent among many migrants I knew, regardless of where they were employed.

When I lived in Beijing in the early 1990s, beauty salons were few and far between, and most Chinese friends I knew either cut their own hair or had a relative or a friend cut it for them. Western hotels had expensive salons, but their location and prices meant that local Chinese did not patronize them. The most prevalent form of "salon" was quite makeshift and practical. On weekend mornings, self-taught barbers, men and women, would set up shop outside along the riverbanks or in parks by bringing a chair, a few towels, a comb, and some scissors. For a nominal fee, they would cut basic unisex styles as customers and friends would hang out chatting, drinking tea, or playing mahjong. These types of outdoor salons are no longer very common in Beijing except on the outskirts, and most of these barbers have either moved on to other jobs or have set up tiny indoor shops. Today, in Beijing there are trendy, fashionable beauty salons everywhere. They usually have large windows so that passersby will take a look inside and decide to get a haircut or a massage. The inside décor is often brightly colored with pictures of western and Asian models hanging on the walls. The employees are mostly young male and female migrants, who often sport spiky, dyed hair and wear blue jeans, stylish t-shirts, and sneakers.

Beauty salons in Beijing thus serve as a very tangible manifestation of the transformations the city has undergone in the last decade and a half. On the one hand, the salons are a result of the market reforms that have ushered in a service economy. On the other hand, they visibly represent a society that has transitioned from one based on collective values and asceticism, and where showing concern for physical beauty was deemed "bourgeois" and could result in an individual being severely reprimanded, to a contemporary landscape where beauty and fashion are revered. This change has resulted from a desire to reclaim "natural" gender differences suppressed during the Mao era as well as from an influx of images of cosmopolitan style that circulate through the Chinese and transnational media.

All but the tiniest of salons—which were more like barbershops and deemed "traditional" (meaning old-fashioned) by the women I knew—presented a microcosm of the essentialized notions of gender and the resulting gendered disciplines, stratification, and power relations that exist in contemporary China, and these were also manifest in mobile phone use in the salons, as I will explain shortly. Beauty salons in Beijing (perhaps like everywhere else) are physical terrains where the performativity of gender is continuously reconstituted through the services requested and rendered that reinstate norms of appearance in line with conventional notions of masculinity and femininity. This observation is similar to those made of African American beauty salons and Korean nail salons in the United States (to give just two examples), and thus in and of itself it is not remarkable.[74] What is exceptional is how the discursive environment of the salons also constructs male and female employees as highly gendered subjects in ways that go far deeper than appearance. For example, in all but one salon I visited, I was told that women were not allowed to be "stylists," meaning they could not cut hair, and interestingly this one exception had a female manager. This unspoken rule can be traced to the old Chinese maxim of "valuing men and belittling women" (zhongnanqingnü), and it persists in the belief that because cutting hair is seen as requiring high technical skill (gao jishu), it is therefore reserved for men.[75] Women, on the other hand, are only allowed to do the practical (shiyong) or unskilled jobs, which include washing and drying hair, applying (but not mixing) hair color, giving massages (amo), cleaning up the salon, and greeting customers and storing their belongings in a locker for safekeeping (see figure 5).[76]

Fig. 5. A young woman greets a customer as male stylists cut hair.

In all of the salons that I have visited, the male employees—who are the "stylists"—tend to control the salon, often giving orders to the women, supervising them, and treating them in a subservient manner. Male stylists absorbed in a card game or another diversion barely glance at a customer who enters a salon because it is the females' job to greet the customer and do all of the preparations up to the actual haircut. On several occasions I observed that even when all of the women in a salon were already occupied with other clients and all of the male stylists were free, a new customer would nonetheless have to wait for a female to wash and comb out his or her hair. The males also had their own physical space—a station with their name often engraved above the mirror—and an ideological space supported by their status, their income (they made two or three times more money than the women), and their "ownership" of time: they had more days off per month and more downtime while at work, which they often spent playing cards, gaming on their mobiles, or going outside for a smoke.

Customers, both male and female, were also more likely to treat the young women working at salons in a demeaning manner. For example, one morning while I was at one of the salons that I frequented, a woman—from her appearance and accent most likely a Beijing resident—came in to ask if the salon offered a certain type of hair treatment. Cui Yiping, the young woman who was working at the time, told the woman she did not think that they offered this service but she would check with the stylist when he arrived (stylists always arrive later in the morning, after the salon has been cleaned). The woman repeated her question, and when Cui Yiping reiterated that she didn't know the answer, the woman berated her, called her foolish (*sha*), and left. This incident is indicative of the type of treatment migrants in general receive from urban residents, and it is also based on the broad perception that women who work in beauty salons are morally suspect and thus not worthy of respect. This is because beauty salons that give massages are associated with prostitution, and massage parlors and some beauty salons are indeed often fronts for prostitution. Though it is easy to tell the difference between a legitimate and "red light" salon, such prejudice and suspicion extends to nearly all women employed in all but the most upscale salons. It should be noted that, as a Korean-style salon, Cui Yiping's salon did not even offer any type of massage service.

The gender stratification and dominant notions of "modern" essentialized masculinity and femininity that were evident in the jobs, behaviors, attitudes, and hierarchy in the salons were also reproduced through mobile phone use. In every beauty salon I visited, male employees had more expensive, high-tech mobile phones with more functions than the female employees had. In fact, during my initial fieldwork nearly every male with whom I spoke had a phone with a music and video player as well as Internet capability, and this was also the case with males I met in other occupations. At the time, going online via a mobile phone was quite expensive in Beijing, but these young men had invariably secured a low fixed rate for unlimited Internet access early on when China Mobile had offered inexpensive packages to entice new customers. For example, while I was in Beijing in 2006–2007 accessing the Internet via cell phone cost about 30 yuan (about US $4) per hour, but the males in the salons often had a deal where they paid 15 yuan per month for unlimited access. The only exceptions were young men who had just arrived from the countryside and were still "in training," and they tended to have inexpensive phones with only basic functions. These were also the only males I ever saw greet customers (unless a stylist was advertising a special promotion), wash hair, or sweep the floor, and this was only at a few salons. The young women, on the other hand, overall had less expensive phones, usually Chinese models, with basic voice and texting functionality and in some cases a camera. Only one woman had previously had a higher-end phone with Internet access (which she had since dropped and broken), but she was clearly the exception. In her own words, she was "like a boy" (*xiang nanhaizi*). During subsequent research, even as many young migrant women could access the Internet via their phones, they still tended to have less expensive models than their male counterparts.

Of course, such differences are partially due to financial reasons. Male migrants usually earn more than females, even when they have the same job, just as urban men make more than urban women in China. However, this phenomenon goes much deeper than finances and is a result of the way dominant gender norms have been reconfigured in the post-Mao era. As discussed in chapter 1, in today's China as a way to repudiate the Maoist past, "modernity" is linked to essentialized notions of gender. In particular, a "modern" woman melds local and globalized standards of outward beauty and femininity. Working in tandem with this reclamation of a more traditional notion of femininity is a consumer culture that emphasizes gender binaries and the sexualization of women's bodies.

Such dominant gender ideologies were manifested in the way my informants understood technology. For example, male migrants often used and displayed their mobile phones as signifiers of their higher status and masculinity vis-à-vis migrant women, and gendered discourses of technology use, exemplifying the performative nature of gender, were pervasive among the men and women with whom I spoke. For example, in 2007 I frequently visited a salon near my apartment in Beijing to have my hair washed and to get a shoulder massage. During these occasions I spoke numerous times to the young women who worked at the salon about their lives in Beijing, their mobile phone use, their goals for the future, and so on. Once while I was at the salon the boss's son (who managed the place in his father's absence) was busy playing an online game on his phone. He was eager to show me his phone—a Nokia smartphone that most likely had cost around 4,000 yuan (over US $520) and that had all sorts of features and applications, which he deftly manipulated with barely a glance at the touchpad. Once he had finished his demonstration, I asked Xiao Wu, who was washing my hair, if she ever played games on her phone or online, and she said that she did not. When I asked her why not, she replied, "Guys like that sort of thing more. They like to show that they are high-tech. Girls don't care about showing off like that. They just like to chat. This starts even from childhood, you know."[77] Just over three years later, in the same salon a different young woman uttered almost the same exact words, and I have met other women in other occupations who discussed men and women's mobile phone usage in similar terms. For example, Tian Ai, a young woman who sold clothing in a market, reiterated that "girls just like to chat and send short messages. Guys like to exchange information and pictures."[78] Still another young woman told me, "It's important for guys to show off and appear cool and up-to-date."[79]

As I was speaking with Xiao Wu, there was a constant popping of firecrackers outside because it was during the two-week Chinese New Year celebrations. As we listened to the firecrackers exploding, Xiao Wu added, "It's like firecrackers. When I grew up in the countryside, girls just watched as the boys played with the firecrackers."[80] Unintentionally and quite simply, Xiao Wu had drawn a link between the most ancient of Chinese technologies—gunpowder and firecrackers—and the most modern of western technologies—the mobile phone, revealing how gender and technology usage are mutually constitutive constructions. As Cynthia Cockburn states, "Gender is a social achievement. Technology too."[81] Just as gender identity is necessarily relational, so, too, "technological artifacts *entail* relations," and these relations "enter into our gendered identities."[82] As a "technology of the gendered body,"[83] a mobile phone is articulated to the production of "modern" female subjectivity underpinned by essentialized notions of gender.

After Xiao Wu explained quite clearly the socially constructed nature of men and women's relationship to technology, she also offered a reason for why women could not cut hair. "It's not the skill [that guys are better at]," she said. "It's that they can see beauty. And, anyway, girls are getting their hair cut for guys to look at, right?"[84] The certainty with which she said these words denied the possibility of questioning the gendered hierarchy of the salon, the heteronormativity of the larger society, or the gendered nature of technology use. The disciplinary practices of femininity therefore not only regulate a woman's body size, gestures, posture, or self-ornamentation. They also pervade usages of technology, and they can once again position women as passive, chatty, and concerned with feelings while men are active, rational, and powerful senders of information.

These discursive constructions of gender and technology were echoed numerous times in my fieldwork. Although cell phones are a "modern" medium that might displace space and time, they do not necessarily disrupt "traditional" notions of gender, particularly when these very notions are conceived of as modern. As Rita Felski notes, "The stories we create in turn reveal the inescapable presence and power of gender symbolism."[85] In my study, the actual phones possessed, their functionality, their usage, and perhaps most significantly, the way they were spoken about all served to strengthen gender norms and differentiation.[86] Though of course some women shared with me their obvious displeasure with their subordinate positions in their jobs due to the fact that they were women, especially in the beauty salons, most still seemed to be resolved to their "fate," confirming once again the power of normalizing discourses and the internalization of a self-critiquing gaze.

## Conclusion

The experiences of everyday modernity cannot be disentangled from a nation's pursuit of development and its citizens' interpellation into modes of governmentality that are gendered and cross-cut as well by class, age, and place. In contemporary China, modernization has meant the pursuit of wealth, beauty, and a comfortable life, and it has brought renewed emphasis on education, knowledge, and technology to boost national and individual *suzhi*. In such a context, mobile phones in the lives of migrant women have become articulated in myriad ways to "being modern."

For migrant women in Beijing, a mobile phone is more than just a material object or a form of cultural capital. It embodies deep emotions and longings for a modernity that is always produced as partial, or what I have called a hybrid rural-urban subjectivity. In 2006 and 2007 in particular, the very act of possessing a phone was a way to assert one's autonomy from an "othered" rural identity and to feel part of a modern, cosmopolitan culture. In other words, mere possession was a form of empowerment. At the same time, mobile phones as technologies of the self have a disciplining function as they are situated within and reproduce a discourse that articulates possession of technology and technological abilities to ideologies of progress, quality, knowledge, fashion, and hipness. They also normalize and demand certain skills, literacies, and etiquette.

My discussion reveals that technology is never neutral and always works as a form of knowledge and power.[87] As Rofel states, "Though being modern is an imagined status, it is not a mere mythical representation. People deeply feel modernity in their experiences precisely because techniques of normalization are secured in its name."[88] In China, as the quest for *suzhi* melds notions of the individual self and the national citizen as being responsible for improvement and "development," governmental power and normalizing discourses and practices constitute notions of modernity. A mobile phone assemblage—made up of a technological artifact and technologies of the self—is thus territorialized in and through such conceptions of modernity.

3

Navigating Mobile Networks of Sociality and Intimacy

If you have a mobile phone, your life is much richer.
—Cui Yiping, Beijing, December 4, 2006

Jia Zhangke's 2005 film *The World* (*Shijie*) revolves around the story of two young adult migrants, Tao and her boyfriend Taisheng, who are both employed at the World Park, an amusement park on the outskirts of Beijing, where superficial cosmopolitanism is embodied in scaled-down, kitschy replicas of famous tourist sites such as the Eiffel Tower, the Taj Mahal, and even the (still-standing) Twin Towers. The fake attractions draw visitors from all over China, giving them and the employees at the park a false sense of having "seen the world." Working as a dancer in the park, Tao appears to live like a liberated, urban young woman: dressing in exotic costumes, dating Taisheng without the blessing of her parents, owning a mobile phone, and spending her free time as she pleases. Yet, while Tao can sit in a grounded airplane at the park, she flies only in her mind, with escape in the film imagined through text-messaged anime sequences. In reality, however, despite the mobile phone's importance in the workers' lives, due to a lack of signal it is practically useless in the cavernous basement area in the park where Tao and the other migrants live.[1] And while the employees at the park are connected through friendships and romantic liaisons, they are, in fact, isolated, alienated, and possibly without hope of ever integrating into the larger "community" of Beijing. As the film unfolds, it becomes clear that while the Chinese government boasts of the nation's bright future, the characters see their own futures as bleak, caught as they are in the margins of society. The film's tragic ending, caused in part by Tao's discovery of text messages from another woman on Taisheng's phone, drives home Jia's point that just as the grandeur of the World Park is but an illusion, the gleaming skyscrapers and other modern trappings of cities like Beijing mask the negative effects of China's wave of development and the many victims that lie in its wake.

*The World* primarily centers on the lives of Tao and Taisheng, yet the mobile phone—despite constraints on its use—plays a significant role in the film, through facilitating relationships (both platonic and romantic), signifying connection, and even signaling betrayal. In this chapter I take up such themes as I explore how young rural-to-urban migrant women use mobile phones for expanding and enriching their social networks, exploring their sexual identity, and forging romantic relationships. Like Tao in *The World*, migrant women maintain friendships and form new bonds via their mobile phones. Compared to her, however, many lead lives that are far more circumscribed by strict work schedules, isolated living conditions, and a relatively contained social world. For these reasons, the mobile phone has become indispensable not only for building social networks, but also for cultivating close relationships and thereby maintaining emotional well-being. A key question, however, is whether through such networked sociality via the phone women are also able to build their social capital in ways that will improve their life conditions.

In the following discussion, I continue to explore the theme of how the mobile phone is part of what James Carey calls communication as transmission and communication as ritual. I also further develop the notion of how the mobile phone allows for "immobile mobility," or the socio-techno means of surpassing spatial, temporal, physical, and structural boundaries. As I discuss migrant women's mobile phone assemblage, I trace changes and continuities that have arisen over time as certain practices have become deterritorialized and new ones have emerged, in particular as most women now regularly access the mobile Internet. While this online access via the phone is an important aspect of digital inclusion, I argue that it demonstrates a form of "necessary convergence" because few migrant women have computers and Internet connections in their homes. I also ask whether in the midst of opening up new possibilities for sociality and intimacy, certain practices possibly reify women's marginalization, through solidifying their status as rural "Others" in the city. To frame this analysis, I first discuss Chinese concepts of selfhood and *guanxi* (relationship) and then relate these to Pierre Bourdieu's notion of social capital. My goal is to illuminate how local socio-techno practices are articulated to larger social and cultural structures and meaning.

The Egocentric Self, *Guanxi*, and Social Capital

Although any culture is widely variegated, and China is in the midst of a profound transformation, Chinese social organization has often been called relationship-oriented, in contrast to the individual-oriented nature of western cultures. In traditional Chinese culture, "the individual is never an isolated, separate entity," and there is no unique "self" outside of one's social relationships and the personal responsibilities they bring.[2] Fei Xiaotong, one of the founders of modern Chinese sociology, thus compared the pattern of Chinese social structure to "the circles that appear on the surface of a lake when a rock is thrown into it," where each person "stands at the center of the circles produced by his or her own social influence."[3] He used the term "differential mode of association" (*chaxugeju*) as an ideal type to describe this pattern and to emphasize that the more distant the circles of relationships from the center (oneself) are, the less significant they are in a person's social network. Liang Shuming, a contemporary of Fei's, wrote that China has a "relationship-based (*guanxi benwei*) social order," where those who are closest are at the center and have a large degree of mutual affection and obligation.[4] Both of these scholars formulated their theories of Chinese selfhood before 1949, when China was a predominantly rural society. However, despite various transformations as a result of communism, industrialization, and urbanization, as well as increasing individualization, many scholars still argue for the persistence in China of a sense of self that is predominantly relationally focused.[5] In numerous conversations, my informants confirmed this relational orientation.

Chinese society, then, is primarily neither individual-oriented (and thus not focused on individual rights or the concept of equality) nor group-oriented, but is "egocentric."[6] The differentially categorized circles of social relationships "form a network composed of each individual's personal connections," and because these stress differentiation and hierarchical distinctions, they imply different obligations, norms of reciprocity, and moral demands.[7] At the same time, such circles are discontinuous and highly elastic. Aside from what are seen as "natural" relations—for example parent–child— "nonnatural relations are voluntarily constructed with the individual self as the initiator."[8] Further, an individual has a large degree of autonomy in deciding whether or not to enter into such "voluntarily constructed" relationships, of which he or she is the architect.[9] In theory any two people can form a connection either through a shared relational category (such as colleague or classmate) or through an intermediary.

Closely associated with this relationally based self-orientation is *guanxi*, a ubiquitous yet ambiguous word that literally means "relationship" but often is interpreted as " 'personal connections,' 'social networks,' or 'particularistic ties.' "[10] According to Gold, Guthrie, and Wank, *guanxi* ties:

> are based on ascribed or primordial traits such as kinship, native place, ethnicity, and also on achieved characteristics such as attending the same school . . . having shared experiences . . . and doing business together. Particularly in the last instance, potential business partners may consciously establish or seek to manufacture *guanxi* when no prior basis exists, either by relying on intermediaries or establishing a relationship directly. While the bases for *guanxi* may be naturally occurring or created, the important point is that *guanxi* must be consciously produced, cultivated, and maintained over time.[11]

Within the realms of business and politics in China, *guanxi* is often equated with corruption, bribery, and using others for one's personal or political benefit.[12] The Chinese Communist Party has always associated *guanxi* with "feudal" thought and has conducted propaganda campaigns and instituted various policies to replace the importance of kinship and locality-based ties with a system of normative "socialist morality." Despite such efforts, however, during both the planned economy under Mao and the current era of marketization, the importance of *guanxi* has remained.

In contrast to a purely instrumental view of *guanxi*, scholarship on *guanxi* in the countryside has emphasized its expressive features and its association with friendship and feelings. In rural contexts, the cultivation of *guanxiwang* (personal networks) has been understood as producing one's subjectivity, because a relationally based notion of the self implies that "relationships are constitutive of one's self."[13] Yan Yunxiang argues that one's *guanxi* networks of personal relations can also be thought of as one's local world, made up of concentric circles of relationships categorized into three zones: the "personal core" made up of family members and very close friends; the "reliable zone" consisting of good friends; and the "effective zone," which is larger and more open and can include all friends, coworkers, relatives, and even potentially (but not likely) all fellow villagers.[14] Some scholars believe that more traditional notions of *guanxi* still prevail in the countryside because the roots of *guanxi* can be found in rural culture "where kinship ties and a tradition of labor exchange and mutual aid and obligation have always been dominant."[15] However, even these scholars acknowledge that economic development has changed *guanxi* practices in rural areas, at least in terms of how villagers deal with outsiders with whom they do business.[16] Moreover, such emotionally based *guanxi* is the result of interpersonal relationships fostered over a long period of time in a tight-knit, stable (non-mobile) community, yet rural-to-urban migration has clearly affected the stability of rural life.

*Guanxi* has been likened to Pierre Bourdieu's concept of social capital, or "the aggregate of the actual or potential resources which are linked to possession of a durable network of more or less institutionalized relationships of mutual acquaintance and recognition."[17] Bourdieu emphasizes the uneven distribution of social capital, its reproduction in the social sphere, its exclusionary nature, and hence its role in maintaining both privilege and inequality. To Bourdieu, one's position in society both enables and constrains access to social capital, and those who are linked to others who have a large quantity of various forms of capital—money, knowledge, position, prestige—will have an advantage in the "game of society."[18] Bourdieu also underscores the necessity of continuous efforts to build and maintain relational networks through conscious and unconscious strategies that are aimed "at transforming contingent relations, such as those of neighborhood, the workplace, or even kinship, into relationships that are at once necessary and elective, implying durable obligations subjectively felt (feelings of gratitude, respect, friendship)."[19]

Both *guanxi* and Bourdieu's notion of social capital thus entail reciprocity, mutuality, long-term cultivation, and group boundaries. However,
there are important differences between these two concepts. First, the
mutual benefits and interests entailed in *guanxi* must be implicit, rather
than explicit.[20] Second, *guanxi* is different from social capital in that while
it usually does involve a material aspect of some sort, it is also supposed
to include feelings and morality; thus, "instrumentalism and sentiment
come together in *guanxi*, as cultivating *guanxi* successfully over time creates a basis of trust in a relationship."[21] Andrew Kipnis, in his research
on rural *guanxi* practices, most explicitly troubles the binary often drawn
between "modern" western cultures that are based on universal ethics and
where gift giving is supposed to be disinterested exchange, and "traditional" Asian cultures based on particularism, ritual, and favors, stating,
"In *guanxi*, feeling and instrumentality are a totality."[22] Thus, "*guanxi* can
be seen as unifying what Western bourgeois relationships often separate:
material exchange and affectionate feelings."[23] When I use the term *guanxi*
in the remainder of this chapter, I tend to focus on its positive, expressive
dimensions, but, like Kipnis, I reject a strict separation between instrumentality and affection.

Mobile Phones and the Social World of Migrant Women

To trace the significance of mobile phones as they are articulated to various modes of networked sociality for young migrant women, it is instructive
to take a historical perspective and consider some of the most basic communication needs that mobile phones meet for those who have traditionally
been marginalized by China's telecommunications policies. Many women I
knew grew up without fixed-line phones in their family homes until the early
2000s, and mobile phones did not become widely accessible to low-income
people in many Chinese cities until around the mid-2000s (and not in many
rural areas until the late 2000s). In 2006, when I first started the bulk of this
research, most young migrant women had had to work for several months
before they could purchase phones, as discussed in the previous chapter.
Prior to such ownership, they had to use either a pay phone in their dorms or
a phone at a public "call bar" (*huaba*).
    Considering this lack of previous easy access to telephony, it is no wonder
that their initial reason for buying a phone contrasted markedly with that

of females (young and old) in other (primarily western) contexts. Numerous surveys have revealed that when members of the latter group have been asked about their primary motivation for buying a phone, the reason given is often related to safety or security.[24] Young migrant women, on the other hand, despite being in a new environment away from parents and most other family members and friends, never mentioned safety as a main motivation for buying a phone; instead, they invariably stated that it was for "convenience" (*hen fangbian*). To get a sense of what convenience means for them, we can consider the example of Zhang Xiumei. From 2001 to 2003 she had worked in a factory in Guangzhou, where her dormitory installed two public pay phones (which only took incoming calls) for its eighty residents only during her last year there. Zhang Xiumei moved to Beijing in 2004, and she bought her first phone in 2005. As she told me:

> When I was at the factory in Guangzhou, I wrote a letter to my family about once a week. My family didn't have a phone [until 2003] but our neighbors at the front of the village did, but it was far for my mom to walk, so I only called them from a public phone about once a week. They didn't usually call me. [Now, with a mobile phone] it's very convenient. Before no one knew where I was, for example. So, for a long time I didn't keep in touch with a lot of people. So, now with a mobile phone, it's really convenient. You can send a text message, or call, chat. It's good. Now people know where you are. Before, [when you went out to work] no one knew where you went.[25]

Zhang Xiumei's words are telling in many ways. First, as might be expected, regardless of where she was located geographically, she kept in touch with her family. However, such communication entailed much effort for both her and her parents—composing letters, scheduling calls, using pay phones, traveling some distance, maintaining good relations (*guanxi*) with neighbors. Zhang Xiumei's family's efforts toward keeping in touch were eased once they got their own landline, but hers were not until she owned a mobile phone. Her story also reflects the difficulty she had in maintaining ties with non-family members once she left home due to various movements across worksites, cities, and provinces.

Xiao Sui, who worked in a small company, also emphasized the convenience of a mobile phone:

xs: If I didn't have a mobile phone and you wanted to find me, I could only give you my work unit's phone number or my dorm phone number. If I wasn't at my work unit or my dorm, then what? You definitely wouldn't be able to find me. Right? If you had this situation you wouldn't be able to find me.

cw: Can your friends call you at work on the work phone? Does your boss care?

xs: If it's something urgent [*ji de shiqing*], then they can call me at work and the boss won't care. But if I wanted to call I would have to go outside to use the public phone.

cw: Before you had a mobile phone you had to use the public phone?

xs: Yes.

cw: Did your dorm have a phone?

xs: No, just the work unit.[26]

As found with similarly marginalized populations across the globe, for migrant women without easy access to landlines and personal computers, a mobile phone thus provides a means of keeping in touch with friends and maintaining one's various social networks that was previously impossible.

*Expanding Social Networks*

In addition to the convenience of mobile phones for maintaining communication within established relationships, how do mobile phones help migrant women negotiate new social relationships, given the constraints on time and space they face in the city? In almost all instances, rural-to-urban migrants rely on some type of connection—usually a relative or a friend in the destination area, but sometimes an institutional intermediary such as a school or job recruitment agency—to facilitate their move by providing help with employment, housing, and bureaucratic requirements such as temporary work permits and identification cards. Once in the city, however, they often live "isolated lives."[27] As Zhang Xiumei stated, "My social circle is very small. I usually just go to work, get off work, go home, sleep, wash clothes, and sometimes go to Facilitator [short for the Culture and Communication Center for Facilitators, a non-governmental organization (NGO) that serves Beijing's migrant community]. My circle is very small, my life circle. I don't really go out."[28] Like Zhang Xiumei, most of the migrant women I knew led lives that revolved within a very small social world for a number of reasons, including long work hours (ten or twelve or even fourteen hours a day) and very little time off—some women have one or two days off a month and others only get time off for the annual Spring Festival holiday. In restaurants and hotels in particular, there are also frequent demands by bosses for employees to work overtime, and in all types of service work there can be mandatory training or "teamwork" sessions that employees are expected to attend.

Not surprisingly, then, precious time off is often used for doing mundane tasks like laundry, food shopping, and sleeping. This small social world is also reinforced by the women's housing situation—tiny apartments or cramped dorm rooms provided by an employer with curfews enforced, or with a relative (often an uncle or older sibling who serves as a surrogate parent). Some migrant women have substantial daily commutes because cheaper housing is available outside the city center, yet aside from going to work many are reluctant to venture out of their local neighborhoods for a variety of reasons. The discursive context that forms their gendered, classed, and placed subjectivity also locates them culturally and ideologically as outsiders in Beijing, marked by their accent, appearance, and mannerisms. I knew several women who were fortunate to have housing near their workplaces in the city center; nonetheless, they rarely ventured much further than a half-mile radius from where they lived or worked.

Given these circumstances, how do migrant women use mobile phones to expand their social networks beyond the small social world they occupy in the city? Of particular interest is how mobile phones enable immobile mobility, or a means of surpassing constraints of space, place, gender, and class in building social capital through cultivating *guanxi*. Based on fieldwork in southern China, Patrick Law and Yinni Peng found that mobile phones helped migrant factory workers not only "to maintain existing kinship relationships in expanded spatio-temporal contexts, but also to prolong new social relationships developed in the workplace."[29] As they note, in the factories and dorms, migrants mix with others from different provinces, which has helped to break down previous notions of insider/outsider; moreover, such relationships continue via the phone even after workers change jobs.[30] What is less clear, however, is the degree to which such relationships transcend not only place-based but also class-based notions of inclusion and exclusion. When young migrant women who are not located in this "dormitory labor regime" use mobile phones to expand their social networks, do they do so in ways that both challenge and adhere to normative *guanxi* principles? These questions are even more pertinent as the mobile Internet has become affordable for migrant women, thus giving them greater ability to connect with friends and strangers, particularly via QQ, which is an instant messaging, gaming, and social networking platform that is especially favored by young adult migrants.

One way I attempted to explore such issues was to view the contents of the women's mobile phone address books. As might be expected, these almost always contained the names of current and previous coworkers as well as former classmates at home or out laboring in other parts of China. The address books also had the names of a few family members, usually siblings or cousins. If a woman had the phone number of a Beijing resident or someone from a different social class, in most cases it was for an employer, a supervisor at work, or a staff member at one of the NGOs that serve Beijing's migrant population. Although many women had only around ten contacts total in their phone, some had more than fifty. Regardless of the number of contacts, the interactions via text and voice were primarily with three to eight migrant peers or siblings, and to a lesser extent with parents or other relatives. Some used their mobiles to communicate with bosses or coworkers, depending on their job.

Once women began widely using QQ, compared to the mobile phone address books, informants' lists of QQ contacts presented a slightly different picture. Some names in their QQ chat lists overlapped with the contacts in their phone address books, except that there were fewer coworkers and rarely employers. Nearly every woman in this study also participated in QQ groups, and these groups were distinguished as consisting of friends, classmates, relatives, and people from their home villages or provinces (there could be overlap between members of some of the groups). While some women said they refused to interact with strangers on QQ, either through chat or groups, many women had "net friends" (*wangyou*) that they had met online, especially through a hometown group, but they often had not met these net friends face-to-face.[31]

In many ways, the names in the phone books and the contacts in QQ followed the Chinese patterns of *guanxi* building discussed earlier. That is, apart from kinship ties, relationships were usually established when there was some type of shared identity or personal experience, which then remained as the signifier of the relationship. Thus, rather than calling all those in their phones "friends" (*pengyou*), women almost always differentiated relationships with terms such as "classmate" (*tongxue*), "colleague" (*tongshi*), or someone from their home village (*tongxiang*). As Mayfair Yang explains, in Chinese "the word *tong*, meaning 'same' or 'shared,' is used to designate a whole set of close personal relationships which serve as guanxi bases."[32] Although some names in the address books and QQ contact lists were designated as those of "friends" and these could potentially overlap with classmates, colleagues, and so on, clearly women were using their mobile phones not only to keep in touch with friends and family, but also to build their *guanxi* bases. Following the terminology of Yan discussed earlier, as representative of their "local world," their mobile phone contacts were made up of those in their "personal" and "reliable" zones and could be expanded to include those in their "effective" zones. For most women, however, the number of those in their personal zones was quite small. For example, once when I commented on the large number of friends a woman had in her mobile phone address book, she replied that they were mostly "ordinary friends" (*yiban pengyou*), meaning they would fall within the effective zone.

Even when there is not an obvious shared (*tong*) identity as a basis for a personal relationship, the phone can still come in handy to produce *guanxi*. Kwang-kuo Hwang has stated that when a person seeks to establish *guanxi* with someone whom she does not know, she must "altercast" the relationship; in other words, she needs to find a link where there formerly was none. For this reason, "interpersonal fatalism" is a common practice, where a new relationship is interpreted as one that was "meant to be" because two people have a "natural affinity" (*yuan*).[33] If both sides view their meeting as predestined, then they are likely to incorporate one another into their personal social web. The following chain message, sent by a young migrant woman to a young male migrant worker from another province whom she had met when they shared the bulk of a seventeen-hour train ride home during Spring Festival, demonstrates this idea of the role of fate or destiny (*yuanfen*) in bringing two people together:

> Having many friends is meaningless. If you have one really close friend, they are worth hundreds of others. You cannot judge the value of your friendship based on how long you've known each other. If you have a good friend, and you spend one day together, the friendship may last for one

thousand years. You cannot choose the timing to make a friend. If you can make a really good friend they will help you your whole life. Having you as a friend is fate, luck, and a blessing.

As conveyed in the message, the two had only spent this one time together, but they continued to cultivate their relationship (which was strictly based on friendship according to the young woman) via the mobile phone, feeling that it was fate that they had met.[34]

On the other hand, some women used their phones to engage in new modes of relationship building that did not necessarily adhere to traditional *guanxi* norms. Chatting with strangers on QQ was certainly one instance of this, yet often the strangers who became their *wangyou* were from their home province. QQ groups also brought new opportunities for expanding relationships. Again, though most women were members of groups that still followed typical *guanxi* principles (groups for relatives, hometown people, etc.), where a "natural" affinity made it more likely for the members to bond, others joined groups based on common extrinsic interests, such as a group devoted to pop star "Super Girl" Li Yuchun. In such groups, however, the common interest did not necessarily generate what would be considered a "true" friend in China. Moreover, some women had joined groups based on hometown affiliation or interest but eventually left such groups, finding them either too "chaotic" (*chao*) or too much of a burden to maintain given their work schedules.

In general, then, migrant women are using their mobile phones to generate what Barry Wellman calls "network capital," or the "relations with friends, neighbors, relatives, and workmates that significantly provide companionship, emotional aid, goods and services, information, and a sense of belonging."[35] But are mobile phones helping women to expand their social capital in a Bourdieuian understanding of the concept? This is a more difficult question. Although women have enlarged their social networks and, especially via QQ, have connected with people they would not have connected with before, for the most part the people whose names were stored in their mobile phone address books and QQ contact lists were like them—migrant workers, classmates, family members—almost all with rural *hukou*, thereby affirming their identity as "not Beijing people," as one of my informants termed it. Thus, in some ways mobile phones reinforce Bourdieu's notion of social capital as exclusionary, serving to uphold distinct boundaries based on class and income, and thereby maintaining inequality in society. Given the increasing social stratification in China discussed in chapter 1, this finding is not surprising. Though migrant women have greater agency via mobile phones to maintain and forge new voluntary relationships, these are circumscribed by what Linda Martín Alcoff calls their "positionality," which is marked by the intersections of their gender, class, age, and rural origin and which then situates them within cultural, political, and economic networks that lack power.[36] Immobile mobility enables migrant women to overcome certain structural constraints but clearly it cannot erase these completely. At the same time, while established norms of sociality and relationship building may affirm their "ruralness," the mobile phone in particular allows migrant women to expand their social networks in ways that would not be possible—or at least would entail much greater effort—without one.

*Enriching Social Networks*

Aside from expanding networks, how are mobile phones used to enrich the quality of relationships in the face of severe constraints due to distances and a lack of leisure time, and given the fact that migrants in the city, whether newly arrived or veterans of several years, can experience loneliness and homesickness? As one of my informants said, "When I first moved to Beijing I was so lonely. I cried every night. Sure I had my aunt and uncle, but I didn't want to share these feelings with them."[37] Many migrant women must also endure extreme isolation and/or boredom at work, or what I call regulated drudgery, depending on the type of job they have. The long work hours and minimal free time discussed earlier mean that many women have little opportunity for face-to-face interactions with friends outside of colleagues. Even on the rare occasion where two friends have the same day off, if they live in different parts of the city it can be very difficult to meet up due to long bus commutes. Thus, on a precious day off, no matter how much one desires face-to-face sociality, a choice might be made to stay home and sleep instead.

Such temporal and spatial constraints, however, were overcome through the immobile mobility provided by the mobile phone. That is, many women had friendships that were nurtured *almost strictly through their mobile phones* rather than through face-to-face contact. This use of the mobile phone presents a striking contrast to the way phones are often used by more affluent populations in developed countries. For example, Rich Ling cites a European-wide study that found that mobile voice calls and text messaging "are nearly a proxy for face-to-face interaction with a person's social network."[38] In other words, these three types of communication—texting, calling, and speaking while physically co-present—tend to revolve around friends who live in the same local area. He concludes that "there is immediacy in mobile interactions. They are not used to maintain the more [geographically] remote social relations."[39] Scholars researching in other western European countries and urban Japan have reached similar conclusions.[40]

For this reason, in other contexts the mobile phone has been called a "supportive communication technology" utilized to sustain relationships that are primarily grounded in face-to-face contact.[41] Among young migrant women working in the low-level service sector in Beijing, however, the mobile phone is what I call an "expansive communication technology," used not only for maintaining ties with friends who are now spread all over China, but also with those who, although in the same city, are nonetheless geographically unreachable. In this way, the mobile phone again affords migrant women with immobile mobility, a virtual means of traversing the boundaries of long work schedules, cloistered living situations, and far distances in order to sustain their social networks.[42]

This is not to say that women do not use their phones to communicate with colleagues whom they see on a daily basis. They do, but such communication is often dismissed as merely for fun (*wan*). On the other hand, several women said their close friends were not in Beijing. Those who worked in the relatively isolated stalls in the marketplaces were likely to say they did not have *any* friends in Beijing, though they might have a sibling. Moreover, they were acutely aware of the cultural differences between themselves and Beijing residents. As one young woman said:

> It's very hard to make friends in Beijing, or to find a boyfriend, because I work such long hours, and my fellow villagers don't work near here. I don't like Beijing people. They are too proud and they look down on outsiders. They are also so picky about the smallest things. They always have to correct you.[43]

Women who were involved in an organization such as the Migrant Women's Club or Facilitator, which sponsor activities specifically designed to encourage social interaction and friendship building among rural migrants

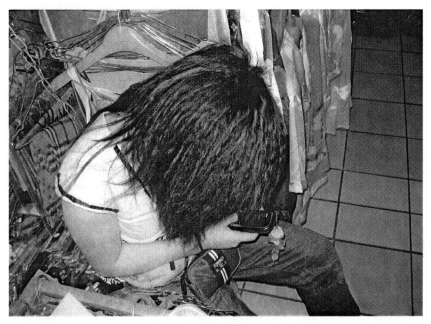

Fig. 6. A young woman responds to a "digital gift" at work.

in the city, tended to have at least a few friends in Beijing. But many of the women I knew were not involved in such groups for a number of reasons, including restrictive schedules and a fear of further stigmatization.

To enrich their relationships, migrant women often use their mobile phones for what has been called "hyper-coordination" or "digital gift giving."[44] Prior to their widespread use of the mobile Internet (specifically QQ), such "social grooming" was often done via text messages that either had minimal content—asking about work or how one was doing—or were prewritten (chain) messages and contained greetings, jokes, or sentimental feelings (as in the message discussed earlier). In sending such messages, migrant women followed norms of reciprocity; in other words, a digital gift always had to be reciprocated and without significant delay (see figure 6). Perhaps reflecting the difficult circumstances migrants face, I found that often such messages expressed a desire for a simpler existence or to be able to leave one's worries behind. Such themes again reveal how the mobile phone can be used for achieving immobile mobility or escaping from reality, even if temporarily. In this way, text messages can become like the lyrics of a song, which listeners use both to construct themselves and to mediate between their private inner selves and the larger social world. Other prewritten messages can be humorous and playful.

Though prewritten messages are still sent, especially on holidays, many women now view texting primarily as something to be used only for a particular purpose, such as to ask about a meeting or to let someone know one is arriving at a destination. In a relatively short time span, QQ has supplanted texting as a means for migrants to enrich their social relationships. There are practical reasons for this shift; for example, many informants said they found it easier to input characters on the QQ interface compared to texting. As one women said, "If I really want to express myself, if I text message, it might be unclear, but with QQ chat I can express myself more clearly."[45] Also, unlike mobile numbers that are changed (to avoid higher fees) when a user moves outside a specified geographic area, QQ numbers are not dependent on a physical place (though they can expire if left dormant for a while). QQ is also cheaper because the cost is based on the amount of space used and not on the number of messages sent or voice calls made. Some women leave QQ on whenever they are not at work, and others who are allowed to have their phones on at work never log off.

Aside from such practical reasons, there are also social reasons for QQ's popularity, including the fact that users are able to chat with many people at a time, can upload and share photos, and can participate in various types of social games. QQ has also brought new forms of digital gifting as well—many women use QQ to share songs and videos. While this practice raises questions of intellectual property rights, an equally important issue is how such sharing fills a void left by China's mainstream entertainment media, which are geared primarily toward an elite, middle-class audience.[46] Several migrant women also said they often read romance novels via QQ, a practice that shows much continuity with their consumption of print media prior to their use of the Internet.[47]

Mobile phones have been said to enable users to achieve various emotional goals,[48] and a newer way migrant women enrich their social relationships is through expressing their feelings through their status updates on QQ's Qzone. Such updates can be seen as similar to those used on Facebook, yet while many Facebook users update their statuses with posts of news or events, none of the women I knew used their status updates for such a purpose. Instead, the space was seen as a site for conveying their emotions only to a select group of close friends. These friends were expected to respond to such posts with similar emotion and empathy. The significance of QQ in enriching relationships, and correspondingly women's own emotional health, is seen in Yan Qiyun's statement that "QQ is part of my life. If it's not there I would be missing something."[49] A young male migrant also said in an interview, "If I don't go on QQ [everyday], my heart feels empty."[50]

Though QQ has become articulated to emotions and feelings among migrant women, the program is not without controversy in China. QQ is known as being a tool for anonymous sexual solicitations, and it is therefore viewed with disdain in official and popular discourse.[51] There is also a digital divide of sorts between QQ, which is heavily populated by migrant workers and rural youth, and social networking sites like Renren and Kaixin001, which are explicitly geared toward university students and white-collar workers, respectively.[52] Such a social networking divide also has implications for social capital. In that users segmented by class and place offline are similarly separated online—both by design and through their own socio-techno practices—we see more evidence that a Bourdieuian notion of social capital as exclusionary operates via typical modes of *guanxi* building, which then inform networked sociality.

Migrants' QQ use also reflects what I call "necessary convergence." That is, unlike more affluent users who have multiple Internet access methods— desktop and laptop computers and tablets like the iPad in addition to mobile phones—many migrants' only means of going online (outside of Internet cafés) is with Internet-enabled mobile phones. Although such access is certainly important in alleviating digital inequality, it still results in certain constraints. The few migrant women I knew who had convenient access to an Internet-enabled computer through, for example, sharing costs with roommates or illegally tapping into a neighborhood wireless account, all insisted that given the choice they would access QQ via a computer and not a mobile phone due to the ease and convenience of use of the former. Thus, although western market researchers and tech commentators might celebrate how "for many people in China, the mobile Web is the only one they need," such proclamations miss the inequality underlying such usage. Mobile phones converge functions on one device, but they cannot substitute for the requisite digital fluency and technical skills needed in the job market.[53]

## Mobile Phones and Romance

Although my focus thus far has been on how mobile phones are used to expand and enrich relationships among friends, family, and various acquaintances, another important part of migrant women's mobile phone assemblage is the phone's role in dating and sexually intimate relationships. In such cases, the phone is not just used as a device to transmit thoughts and feelings; rather, the phone also signifies deep emotional investments. Before discussing this aspect of the phone, however, it is first necessary to describe how courtship and marital patterns in rural and urban China have transformed over the last couple of decades. Despite such changes, marriage has endured as a nearly unquestioned institution and a significant milestone in young adults' lives.[54]

*The Transformation of Marital Patterns*

Although completely arranged marriages were abolished long ago, and China's marriage law was updated as recently as 2001, in reality contemporary rural marriage practices vary greatly by region. Arranged marriages, selling daughters for marriage, and even child betrothal have reappeared in certain areas in the reform era.[55] At the least, in many rural areas it is presumed that children will comply with the expectations of their immediate families when selecting spouses, although to what extent marriages are "arranged" or "free choice" depends on a number of factors, including the specific region, the wealth and status of the family, and the age of the couple.[56] When economic cooperation among members of peasant households is stressed and marriage is seen as a significant factor in the household economy—and thus a means of enhancing the family's economic and social capital—young people may be able to choose their spouses, yet go-betweens are often used to connect families with children of marital age, and members of the kin group take part in marriage negotiations.[57] In the poorest rural areas, however, near-complete parental influence over a child's (especially a daughter's) marriage can still be prevalent.[58] Even among China's urbanites, though arranged marriages are nonexistent, some type of intermediary is also quite frequently a factor in marital arrangements, yet this is more often than not a friend or relative of the same generation rather than a parent.[59] In a recent survey of marriage patterns in China, only about 30 percent of urban couples who had married after 1990 met without the aid of some type of intermediary.[60]

Such differences in urban and rural marital patterns should not be interpreted as reifying a notion of rural women as "traditional" chaste females in contrast to their "modern" urban counterparts. Several studies have shown a high incidence of premarital sex and cohabitation among migrants in the city and among unmarried couples in certain rural areas, though cohabitation usually occurs once a couple is engaged.[61] Evidence from my own fieldwork concurs with such findings. Moreover, conservative sexual attitudes expressed by urban women versus urban men are also a common finding in research on sexuality in China, despite a rash of sexually explicit storytelling by young urban women (e.g., *Shanghai Baby* by Wei Hui, and Muzi Mei's sex blog).[62]

## Migration, Dating, and Marriage

In China, due to local custom, young rural women tend to marry and bear children at a younger age than their urban counterparts.[63] Nearly all of my informants who were twenty or older (and some who were younger) reported that their female friends in their home villages were already married and that many had already had children. Xiao Sun, who was twenty-four and had been in Beijing for six years working at a variety of jobs, was typical in her response when I asked her how her life would be different if she had never come to Beijing:

> It would be very different. I would be married by now and have a child. . . .
> Many of my friends—their whole life is being a mother. I am definitely
> different from them. I don't want to live that kind of life because that kind
> of life, if I have to take care of kids and cook, I'm not used to it. I definitely
> prefer to go to work.[64]

Like Xiao Sun, most young rural women involved in labor migration are more likely than their rural peers to postpone marriage.[65] In fact, delaying marriage or avoiding an unwelcome arranged marriage are frequently cited by rural women as reasons for migration. Moreover, migrant women are more likely than those who never leave home to choose their own boyfriends and husbands.[66] Rural-to-urban migration has thus challenged Chinese norms regarding unmarried rural women's chastity and parental authority in marriage. Unlike males who often migrate after they are married, one-third to nearly one-half of all female migrants leave home before they are old enough to marry.[67] The expectation is that once they reach marriageable age (in their early twenties), they will return home to wed and start a family.[68]

Those who delay return (in their mid- to late twenties) are potentially seen as "old maids" back home. Nevertheless, more and more migrant women have been prolonging their stay in urban areas, and some may never return home.[69] Their urban experiences, changed values, and increased knowledge of the world make them less tolerant both of the conditions back in their home villages and of the males there who are their potential partners.[70] Many of the women I knew expressed such concerns, and for some the anxiety about the possibility of finding a suitable partner weighed heavily upon them.

*Mobile Intimacy*

The small social circle that most migrants occupy in the city means that they have always used various tactics to meet potential romantic partners. For example, prior to their widespread use of mobile phones or the Internet, young migrants sought "pen pals" (a euphemism for a boyfriend or girlfriend) through classified ads in print media geared toward migrants. This practice still exists, and a mobile phone makes sustaining such a relationship tremendously more convenient, yet none of the women I knew said they used such ads, nor did they acknowledge ever responding to a sexually provocative text message sent by a complete stranger.[71] This is not to say that intimate or even sexually explicit messages were not sent among couples.[72] Moreover, some women are using QQ on their mobile phones to try to find suitable partners, often through relying on the types of shared identity mentioned earlier, such as a shared geographic region.[73]

Migration thus enables new freedoms in pursuing relationships, as do new media technologies. However, in the city young rural-to-urban migrant women do not necessarily discard cultural norms regarding intimate relationships, nor does technology completely change people's values and practices. Rather, what I observed was most often a mixing of established norms and new media technology, or a blend of culture and communication tools, in women's dating relationships. In the remainder of this chapter I first relate two narratives that, while slightly different, together form a portrait of the way socio-techno practices arise within existing social and cultural meanings.[74] A third story shows how technology use coalesces with both cultural patterns and transforming institutional structures to create expanded possibilities for the forging of intimate relationships. All three narratives continue to raise questions about the connection between technology and social capital and to illuminate how mobile phones are articulated to *guanxi* principles.

### A HUMAN INTERMEDIARY

Chen Weiwei was from a village in Hebei province, and when I first met her in 2007 she had been in Beijing for about a year working in a small beauty salon. Like every woman I knew, her work schedule meant (in her words) that it was "nearly impossible to meet a friend [meaning boyfriend] in Beijing."[75] So, when a relative at home wanted to introduce her to a young man named Li Kang from a neighboring town, Chen Weiwei was quite amenable to the idea. With Chen Weiwei in Beijing and Li Kang in Hebei, an introductory meeting was arranged via a webcam at an Internet café. As Chen Weiwei said, "We met this way a couple of times, just to see what each other looked like and get a first impression."[76] A few virtual meetings were enough for them to decide that they were suitable for a relationship, and due to the inconvenience and costs associated with going to an Internet café, all future "dating" took place via the mobile phone, with text messages sent throughout the day and long conversations until late into the night.[77] After four and a half months, Chen Weiwei and Li Kang finally met face-to-face. They then maintained their relationship via the mobile phone, with periodic face-to-face visits, until eventually Li Kang moved to Beijing.

Though romantic relationships sustained via a mobile phone have been observed in other contexts,[78] Chen Weiwei and Li Kang's story illustrates several characteristics of Chinese social relationships. These include the importance of a common (*tong*) identity in forming the basis for establishing a relationship (here a common province implies common experience), the role of intermediaries in potential marital arrangements, and how rural couples tend to decide rather quickly on one another's suitability. Despite these conventional aspects of their introduction, Chen Weiwei and Li Kang used their mobile phones to achieve a large degree of autonomy in pursuing an intimate relationship. In the salon, Chen Weiwei was sometimes teased by her colleagues that she was "always with her boyfriend" or "always dating" because she was often texting Li Kang or had her mobile phone with her even when she wasn't using it. Rather than understanding this situation as "perpetual contact" or "dependent presence,"[79] however, we can see Chen Weiwei and Li Kang's use of mobile communication as illustrating how once again the immobile mobility achieved through the phone is as much a technological practice as a social and emotional mode of being and being in relationship with others in the world.

### A VIRTUAL INTERMEDIARY

At twenty-five, Zhang Meili was one of the oldest migrant women in this study, and she had also been living in Beijing the longest (seven years). In the past, she said, she had felt pressured by her family to get married so that villagers would not gossip about her being a "shameful" woman. Single migrant women who remain "out to work" beyond the customary marriage age are often the target of such gossip in their home villages, with the assumption being that their reason for remaining in the city is that they are either doing some sort of illicit job (such as sex work) or are engaging in a sexual affair, or both. By the time I met Zhang Meili she already had a boyfriend named Xiao Zhao. They had met in a manner that reveals not only certain particularities of Chinese culture but also the limitations as well as possibilities of the inferior technology that rural-to-urban migrants often use.

Zhang Meili had a friend named Sun Li who was engaged and who several months earlier had had to return to her home in Sichuan province to prepare for her wedding. Sun Li had a "Little Smart" phone (*Xiaolingtong*), a less expensive mobile phone with limited mobility. Because her Little Smart only worked in Beijing, Sun Li had asked Zhang Meili if they could temporarily trade phones. Borrowing or swapping phones was quite common among the migrant women I knew in Beijing, and it was rather different from the copresent sharing of mobile phones observed among youth in other settings.[80] If a friend or relative needed a phone and didn't have one (e.g., because it was broken or stolen, or she couldn't afford one), my informants would lend that person her phone as a matter of course. On numerous occasions I sent text messages to migrant women friends only to have their reply come from a phone other than their own, or from a sibling or friend explaining their temporary use of the phone (those who borrowed the phone always passed on messages). These acts of swapping, lending, and borrowing of phones reflect the cultural norms of obligation and reciprocity explained earlier as well as the often very practical use of mobile phones by migrant women.

Thus, Zhang Meili traded phones with Sun Li, and she explained the rest of her story as follows:

> Sun Li's fiancé was in the army and he had a friend named Xiao Zhao who had just bought his first mobile phone. Xiao Zhao complained that he had no one with whom to exchange messages, so Sun Li's fiancé told him to contact her, maybe she could help. Well, when Xiao Zhao finally sent a message, Sun Li was in Sichuan and I had her phone. When I received his text asking for help finding a friend, I was kind of interested, you know [laughs]. So, I asked him who he was, how he knew Sun Li, and so on. I thought his answers were acceptable, so I told him we could be friends. After that we started exchanging messages on a daily basis, then several times a day, and of course we called each other, too.[81]

This relationship began via new media technology, yet early on Zhang Meili and Xiao Zhao also incorporated more "traditional" forms of courtship, including writing letters and mailing photos. As Zhang Meili said, "I had to make sure he looked alright." Eventually they started dating solely through the mobile phone, and like Chen Weiwei and her boyfriend, they did not have their first face-to-face meeting for several months. After nine months they became engaged, and because Xiao Zhao was in the army with minimal leave time, they had actually only seen each other a handful of times prior to their engagement. Before they became engaged, Zhang Meili's mother had gone to Beijing to meet (and approve of) Xiao Zhao.

In Chen Weiwei and Li Kang's story, a relative acted as an intermediary in a customary fashion; their shared province entailed a "natural" bond between them; and technology then enabled immobile mobility, or for spatial constraints to be overcome, though not entirely erased. In Zhang Meili and Xiao Zhao's story, the technology itself served as the intermediary through a confluence of several factors. In following Chinese norms of friendship based on reciprocity and obligation, Zhang Meili and Sun Li swapped phones. Sun Li's phone then became an intermediary only because Zhang Meili did not perceive of Xiao Zhao's text message as coming from an anonymous stranger with whom she had no shared (tong) identity, but from someone with whom Sun Li's fiancé must have had good guanxi. Zhang Meili thus felt comfortable responding to Xiao Zhao's messages and pursuing their relationship.

It is important to point out, however, that few people in China have a Little Smart phone if they can afford a standard mobile phone. The Little Smart's reception quality is often poor, and it is inconvenient due to limited range, which is why Zhang Meili and Sun Li traded phones in the first place.[82] People may borrow and lend phones for a variety of reasons, yet Zhang Meili's story demonstrates how cultural, social, and economic factors give rise to contingencies that are particular to the lives of China's migrant workers. At the same time, although she and Xiao Zhao lacked economic capital and cultural capital (objectified in minimal leisure time, for example), his position in the army could possibly bode well for their future.[83] In this regard, her phone did help her build her social capital, although I do not mean to imply in any way that this was the primary reason she began a relationship with him.

### NO INTERMEDIARY

It has been well documented that many migrant women hope to marry an urban resident in order to improve their life circumstances, yet for most rural women the chances of this happening are rather small given the constraints on their interactions with urban men, the negative stereotypes urbanites have of female migrants, and the fact that, proportionally, migrant women outnumber single urban men in their age group.[84] There is also a widely held perception that a "good" urban male would not want to marry a migrant, and that if such a marriage took place, the difference in the social statuses of the husband and wife could result in the wife becoming a victim of domestic abuse.[85]

While these perceptions and actual constraints still exist, small transformations, both cultural and structural, have been taking place that may help slowly to erode the barriers between migrants and urban residents. For example, cities such as Beijing have gradually expanded their boundaries, incorporating what were formally rural areas into new city districts. It is possible, but certainly not inevitable, that residents in those outlying areas will not be as prejudiced against migrants as those who consider themselves "old Beijing" (meaning the family has roots in a small central area of Beijing), since, until recently, they themselves were considered "outsiders." In addition, the government's more sympathetic official stance toward migrants and rural peasants has the potential to "trickle down" to the populace. Others have also noted that migrants' persistent presence in the city acts as a subaltern liminal politics, whereby their expenditure of time, energy, and labor operate to erode the barriers against them.[86] All of these issues are potentially at play in the last narrative I include about dating.

Fang Hua worked at one of the large marketplaces in Beijing, selling scarves to both Chinese and foreign customers. In 2008 she had been introduced to another migrant worker in Beijing, and they had used their mobile phones to "date" because they did not have a lot of time to see one another. However, just like Tao in the film *The World*, Fang Hua eventually learned her boyfriend was cheating on her when she saw text messages that another girl had sent him. She broke up with him and refused his plea for forgiveness. In 2010 when I saw Fang Hua, many changes had occurred in her life. She had a new job and a new haircut, and she was engaged to Hu Shen, a university-educated Beijing resident from Tongzhou, a district of Beijing that had been incorporated in the late 1990s. They had met when he went to the marketplace to buy a gift for a friend, and they both said it was "love at first sight." Before leaving the market Hu Shen had asked Fang Hua for her mobile number. He then asked her to dinner; because his family's home was not too far from where Fang Hua lived, he began meeting her after she got off work at 7:00 p.m. every night. They would eat dinner and then he would walk her home. They also called and texted constantly, but because Hu Shen often used his parents' landline to call Fang Hua, the bill became very expensive. After about six months, Hu Shen's father, who used China Mobile's GoTone service (discussed in chapter 1), added Fang Hua to his family plan, making the numerous calls between Hu Shen and Fang Hua free. After ten months, Hu Shen and Fang Hua became engaged, and she moved into his family home. They are now married and she is working at a small company and taking night courses to receive a university degree.

I relate Fang Hua and Hu Shen's story not to imply that Fang Hua's future happiness depends on her marrying a Beijing resident. On the contrary, aside from the potential problems caused by differences in status mentioned above, in cases where *dagongmei* have married Beijing men, there are further difficulties brought on by the restrictions on legal residence, housing, family planning, and, if they have a child, the child's education.[87] Instead, Fang Hua and Hu Shen's story reveals that not only access to communication technology but also transformations in the attitudes and values of China's young people, along with structural changes in city boundaries and thus notions of insider/outsider, are contributing to small but significant changes in how migrants might fare in the city. It also shows that Bourdieu's notion of social capital can be too rigid. On the other hand, it is significant that Fang Hua had finished senior high school prior to arriving in Beijing and that she was from Hebei, the same province as Hu Shen's grandparents. Thus, in their case *guanxi* principles were flexible but did not entirely disappear. Perhaps their relationship is merely the exception that proves the rule, or, perhaps in the future, as further barriers between migrants and urbanites are broken down, Fang Hua and Hu Shen's story will be as mundane as two Beijing university students going on their first date.

In addition to the narratives of Chen Weiwei, Zhang Meili, and Fang Hua, my research yielded numerous examples of dating via the mobile phone. When informants were asked if these relationships would have been possible without a mobile phone, they never said "no," but many thought it would have been rather difficult. For the most part, my informants did not use their phones to actively search for a suitable partner although, as mentioned earlier, some migrant women are using QQ for this purpose. The majority of the time, except in Fang Hua's case, when my informants used technology to enhance their dating lives, there was still an intermediary, just as in traditional Chinese culture. Significantly, relationships were maintained primarily through text messaging (and, more recently, online chat) supplemented by voice calls, with face-to-face meeting occurring long after the relationship had been solidified via the mobile phone.

In considering transformations in how young Chinese people establish intimate relationships, it is important to note that market reforms have brought an abundance of western fast-food chains, shopping malls, trendy bars, and coffeehouses that provide a place for adolescents and young adults to have a "private" life in public, away from the prying eyes of parents and other authority figures.[88] However, migrant women in Beijing cannot access these public spaces because they clearly cannot afford them and they have minimal leisure time. A mobile phone thus offers them a "private" life in a public space (a workplace, a dormitory) and affords them privacy perhaps heretofore impossible because they tend to live in communal areas where, even if there were a phone, it would be difficult to use, and conversations would be anything but private. Mobile phones do not determine culture yet they do allow for heretofore desired but unrealizable freedom and autonomy in establishing and maintaining intimate relationships.

Conclusion

Rural-to-urban migrant women's technological mediations of *guanxi* and social capital, which I have outlined in this chapter, reveal that the mobile phone has become integral to the way that these women navigate myriad social relationships in Beijing. At the most basic level, the mobile phone is a convenient device for keeping in touch with friends and family who are far away, because it alleviates the hassle of scheduling phone calls and relying on public telephones. It has also become articulated to building network capital, primarily as it is used to expand horizontal networks of sociality and develop potential *guanxi* bases. Kenneth Gergen has postulated that the cell phone challenges the western sense of the "bounded self" through emphasizing the relational and "underscor(ing) the importance of connection as opposed to autonomy, looking outward rather than inward, toward network as opposed to self-sufficiency."[89] In China, the mobile phone seems to supplement cultural notions of self and autonomy that have long been in place.

Beyond the phone's use as a transmission device, it also performs a significant role in rituals of communication when it is articulated to such practices as "digital gift giving" of messages, songs, videos, and novels as well as through the borrowing and lending of phones among friends. Such practices did not arrive with the phone but rather show continuity with the relational mode of Chinese society. In the same way, the dating practices that have emerged via the phone blend both the traditional and technological, while challenging established norms and patterns. Most importantly, the immobile mobility accessed through the mobile phone allows migrant women to transcend myriad barriers of space, place, and time to expand and enrich numerous types of relationships.

If the value of social capital is not only found in its relational purpose, but also in whether it can be translated to other forms of capital, then in general this chapter argues that mobile phones are not going to be articulated to substantial changes in migrant women's material conditions. As shown throughout, in the majority of instances, and in line with typical *guanxi* norms, those in the women's expanded and enriched social networks are like them, or "not Beijing people." However, given the mode in which social relationships are established in China, and the vast evidence elsewhere against technological determinism, we shouldn't expect otherwise. In other words, immobile mobility does not equal social mobility. However, because both social change and technological change are mutually constitutive, we can hope that mobile phones will continue to be articulated to modes of relationship building that push for inclusion rather than exclusion in the highly stratified yet dynamic assemblage that constitutes contemporary China.

# 4

## Picturing the Self, Imagining the World

What I want, in short, is that my (mobile) image, buffeted among a thousand shifting photographs, altering with situation and age, should always coincide with my (profound) "self"; but it is the contrary that must be said: "myself" never coincides with my image.
—Roland Barthes, *Camera Lucida*, 12

One spring day I went to visit Li Yun, a friend who worked in one of the large marketplaces in Beijing. It was relatively early in the morning, and the lack of customers meant it was an ideal time for talking with Li Yun and her colleagues. On this particular day Li Yun introduced me to Zhao Ning, who had come from a small village in Henan and had been in Beijing for a couple of years. "She loves to play with her phone. You'll like her," Li Yun said. Zhao Ning smiled and agreed that she did indeed love her phone. Over the next hour or so as the three of us chatted about various topics, Zhao Ning had me listen to several songs stored in her phone (acquired through friends rather than downloaded, which would have been cost prohibitive), showed me a few of the phone's pre-installed games, and had me view dozens of the photos she had taken. Eventually the market started to get busy, so I told Li Yun and Zhao Ning I should get going. As I was about to leave, Zhao Ning said, "Wait, let me have your phone. I want to give you something." Before I knew it she was manipulating the Bluetooth in both of our phones. "Look," she said, "a remembrance." On the screen of my phone was a picture of Zhao Ning, her chin resting on her folded, well-manicured hands, her hair combed perfectly, and her eyes gazing straight ahead as she smiled demurely. "Now let me take one of you," she said. I suggested that all three of us be in the picture, but she and Li Yun told me they didn't want to be photographed in the orange vests they had to wear during work. Zhao Ning snapped a picture of me with her phone, asked me to check that it was acceptable, and then we all said good-bye until next time.

My photographic encounter with Zhao Ning and Li Yun—viewing cam-era-phone images, snapping pictures, posing—was similar to interactions I had with several migrant women during my fieldwork. The carefully con-structed picture that Zhao transferred to my phone also resembled the style and form of other women's self-images that were stored in their phones. The way the camera phone was used—for sociality, memory, and self-pre-sentation as well as for spontaneous image making—has been explored in research on camera phones.[1] This emerging body of scholarship has shown that camera phones should not be understood as "just another kind of cam-era" due to the fact that the phone's camera is embedded in a communication device and is often carried on the body.[2] However, with few exceptions most of these studies have been conducted in developed countries among youth and young adults with easy access to computers and digital cameras in addi-tion to their mobile phones.[3] Thus, little is known about the everyday use of camera phones by marginalized youth and young adults.[4]

Like the Kodak camera before it, a camera phone further democratizes photographic practices, particularly as these concern personal imaging.[5] Because camera phones are potentially always at hand, they are said to extend "existing personal imaging practices" and enable "the evolution of new kinds of imaging practices."[6] This assertion may be true, yet "extend-ing" and "evolving" imply a basis in, and prior experience with, conventional cameras. What types of imaging practices emerge when a camera phone is the first camera that a person has ever had? Moreover, though there may be similarities in usage across different contexts, what are the implications of such a device for those who face highly constrained material circumstances? For example, in much of the existing research, camera-phone images are said to be "fleeting" or transitory; their poor image quality means that for special occasions the preference is to use a conventional digital camera.[7] How are the terms of usage different without the assumed choices between a digital camera and a camera phone and without convenient access to a computer for storing images?

The questions above lead to the main theme of this chapter: the imaging practices of migrant women and the kinds of cultural work such practices achieve. As with the other socio-techno practices explored thus far in this book, it is not only the activity, in this case taking a picture, that is important, but also the numerous emotions, sensations, imaginings, and desires that are articulated to express what could be called a particular mobile constellation. To map this territory, I examine how young migrant women use camera phones to document their lives in, and imagine a world outside of, Beijing. In order to situate my analysis, I first discuss the rise of commercial and personal photography in China in the reform era, and I follow this discussion by an overview of the technical limitations of my informants' camera-phone use. I then consider some of the larger theoretical issues surrounding photography and camera phones before exploring how migrant women use camera phones for representing the world, constructing the self, transcending limited circumstances, envisaging new possibilities, and planning for the future. Though I divide camera-phone use into these five categories for analytical purposes, I argue that ultimately all of these imaging practices are about self making and actively deploying the imagination, or what Arjun Appadurai defines as "an organized field of social practices, a form of work . . . and a form of negotiation between sites of agency (individuals) and globally defined fields of possibility."[8] Thus, although I focus on socio-techno practices specific to migrant women, these must be understood within a broader global visual economy perpetuated through electronic media and heightened in the era of digital technology. In discussing imaging and imagining, I build on themes in previous chapters, including consumption practices, the constitutive nature of subjectivity and technology, the phone as a technology of the self, and the affective dimension of mobile phone use. I also continue my elaboration of necessary convergence and how mobile phones enable immobile mobility, or a virtual means of traversing myriad structural, temporal, and spatial boundaries.

In their early work on camera-phone use in Japan, Daisuke Okabe and Mizuko Ito noted "technosocial situations" of camera-phone use that they saw emerging from pre-existing social and cultural meaning systems and structures.[9] My analysis as well is grounded in the belief that socio-techno practices materialize within specific social and cultural contexts. In discussing the camera-phone use of the migrant women in this study, I therefore insist on the salience of their gender, class, age, and rural backgrounds. As *dagongmei* (working little sisters), they faced economic constraints that limited the technology they could acquire and, combined with minimal free time, restricted the experiences they captured with their phones. The relatively contained social world of many migrant women was often reflected in the pictures snapped and stored in their phones, yet the phones were also used to resist these inequitable conditions, thereby exemplifying Sarah Kember's assertion that photography "is clearly much more than a particular technology of image-making. It is also a social and cultural practice embedded in history and human agency."[10] Through analyzing my informants' camera-phone images as part of their mobile phone assemblage, at times I highlight how the actual technology informed such practices and led to necessary convergence, but my larger aim is to show how these women's imaging practices, though not wholly unique, were a means of creatively "making do" and empowering themselves within the constraints of their lives.

Photography in China from Mao to Now

Despite a burgeoning literature on art photography, surprisingly little has been written on personal and commercial photography in contemporary China.[11] However, developments in everyday photographic practices should be understood within the context of the rise of a consumer society and leisure culture in China. For example, when viewing images from the Mao era, it is easy to find familiar subjects—families, couples, children—yet framed in rather utilitarian or proletarian ways in line with the socialist aesthetics of the time. Individuals wear "Mao suits" or plain white blouses or dress shirts and dark trousers, and they often stare straight into the camera without smiling. Women eschew such "bourgeois" elements as makeup or jewelry. However, within the image realm of contemporary China, such pictures look particularly archaic.

Indeed in China today, it is not just images—both official and individual—that have been transformed, but also people's ability to construct their *own* images has evolved. This is true elsewhere in the world, given the rapid diffusion of technologies for personal image making: handheld video recorders, digital cameras, and photo-editing software. However, in China this transformation is particularly noteworthy when placed in historical context. Throughout the Mao era, some urban families might have had cameras, but most did not, and individual cameras were certainly a rare sight for those residing in the countryside. For special occasions people could go to state-run studios to take black-and-white portraits, which were then prominently hung on living room walls. If a person happened to have a friend with a camera, he might be able to rely on him or her to snap family pictures. Yet it wasn't until the early 1980s that personal photography started to enter the domain of the everyday. As sightseeing became more common, at popular tourist sites people could rent a camera, purchase a roll of film, take pictures, and then develop the film on-site before returning home, where the negatives could be taken to a local shop to be printed.[12] By the early to mid-1980s, more families and individuals were able to buy cameras, which were inexpensive Chinese analog cameras or Japanese and Korean imports. Some people, especially students in cities like Beijing, created makeshift darkrooms and developed their own film as a hobby and a way to save money.[13] By the early 1990s, reflecting the changes brought about by the economic reforms, it was common for families in major urban areas to own a camera and to take photographs to document occasions of all kinds.[14] In the mid-1990s digital cameras became available, and while at first the cost was prohibitive for most people, now, as elsewhere, digital cameras are the norm for China's middle class. Teenagers from well-off families, especially in urban areas, usually have their own digital cameras. In contrast, most rural teens or young adult rural-to-urban migrants do not have the financial means to own digital cameras.

In addition to the growth in personal photography, commercial photography studios have proliferated in cities and towns in China since the 1980s. In Beijing, for example, there is an abundance of studios offering everything from quick photos for passports and other identification cards to quite elaborate photo shoots involving costumes, makeup, and props. For a hefty fee, "common people" (*laobaixing*) can indulge in a photo shoot and leave with an array of pictures to display in their homes or offices and to distribute to friends and family.[15] Noteworthy as well in China, as in much of Asia, are the commercial wedding photography studios that emerged in the 1980s. These have created a custom that differs in significant ways from wedding photography in the United States, where the bride and groom have posed photos taken of themselves before (or sometimes after) the ceremony and candid

Fig. 7. A wedding photography promotion in a Beijing shopping mall.

shots throughout the ceremony and reception. Instead, wedding photography in China involves an elaborate process that is separate from the actual
ceremony. The bride and groom are photographed in various locations,
wearing different outfits, and, in the case of the bride, often donning a different hairstyle or makeup.[16] Couples often take two sets of wedding pictures:
one with the bride decked out in western wedding garb (white dress, veil,
flower bouquet, etc.) and the other with her in "traditional" attire (silk shoes
and a red *qipao*, a traditional Chinese dress, very form-fitting with a slit skirt
and a high collar). After the ceremony, poster-size color prints of the bride
and groom are likely to adorn the walls of their new home. In cities like Beijing such wedding photography is big business (see figure 7).

I detail these newer modes of personal and commercial photography to
emphasize how omnipresent image making has become as part of the middle-class leisure and consumption culture that has emerged in China in the
last few decades. Like elsewhere, today personal and commercial photography are linked to notions of modernity and pleasure in much the same way
as commercial studio photography was in China's major cities at the turn of
the 20th century.[17] This ubiquity of image making should also be understood
within the overall transformation in the realm of images and image screens
in China that has been quite profound. Once shared by several families in

villages, a television now appears in nearly every rural home. As well, satellite dishes (many illegal) grace the mountainsides of the most remote areas, and everywhere computers are increasingly common. Advertising images are also ubiquitous and blanket space that was formerly filled with government propaganda slogans. And, not surprisingly, images—of beauty, wealth, and happiness achieved through consumption—abound and have created new ways for people to construct themselves and their relationship to the world. This abundance of images is obviously not unique to China but accords more generally with what W. J. T. Mitchell has termed a "pictorial turn," or the way pictures surround, transform, and shape the world and our notions of self.[18] Camera phones certainly fit within this broad "pictorial turn" as they give rise to socio-techno practices that are articulated to shifting notions of modernity and consumption as well as configurations of self and world.

Situating Migrant Women's Camera-Phone Use

In China, with the diffusion of mobile phones, it is now practically taken for granted that a mobile phone, even a basic one, comes equipped with a camera, and this expectation has occurred rapidly. However, when I was first conducting fieldwork in the fall of 2006, camera phones were not widely used by my informants, or even among many Chinese friends and acquaintances in Beijing (although many urban youth and young adults were using camera phones). Yet within a two-year period, the use of camera phones had expanded dramatically. In what follows, I focus primarily on the camera-phone use of about twenty migrant women over the course of my fieldwork during 2006 and 2007 and during follow-up trips in 2008 and 2009. The discussion is based on viewing these women's camera-phone images on the screens of their phones and talking about the images and their general picture-taking habits. It also derives from observations of their uses of camera phones and in some cases from their entries in their mobile phone diaries.

Before proceeding, however, a bit of contextualization is in order. First, as with nearly all of the women in this study, none of the women owned a digital camera. Second, most did not use multimedia messaging service (MMS), and those who sent or received MMS messages did not do so on a regular basis. This lack of MMS usage was due to technical as well as financial reasons.[19] Third, women like Zhao Ning, who had higher-end phones

occasionally used Bluetooth to send photos, but this usage was also constrained because their friends and family did not necessarily have similar technology on their phones and because using Bluetooth necessitates
physical proximity to the phone that is receiving the image. Fourth, because
none of these women owned computers, photos were rarely uploaded to
hard drives for storage.[20] For the most part, these women used their mobile
phones to take and store photos, much like if someone were to have a digital
camera but no computer. Thus, their usage was characterized by necessary
convergence, in that the phone had to function as a camera and a storage
device with limited capacity. For this reason, navigating the camera phone
meant that choices had to be made, not only in terms of which pictures to
take, but also which ones to keep. Such constrained usage was illuminated
for me when a migrant woman I knew named Chen Jiefeng went home for
Spring Festival with one set of images in her phone and returned to Beijing
with a whole new set, save for one earlier picture of her dog. She had, "regret-
tably" in her words, deleted the previous photos to make room for the new
ones.

## Camera Phones: Representation, Ideology, and Fantasy

In her work on photography, Susan Sontag has stated that photographs in
general offer "an ethics of seeing."[21] In other words, our worldview is reflected
in our creation of and response to photographs of the extraordinary as well
as the mundane. Moreover, our beliefs about ourselves and others, and the
way we accept or challenge conventional cultural codes regarding gender,
class, race, nationality, and so on, are intricately related to how we "see." An
"ethics of seeing" is amplified even further in the case of camera phones for
several reasons that derive from their extremely personal nature. In the same
way that mobile phones have been called an "extension of the hand," one
could argue that a camera phone offers an extension of the eye.[22] This intimate quality has been noted in prior research in a variety of contexts, where
the camera phone has been found to be an "expressive device"[23] for users to
assert their sensibility about the world around them and to take spontaneous
shots of interesting views or mundane objects that may only have meaning
or bring pleasure to the user.[24] Camera phones allow each user to create a
"personal visual archive,"[25] a "digital wallet,"[26] or a "digital 'flipbook'"[27] that
stores images of her friends and family as well as her viewpoint on daily life.

Representing the world through pictures is not only an act of "see-ing"; however, it is also about knowing. While scholars such as John Tagg and Allan Sekula have focused on the connections between photography, documentation, and state power, personal photography as well places the one wielding the camera "into a certain relation to the world that feels like knowledge—and, therefore, like power."[28] This power derives from the abil-ity to determine what goes in and what is left out of the frame of the photo, to render photographic subjects as objects, and, through these processes, to authenticate one's own perception and creation of reality. Geoffrey Batchen notes that through mapping and materially producing bodies and objects in time and space, photography is a form of power-knowledge (in Foucault's sense) that constitutes subjects—both the photographer and the subject of a photograph.[29] Because pictures do not so much represent reality as con-struct reality, Victor Burgin argues that all photographs are manipulative and, as such, ideological. However, when he asserts that "manipulation is the essence of photography," he does not mean that all pictures are instruments of deceit, nor is he referring only to production techniques employed in the studio (magnified tenfold in our digital era).[30] Rather, he is drawing atten-tion to the relationship between the viewer and the actual photo, and how this is never outside the social and cultural politics of representation, where complexes of signs create meaning just as much as they communicate it. In capturing the mundane, the immediate, and the extremely personal, cam-era phones intensify this ideological aspect of photography. However, it is important to note that while the actual *photograph* that is produced by cam-era phones may be mundane or personal, camera phones are also used in *moments* of the mundane and personal, as in my exchange with Zhao Ning discussed earlier.[31] Both images and image making are context-dependent; hence, the social *processes* underlying image making with camera phones are no less ideological than the final *product*.

Given my concern with both process and product, in addition to the rep-resentational and ideological, it is also important to consider how pictures draw on deep desires often below the level of consciousness. In Simon Wat-ney's discussion of the institution of photography, he argues that modes of production and consumption of commercial photography adhere to domi-nant notions of gender, class, and race in how they tether meanings to images, and how both ideological and psychological factors are at play.[32] He insists that looking at social influences in photography must be supplemented by discussions of desire and fantasy. As he states, "Photographs are no more, and no less, than fragments of ideology, activated by the mechanism of fantasy and desire."[33] Though his focus is on institutions, personal photography as well is a means of projecting desires and instantiating norms regarding gendered, raced, and classed bodies; the ideal family type; and socially constructed modes of public display.[34]

## Imaging and Imagining Self and World

The pictures stored in numerous young migrant women's phones illuminate the importance of the situated analysis of Okabe and Ito mentioned earlier as well as the representational, ideological, and psychological aspects of photography. In the following discussion, I demonstrate how women used photography to reflect as well as to create a particular view of reality and to construct personal meaning. I also show that while their camera-phone usage at times converged with conventional camera practices and camera-phone use documented in other contexts, their particular socio-techno practices should also be understood as emerging from their positionality in gendered, classed, and "placed" power relations. The categories delineated below are thus not meant to be universal, nor are they completely discrete because certain practices can arguably fit into more than one category. I offer them as a means of broadening our understanding of how people evince creativity and determination through pictures and imaging, and how they use technology to manage, resist, and transcend the constraints of their everyday lives.

### Virtual Mini-World

One of the most consistent features of the images stored in my informants' camera phones was that they offered a virtual version of the women's social world, which was very small. The most common pictures were of colleagues, boyfriends, and family members as well as "fictive kin" (close friends addressed by kinship terms, such as "big sister"), and all of them were, like the women, holders of rural *hukou* (except in the case of bosses, discussed below). Women were very precise in how they identified their various social relationships, differentiating them in terms of what they had in common, in accordance with the *guanxi* principles discussed in chapter 3. Thus, when showing me their pictures they invariably specified whether a photo was of a "friend," "classmate," or "colleague." Because they saw their colleagues nearly every day, there were usually more pictures of coworkers than of those whom they called friends. This distinction was evident not only because the women designated them as such while showing me their pictures, but also by the backdrop for the photos: pictures of colleagues were almost always taken at the workplace or in a dormitory and rarely at another location in Beijing. The fact that these women had so little time off meant that the phone was often used at work with colleagues during downtime—in contrast to the usual association between snapshot photography and leisure activities.[35] Furthermore, although the social aspect of camera phones has been emphasized, where snapping photos of friends and sharing images, often face-to-face, has become an important group activity embedded in the maintenance of relationships, many women told me they used their phones with their colleagues merely to relieve boredom.[36] An exception was found among the women who were involved in the Migrant Women's Club or Facilitator, as they tended to have pictures of other members or the leaders of these organizations taken during meetings or various activities.

In some cases, women who had cultivated "good" relationships with their employers (to whom they were not related) had pictures of them in their phone. Some even had pictures of a boss's spouse or child, again taken at the workplace. These photos were quite surprising to me, given the extensive documentation and my own witnessing of mistreatment and exploitation of migrant workers at the hands of their employers. Such pictures reveal the complicated terrain that migrant workers must negotiate in the workplace, where even in so-called good relationships the power differentials are considerably uneven.

Zhang Xiumei, who worked as a "greeter" at a photography studio, had several pictures in her phone of her boss decked out in fashionable clothing. When I asked her why, she told me that she liked her and that she was a "good person" (*hao ren*). A simple explanation for Zhang Xiumei's understanding of her relationship with her boss is that she is blind to the structures that maintain her subordination (in particular because her boss often asked her to work overtime). The photos, then, provide more evidence for the way that employers position migrant workers in parent-child relationships that necessitate the workers' filial obedience while offering them little in return, both emotionally and materially. Rather than seeing Zhang Xiumei as having "false consciousness," however, we can understand her perception of her relationship with her boss as a trace of her own creative negotiation of her environment. If a "harmonious" relationship with an employer is cultivated in part through the act of photography, then it is possible to read these pictures not merely as a representation of the immediate or mundane, but as a strategic practice, whether the strategy is intentional or not. If shared with friends or family back at home, the photos could also enable Zhang Xiumei to demonstrate that she is faring well in the city.

Aside from friends or colleagues, one of the most common uses of personal photography in general is for capturing images of the family. To Bourdieu, cameras have been a key means of shoring up the nuclear family, while to Barthes the photograph provides crucial evidence that a loved one, now passed away, did indeed exist.[37] When women had photos of family members in their phones, these tended to be of siblings, nephews, or cousins. In other words, a woman's social world, as it was reflected in her phone, was primarily oriented toward the peer group and the younger generation. In this way, the camera function supported the same sorts of ties that text and instant messaging did. Even when women went home for their annual visit during Chinese New Year, they returned with pictures of cousins, siblings, perhaps an uncle, and the family dog, but usually not parents. Some women told me their parents did not like to have their picture taken because they were embarrassed at their "rustic" appearance, revealing once again how the denigration of the rural in contemporary China is reproduced through rural residents who have internalized the dominant discourse that equates rurality with backwardness. Others said they hadn't thought about taking a picture of their parents. One of the most poignant reasons for not having any pictures of parents was given to me by a young woman who called herself Lois. She said she missed her mother so much that it was too painful to look at her in a photo.

In addition to preserving memories of family and friends, conventional cameras are said to play a central role in documenting special ceremonies, holidays, trips, and vacations. Research on camera phones tends to stress that although they can be used to memorialize certain events, digital cameras are preferred for preserving special memories.[38] Most of the images I viewed in women's phones were of their immediate surroundings; in other words, they revealed their small social world. Nonetheless, rare trips to a park or other sightseeing destination in Beijing, birthday celebrations, and annual trips home were all captured and stored in the camera phone. There was no need for these women to make a technical distinction about which camera to use because they only had one choice. In this regard, the camera phone enabled necessary convergence. That is to say, unlike the "selective convergence" of more privileged users of camera phones, who may choose their phones rather than digital cameras to document a special occasion or may use convergent functions as a matter of convenience, these women's necessary convergence was about overcoming the constraints of their everyday lives. As with accessing the Internet through the mobile phone, in dealing with numerous constraints, necessary convergence should be seen, to slightly revise Appadurai, as a tactic "of negotiation between sites of agency (individuals)" and *locally* "defined fields of possibility."

*Constructing the Self*

In chapter 2, I argued that, for migrant women, a mobile phone is articulated to processes of subjectification in the city. This articulation is produced partly through possession of a device that outwardly reflects contemporary Chinese notions of femininity, through, for example, the color or the addition of personal touches like rhinestones. Because camera phones extend modes of mobile customization from those that focus on the exterior to the interior of the device, they add an additional resource through which young people construct the self.[39] One way that users shape and reflect upon their identity through camera phones is by using the phone to store pictures of themselves—either self-portraits or those taken by others—for what has been called "self-presentation."[40] My informants engaged in such self-presentation, as exemplified in the following excerpt from my fieldnotes in August 2008:

> We were sitting in the corner of the tiny, windowless shop during Xiao Chen's lunch break. As her boss haggled with a buyer over the cost of sweaters bought in bulk versus those sold individually, Xiao Chen took out her mobile phone and said eagerly, "I want you to see a few pictures." Smiling, she thumbed through the memory of her phone until she found the appropriate folder. "Have a look," she said, as she handed me the phone. The first picture was of Xiao Chen decked out in a bright yellow silk blouse. She appeared to be wearing makeup, in contrast to her everyday appearance, and her hair had been styled so that it clung to the edges

of her face. Her head was tilted and she smiled seductively. "You look very pretty," I said, to which Xiao Chen responded "Really?" The next twenty or so pictures were variations on this theme, with Xiao Chen smiling, pouting, or sticking out her tongue. As we looked at the photos together, Xiao Chen made comments about herself, telling me which pictures she liked, which ones looked "silly," which ones looked pretty, and so on. After viewing 120 pictures of Xiao Chen, I handed her back her phone and told her I enjoyed seeing the pictures. "Really? Thank you," she said, beaming.[41]

Xiao Chen told me she had taken these pictures "just for fun," but the images clearly document the modes of self-fashioning that many migrant women undertake once they have left home. For migrant women, "developing oneself" through residing and working in the city means gaining skills and income as well as modifying one's physical appearance to comply with norms of dress, makeup, and hairstyle that signify a "modern" feminine construction of self, as discussed in chapter 2. Such "disciplinary practices of femininity"[42] obviously are not unique to China, but they are especially powerful in processes of self-transformation by rural women. Xiao Chen may have had a larger number of images of herself in her phone than other women did, but her use of the phone in this regard was not unique. In fact, in almost every case where I asked to see women's phone photos, the first pictures I viewed were of the migrant women themselves, usually in glamorous poses. And like Xiao Chen, when showing me the images and seeing my reaction, the women conveyed a mixture of self-consciousness and pleasure. Though many women would frequently show me pictures of themselves and comment on how "ugly" or "funny looking" they were, they clearly took satisfaction in their appearance, which had usually changed significantly from the time of their arrival in the city to the time they were able to purchase a mobile phone. "Self-portraits" were not only contained inside the phone; many women had stickers of pictures of themselves (alone or with a friend) affixed to their phone via the "sticker clubs" that can be found in stores all over Beijing.

Teresa de Lauretis has argued that film images and literary discourses are "technologies of gender" and that gendered subjectivity is "the product and process of both representation and self-representation."[43] De Lauretis's assertions apply as well to camera phones. For example, in her research in Seoul, Korea, Dong-Hoo Lee notes that the young women in her study enjoyed taking pictures of themselves and used these to evaluate their appearance in conformity with patriarchal, capitalist values that position women's bodies as objects of male consumption.[44] At the same time, the women challenged the typical structure of the male gaze in that they were both subjects and objects of their self-portraiture. The same could be said of my informants; however, their images revealed adherence not only to norms governing gender but also gender as it is cross-cut in contemporary China by ideas about urban cosmopolitanism in opposition to rural backwardness. In Xiao Chen's and the other women's self-images, the camera function was deployed to reflect upon, work on, and transform the self in accordance with modes of neoliberal governmentality. In conducting this transformation of self, migrant women have internalized the discourse of *suzhi* (quality), in which compliance with urban norms of feminine conduct and demeanor is supposed to be the manifestation of a corresponding inner self-awareness, knowledge, and worth. Thus, the phone once again is shown to be a literal and figurative technology of the self, as the ideology of *suzhi* found its expression in the representation of the rural, female worker's body, which desired modern subjectivity. To return to the picture of Zhao Ning discussed earlier, her perfectly manicured hands, so prominent in the photo she transferred to my phone, signified her status as someone not engaged in agriculture just as her refusal to be photographed in her orange work vest was an attempt to elide her status as a *dagongmei*, or "working little sister."

In her discussion of camera phones and the gaze, Lee ultimately concludes that while camera phones trouble the conventional male gaze, they also encourage a narcissistic gaze.[45] Although I agree that such self-imaging and presentation contain elements of narcissism, it is important to keep in mind that there are cultural differences regarding what are deemed appropriate displays of pictures of oneself. In China, urban residents prominently exhibit framed pictures of themselves (usually alone, in various poses taken at different locales) around the home. In the case of married couples, the photos are just as likely to be of the couple together as apart. At the workplace it is common for people to have pictures of themselves, framed and sitting atop their desk or unframed and placed below the glass covering their desk. Such self-presentation is not merely about individual ego or taste but also about the self as a work in progress. While in the past the "new socialist man" was the desired outcome, now China's pursuit of market reforms has produced modes of neoliberal governmentality in which one's economic status and level of consumption are not only markers of a desired lifestyle but also are articulated to notions of quality and worth. As such, the display of oneself should not merely be read as absorption with a reified self; rather, it indicates the self as an achievement *and* a process.

Obviously those at the lower end of the socioeconomic strata are not able to participate in this lifestyle, and they can only minimally engage with these forms of self-display. In many rural homes I have visited, unless the couple is young the number of photographs on display in the main living area is relatively small, and these are likely to be supplemented with inexpensive posters of models or movie stars hanging on the wall. If color photographs adorn the wall, these are often gifts that have been given to the family or wedding photos of children who have married after returning from labor migration. As mentioned earlier, none of the migrant women I knew owned cameras, and they did not have the money to visit the professional photography studios that have cropped up all over Beijing in recent years. A camera phone clearly intervenes in this situation and supplies them with one tool for constructing, evaluating, and presenting their selves.[46] In that camera phones are a technology of the self, they enable Sontag's ethics of seeing to merge with Foucault's ethical governing of the self, where self-surveillance and self-fashioning are deployed for the sake of pleasure, fantasy, and regulation.[47] Migrant women's self-images thus can be seen as a form of self-problematization, rather than merely narcissism, governed by dominant discourses of modernity and femininity. As such, they also form part of what Giddens calls the self as a reflexive project, in which a "continuously revised" narrative of oneself is the result of both local and global influences.[48]

*Mobile Transcendence*

If pictures exist within an ideological space, as Burgin notes, then they can also be used to exceed this space. It is in this regard that the intersection between image and affect is perhaps deepest. Though self-presentation and pictures of friends and family made up the majority of the photos in my informants' camera phones, women also used their phones to transcend the limits of their immediate world in Beijing in several ways. One method was by asserting their sense of beauty and aesthetics through their phones, often in distinct contrast to the setting in which they found themselves in Beijing. Several women used their phones to snap pictures of something they considered naturally beautiful, such as a flower in the courtyard outside their dormitory, a favorite old tree or the blue sky in their hometown, or even fresh vegetables. These pictures were more than memories or keepsakes. They were also seemingly kept as a small defense against the alienating urban jungle of modern Beijing.

A few weeks after my conversation with Li Yun and Zhao Ning described at the beginning of this chapter, I visited Li Yun again just before she got off work. Though she had been in Beijing about a year, she did not particularly care for the city, and in her assessment of life in Beijing—that it was alienating, that people only cared about money—she exemplified the estrangement caused by urban life noted over one hundred years ago by classical sociologists like Simmel and Durkheim. Nonetheless, she admitted that she, too, was in Beijing because it was there that she could earn an income. To counter such feelings of urban anomie, she used her phone as a sort of virtual sanctuary by storing images that gave her "peace of mind" (*xinqing yuyue*).[49] Some of these pictures were of friends and family, but of the approximately fifty images she had in her phone, about one-third were of nature. As I viewed these images we had the following conversation:

> CW: Where did you take this picture [of a flower]?
> LY: Outside my apartment. Isn't it nice?
> CW: Yes, it is.
> LY: Not like here [the crowded market].
> CW: Yes, not like here. What is this?
> LY: Cherry tomatoes! Can't you tell? They are freshly washed.
> CW: Oh, that's why they're glittering. Why did you take this picture?
> LY: Because they are pretty, don't you think?
> CW: Yes, they are pretty.[50]

When I told Li Yun that I had never thought about taking a picture of vegetables, she laughed and repeated that they were pretty, asserting her sense of aesthetics.

As mentioned earlier, studies in diverse contexts have also noted the importance of camera phones for expressing a highly personal viewpoint, particularly through users taking pictures of mundane objects.[51] Beyond showing the power of the camera phone for expressing one's personal viewpoint, in many images shot by my informants, beauty and transcendence also merged with memory, as evidenced in the reason Li Yun kept a picture of an old tree from her hometown in her phone. For her, the lush green leaves on the tree were appealing, yet the tree also served as a precious memory of home and embodied a longing and desire for a place, surely idealized, far from Li Yun's current circumstances. "I look at this tree," she told me, "because it's beautiful, but also when I miss my home."

In Bourdieu's classic work on aesthetic taste in France, he contrasts the reactions to artistic images by the working class with those with higher education and status. He asserts that the latter "refuse the ordinary objects of popular admiration," such as a sunset or landscape, and instead prefer photos or paintings to be "made from objects socially designated as meaningless," of which he includes a metal frame, tree bark, and "especially cabbages."[52] But perhaps Bourdieu missed something in so tightly harnessing an image's meaning, or lack thereof, to class status. Li Yun's pictures and other women's phone images are significant because of what they are as well as for what they signify, regardless of whether they depict flowers or fruit. As such, they evoke what Roland Barthes calls the *punctum* of a photo, an element that "pricks" or moves the viewer.[53] For Barthes the *punctum* is achieved through an image containing an accidental detail that arouses emotion and can transport one back in time; moreover, it exists in special pictures, not ordinary ones.

In discussing the *punctum* in relation to camera-phone images, Martin asserts that their poor quality means they cannot evoke the *punctum*. I want to challenge both Barthes' emphasis on the extraordinary and Martin's focus on the technology deployed. In asserting their visual aesthetic, my informants revealed deep feelings through and in relation to the images in their phones. The subjects of their photos were quotidian—no brilliant sunsets or breathtaking waterfalls, but rather ordinary flowers or trees. Furthermore, the emotions the photos evoked and the transcendence they enabled were not the result of an accidental detail or amazing technical quality. Nevertheless, they allowed at least momentary transcendence through their power to signify and transport one to another place. In this way, they provided immobile mobility—the images stored in the phone, and kept on the body, enabled constant access not only to a personal aesthetic but also to places out of reach temporally and spatially.

*Mobile Envisaging*

Sontag states that photographs "lay claim to another reality," by which she is referring to the power of images—in museums, in books, in the media—to sweep away viewers to another world.[54] Emotionally moving images, such as well-known photographs or paintings, can take on a nearly iconic status as they are reproduced as posters and within coffee-table books. Equally important, however, is the way people use personal photography to express desires and insert themselves into possibilities beyond the structural constraints of their everyday lives. In the same way that women used camera phones to transcend their immediate circumstances through viewing a familiar image such as a flower outside their dormitory, they also used their phones to imagine new realms.

Viewing an image of something or some place that touches one emotionally versus taking one's own photograph are often thought of as two different undertakings. However, many of my informants used their phones to merge these two acts. Perhaps nowhere was this more profoundly evident than in something that I came across numerous times, and this was *pictures of pictures* that were stored in the phone. For example, there were images of famous historic sites or of natural beauty such as a field of lilies that had been captured from books or magazines. In all cases, the women had never been to these locations or seen these sites in person. For example, on one occasion I was sitting with Yang Jing at her clothing stall and was viewing the new photos she had stored in her phone. After scrolling through various pictures I came across one of Japanese cherry trees in full bloom. I was quite surprised by the picture because I knew she hadn't traveled anywhere recently. When I asked her where she had gone to take it, she laughed, told me it was a picture of a picture, and then said with delight, "You couldn't tell, could you?" And the fact was, I couldn't.

Perhaps such an engagement with simulacrum is evidence for Baudrillard's contention that the postmodern world is one in which we dwell in the realm of the hyperreal, where the distinction between simulation and the "real" implodes and we are left with nothing but surfaces without depth and copies without originals.[55] While Baudrillard may overstate his case, he nonetheless calls attention to the problem of believing that representation allows access to the "real." Likewise, though decades of analysis had already eroded the "truth status of photography"[56] prior to the arrival of digital technology, digital cameras and graphics software supposedly put to rest any belief in the evidentiary or indexical quality of photographs. Here, however, my concern is not about the loss of indexicality caused by digital photography. My informants were not manipulating or retouching their photos with Photoshop or other software. Their pictures of pictures did capture the "that has been" and attested to what "indeed existed," in Barthes' words, but their referents were once removed from themselves.[57]

How to understand such images? They are not only a depiction of "reality" but of what Kember calls a projection, or "a facet of desire and of the subject's interior world rather than of the exterior world of objects."[58] In the pictures of pictures, aesthetics merged with aspirations, and again this reflected a transcendent immobile mobility afforded by the mobile phone. In essence, the phone was used to make postcards of the extraordinary, not as a treasured memory of a real encounter or journey, but to virtually and vicariously experience a place and a possibility out of reach. If having an experience has been equated with taking a picture as documentation, then perhaps we can say the opposite is also true: photographs are not necessarily "experience captured";[59] rather, they capture experience desired.

Many women showed me such pictures with pride in their ability to circumvent the limitations of their own lives. This affective dimension of photography, where interior desires were articulated to the exterior world, was evident as well in the pictures of various objects, such as designer watches, shoes, and handbags sold daily but never to be bought. There were also pictures of fashion models in magazines, or a favorite actor on the TV screen, captured in this manner because early in my fieldwork downloading from the Internet was either technically or economically unfeasible, thus further exemplifying my informants' enactment of necessary convergence.

Such desires for material goods should not be interpreted simply as these young women blindly participating in the very capitalism that exploits them and incites desires that can never be fulfilled. Like the images of self-fashioning mentioned earlier, such pictures are a form of what Colin Campbell calls "covert day dreaming," where pleasure is derived from the meaning and fantasies associated with certain objects.[60] With images of cherry blossoms or Gucci watches, women were inserting themselves into the realm of that which they desired and to which they aspired. Although I am calling such images "mobile envisaging," they share with images of the self a desire for self-transformation, and they speak to a potential self.

Such desire was illustrated in the pictures of Guo Yanmin, a young woman from an extremely impoverished village in Gansu province. Inside her phone, among photos of her cousin and colleagues, were also images of flowers and trees that she had taken at a small park near her dorm, where she lived in a windowless basement. As I looked at her photos we had the following conversation:

GY: Look at this picture.
CW: It's an airplane. Where did you take it?
GY: It was landing at the Beijing airport. I could see it from outside my dorm.
   I had never seen a plane before.
CW: Really?
GY: No, only on television.
CW: Oh.
GY: That's how you came to China, right?
CW: Yes.
GY: I envy you [plural (*nimen*)].[61]

My status as a foreign scholar, and my location in a class (note her use of the plural form of "you") with access to conveniences and privileges beyond the reach of all of the women involved in my research, certainly is driven home here. It also explains beyond any description I could offer the delicate balancing act that played out in all of my encounters with migrant women between attempting to relate to them on their terms and knowing that there were insurmountable cultural and social barriers that would remain, no matter how close we became. Such issues are extremely significant, and say much about the necessity of reflexivity in ethnography.[62] However, the image of the airplane—and I should note that other women also had stored pictures of airplanes in their phones—also reveals much about migrant women's agency in dealing with severe structural constraints. In Chinese, *xianmu*, the term that I have translated above as "envy," is not used in the negative sense of "to be jealous" but more "to admire." It thus connotes recognition of one's immediate situation and a motivation to surpass one's present circumstances. In "lay[ing] claim to another reality," whether through pictures of pictures or pictures of airplanes, Guo Yanmin, Yang Jing, and other women I knew were using their camera phones to express imagination and admiration, as well as aspiration, a topic I explore in more detail in the next section.

*Mobile Aspirations*

In an early study of camera-phone usage, Kindberg and colleagues distinguish images that are "affective" from those that are "functional."[63] By the former, they mean images of friends and family, images that are employed for personal contemplation, or those that "enrich a shared, co-present experience," while the latter are pictures used to support a mutual, remote, or personal task.[64] Following these designations, much of my discussion thus far has emphasized the affective dimension of migrant women's camera-phone usage. However, I would argue that the affective dimensions of mobile imaging cannot be so neatly separated from so-called functional uses. In other words, longings and desires expressed in migrant women's camera-phone images demonstrate these women's insistence on imagining a world beyond their current situation. As such, they also are a means of moving toward new possibilities for transcending spatial and economic limitations, certainly a first step in individual agency and resistance to inequitable structures and strictures.

That the functional cannot be so easily disentangled from the affective is clearly shown in some women's use of their phones in ways that blended the aspirational with the practical. Most often, such merging was apparent in the way phones were harnessed to plan for the future, particularly future employment. This usage was clearly shown in the imaging practices of Wei Wei, the only female hairstylist I knew in Beijing. In describing her work, Wei Wei compared her job to that of a doctor and took "great pride" in her ability to assess her clients' needs, give them the hair treatments they desired, and make them feel good about themselves. She also felt that, like a doctor, the more training and experience she gained, the higher the position she could obtain. For this reason Wei Wei used her phone to take pictures of hairstyles that she saw in magazines so that she could emulate them. She also felt it was very important to document her progress as a stylist, both for her own self-esteem and so that she could seek a better job in the future. Because she could not afford a digital camera, she used her mobile phone to archive the haircuts that she had done that she was particularly proud of. She explained that cutting hair was not about making money; it was about expressing herself as an artist. Nevertheless, she was effectively using her phone to chart her own development as a stylist and as a sort of digital résumé in order to secure a better job in the future. She told me that in fact her use of the phone as a virtual calling card was as important as the social networking it allowed her to engage in.

In the same way, Yang Jing, who showed me the pictures of pictures of cherry blossoms, had taken photos of some of the fashions that she sold in her stall in the market. These photos were not only her way of asserting a personal aesthetic (she thought some of them were pretty) but also a means of planning for the future. Like many women I knew, she had a dream of eventually opening up her own business—a clothing boutique—back home in the countryside. The photos were thus part of her preparation. She was archiving which fashions sold and which ones didn't, and she regularly took pictures of clothing items that other vendors sold. She was also maintaining a record of clothing prices and, in her phone's address book, business contacts in Beijing.

Earlier I argued that migrant women practice necessary convergence due to the fact that they do not own digital cameras. Through Wei Wei's and Yang Jing's uses of their camera phones to merge camera function and desktop-publishing portfolio, we see another example of necessary convergence. However, to truly advance their careers, images of haircuts and clothing had to be stored and archived in a more permanent form. Because until recently most migrant women did not have computers (and many still do not), and uploading photos to social networking sites is a relatively new phenomenon, saving images outside the phone was a challenge for many women I knew.[65] Both Wei Wei and Yang Jing were able to use their employers' computers to upload their camera-phone images from time to time and then transfer them to a digital memory stick. Other women did not have such easy access to computers at work so they had to go to Internet cafés to transfer and store images, but as discussed in chapter 1, many women rarely went to such cafés. Still others lacked the technical know-how to transfer their photos. Like Chen Jiefeng mentioned earlier, they had to make tough choices about which images to save and which ones to delete to free up the memory in their phones. Though camera phones can enable immobile mobility, obviously they alone will not erase digital inequality.

The Mobile Image and the Profound Self

In the epigraph with which I began this chapter, Roland Barthes expresses a longing for an impossible unity between image and a "real" self. In his ruminations on photography in *Camera Lucida*, from which this quote is taken, he weaves a deeply personal narrative of the way images produce subjective experiences that at once require articulation yet remain profoundly inexpressible. Barthes was concerned with his role as a viewer and object of photographs, yet his eloquent reflections on the connections among images, emotions, memory, and desire extend as well to motivations for personal photography. In this chapter, I explored a range of different practices that touch a series of overlapping themes—documenting the world, fashioning the self, transcending constrained circumstances, envisioning new possibilities, and planning for the future. I have argued that, as subjects, objects, and viewers of images of their own making, migrant women use camera phones to articulate desires, aesthetics, and aspirations that ultimately are about the construction of self and imagining this self in a different world. This construction is grounded in everyday reality and projected into the realm of the imagination; it links exterior with interior and the material with the virtual, and it reveals once again the mobile phone as a tool for immobile mobility and a technology of the self.

Particularly among groups like China's migrants that have limited economic resources and thus no access to conventional cameras or video recorders, a camera phone offers a new means for technological "leapfrogging." It therefore affords a different way of viewing convergence; that is, convergence is not only about participatory culture or how content circulates across multiple media platforms, and it is also not only about technical advancements that render one device into a be-all/do-all tool. Rather, necessary convergence is a socio-techno practice that emerges when users are *not* equipped with an array of technological devices and thus must creatively converge uses within a single device. Because of this necessary convergence, the trivial *and* the significant were captured and stored in my informants' phones.

Camera phones were not deployed by migrant women to change the actual structural constraints of their lives. Nonetheless, they are a tool of empowerment and a form of *hope*, because they allow migrant women in some manner to rework the constraints of their lives. Such "symbolic" resistance is often thought not to matter because it clearly does not change institutionalized inequality, yet images and imaging practices were a means for these women to keep something for themselves, a sense of themselves, and at times, their own sanity. The pictures in their digital archive were clearly a personal and portable aesthetic, captured and displayed in one of the few spaces that a migrant woman can actually call her own.

The images of self, flowers, blue sky, high-end sports shoes, airplanes, and pictures of pictures that were snapped and stored in women's phones reveal the ideological and psychological functions of images mentioned earlier. Images are "manipulative" in that they place the viewer in some sort of relationship, whether it be longing for a home far away and far removed culturally and socially, or desiring the trappings to which consumer society and the ideological underpinnings of urban modernity dictate one should be entitled. As I have argued earlier in this chapter and throughout this book, in their consumption and imaging practices, my informants were not blindly reproducing a system that exploits them. Rather, within the ideology of *suzhi* and dominant modes of governmentality, they were striving for something beyond, within conditions "not of their own making."

5

## Mobile Communication and Labor Politics

> We have worked for one year but we were not paid our wages at
> the end. My boss Zhou pretends to be kind but he is really a man
> without conscience or shame.
> —Sun Heng, "Get Back Our Wages"[1]

"I *must* leave. I can't take it anymore," Zhang Yan Xia said, as she tried to
hold back the tears rolling down her face. Liang Pei Juan stood silently to
the side, her facial expression a mixture of anger and disbelief. Though it
was mid-afternoon and they would normally have been at work, both young
women were dressed in street clothes, and each carried a small, wheeled suit-
case filled with all her belongings. For the previous three months they had
both worked seven days a week at two large restaurants that stood adjacent to
one another a few kilometers from the Fragrant Hills Park, a spacious public
area with forests, gardens, lakes, and ancient pavilions that sat at the base of
the Western Mountains in the northwestern reach of Beijing's Haidian District. The park is a popular tourist site in the spring and summer, when lush
gardens offer a respite from the heat, as well as in the fall, when the leaves
covering the mountains turn a brilliant red. The two restaurants, with their

garish neon signs bearing flowery names and promises of regional specialties such as duck or hotpot, were meant to cater to the busloads of tourists that descend on the park during the busy seasons.

I had visited Zhang Yan Xia, Liang Pei Juan, and several other women I knew at these two restaurants a handful of times before this day. On previous occasions the owner of the hotpot restaurant, Mr. Wang, had always ushered me and whoever accompanied me into a private room designed for large parties. There he would offer tea and chat with us while allowing the women I knew to alternate taking short breaks to come and visit. The atmosphere would be notably strained when he was present, but once he left we would talk about a range of topics. Invariably the exhaustion and isolation the women felt would become part of the conversation.

On this particular occasion, although I had called in advance, when I first arrived it was immediately clear that something was wrong. The women I knew were nowhere to be found, Mr. Wang was quite brusque, and I spent about an hour being shuttled back and forth between the two restaurants while being told, "Your friends are coming soon." When they finally arrived, Zhang Yan Xia and Liang Pei Juan said they were leaving these restaurants because the salary was too low and the hours too long.[2] They had just spent the better part of the afternoon trying to get Mr. Wang and the owner of the duck restaurant to pay them for several weeks' work. In the end, Liang Pei Juan received some of her wages—a portion was taken out since she was leaving early—but Zhang Yan Xia got nothing because Mr. Wang did not want her to quit. Whether they were paid or not, both had already made up their minds to leave and go work at another restaurant where they had some friends and where it was uncertain whether the conditions would be any better.[3]

This story of migrant women living in isolated conditions, working long hours without a day off, receiving substandard pay, and being denied compensation when no longer able to take it is, unfortunately, rather common in China. Compared to workers who are beaten by employers, physically maimed or exposed to toxic chemicals at their worksites, or even die in fires or accidents, the situation of Zhang Yan Xia and Liang Pei Juan is "sadly, not so bad," in the words of one Chinese acquaintance. Although policies have been enacted to protect workers, including a labor law that went into effect in January 2008, worker mistreatment continues, a result of urban prejudices, inadequate legal structures, China's rapid marketization, and the *hukou* system that constructs migrants as second-class citizens in the city.[4]

Given this reality, a crucial question is whether new media technologies like mobile phones have led to greater empowerment in the labor sphere for migrant workers. Is the mobile phone a "technology of freedom" that helps the exploited overcome their marginalized position, or is it utilized to enact and reinforce already existing relations of domination and subordination, or both?[5] In this chapter I map one final terrain of young migrant women's mobile phone assemblage: the labor sphere, where migrant women must contend with myriad power relations that mirror and instantiate their subordinate position in the larger society. To do so I first situate my discussion within a broader conversation that has utilized Foucaultian notions of power to analyze the labor relations of migrant workers. Though some have argued that distinct modes of power prevail in specific time periods or among particular groups, my research on the ground complicates some of these assumptions. I show how in China's low-level service sector, authoritarian control, disciplinary regimes and modes of governmentality, as well as gendered job hierarchies, all operate to produce young migrant women as particular gendered, classed, aged, and "placed" working subjects. This discussion is followed by a brief review of the existing literature on the connection between mobile phones and labor in and outside of China.

I then consider the relationship between mobile phones and labor in four realms: job seeking and social mobility; income generation; employer control and surveillance; and "mobile resistance"—largely symbolic yet nonetheless meaningful—by migrant women in the workplace. Throughout this chapter I demonstrate that mobile phones, as "artifacts with politics," can be used to resist *and* reify asymmetrical power relations, and as such they are central actors articulated within a quotidian dialectic of freedom and control.[6] Though in previous chapters I argued that mobile phones afford migrant women access to "immobile mobility" through various personal and social uses, here I show that the intersections of their gender, age, class, and rural origin produce particular constraints on their capacity for various forms of agency, thus rendering them relatively immobile in the labor sphere. This is not to imply that migrant women tend to stay indefinitely in a particular job, but rather that their mobility is usually characterized by lateral movements across similar types of employment yet with very little change in status, autonomy, or income.

## Discipline and Control in the Labor Sphere

In "Postscript on the Societies of Control," Gilles Deleuze argues that the era of what Foucault called the disciplinary society, marked by institutions of enclosure such as the factory and the prison, and characterized by disciplinary power that produces "docile bodies" that "may be subjected, used, transformed and improved" has receded.[7] In its stead have emerged societies of "free-floating control" that, rather than containing and molding bodies, operate through constantly evolving appeals to self-improvement, competition, and permanent training.[8] In such societies, the corporation prevails, buffeted by the stock market and advertising, and capitalism no longer produces products but the endless perpetuation of services. Deleuze's assertions are certainly compelling, as he points to modes of control—computerized networks, electronic surveillance—that characterize our age. They are extremely ethnocentric as well, for as he concedes at one point, capitalism based on production has not actually disappeared, it has been "relegat[ed] to the Third World."[9] His sweeping pronouncement of epochal change thus intentionally dismisses a large segment of the world and those who labor in it. His grand narrative of a linear transformation from one era to another is also highly suspect. In fact, in much of the Third World and elsewhere, discipline coexists with control, and disciplinary power and governmentality operate according to context.

In her work on neoliberalism outside the West, Aihwa Ong takes issue with scholars like Deleuze as well as Michael Hardt and Antonio Negri, who argue that with the withering of the nation-state and the deterritorialized flows of labor and capital, disciplinary institutions and technologies have receded as "mechanisms of command become ever more 'democratic,' ever more immanent in the social field, distributed throughout the brains and the bodies of the citizens."[10] Ong contends instead that the "logic of exception in global capitalism allows the combination of managerial and labor regimes in transnational networks that carve striated spaces—or 'latitudes'— shaped by the coordination of systems of governmentality and regimes of labor incarceration."[11] In other words, in the global space of flows, those with skills, knowledge, assets, and a "set of flexible capacities" enjoy a "latitudinal citizenship" marked by the ability to adjust to the changing dynamics of the marketplace.[12] Modes of neoliberal governmentality encourage them to continually self-manage and update their skills in order to maintain their privileged position based on talent, wealth, and connections. This managerial and entrepreneurial class cannot exist, however, without factories and "carceral modes of labor discipline," where "ethnicized production networks depend on disciplinary institutions of ethnic enclaves, factories, and families to instill feminine values of loyalty, obedience, and patience, and to mold docile labor," such as in high-tech sweatshops in the United States in places like the Silicon Valley.[13]

Ong's arguments are cogent, in particular her rejection of theories that purport linear, uniform global transformation and her insistence on contextualized analysis. Yet she suggests that the "talented" class (in China those with "high *suzhi*," or quality) operate according to modes of regulatory power, or governmentality, while migrants and unskilled laborers are subject only to disciplinary power. However, as I have shown in previous chapters it is not only those with "latitudinal citizenship" who are compelled to self-manage and self-improve, because the *suzhi* discourse permeates and shapes the subjectivity of all of China's citizens. Rather, disciplinary power and governmentality can function simultaneously to produce subjects, with one mode of power having more force than the other at particular moments in specific contexts.

Like Ong, scholars of migrant factory labor in China have demonstrated that disciplinary power still circulates to mold "docile bodies." In southern China, Ching Kwan Lee and Pun Ngai have both detailed factory environments with a highly gendered and ethnicized organizational chain of command, where male managers exercise patriarchal authority over their female employees through a variety of means, including the use of pejorative language designed to denigrate both the female and the rural identity of the women workers.[14] In a virtual rewriting of Foucault's "Docile Bodies" in *Discipline and Punish*, albeit set in a Chinese electronics factory, Pun describes how female workers are taught to move in a mechanized manner, how they are positioned spatially on the line, how they follow a rigid timetable, and how they are subjected to the panoptic "electronic eye."[15]

In contexts other than factory work, however, scholars have shown that migrant workers are subject to the same modes of neoliberal governmentality, although articulated in distinct ways, that urban residents and so-called high-*suzhi* strata are, as I've also argued in previous chapters. For example, Ann Anagnost contends that because of their supposed low *suzhi*, migrants are undervalued, and the extraction of their surplus value through labor—and the attendant exploitation—then becomes justified in contemporary China. At the same time, the discursive construction of migrants as lacking and inferior supports new modes of governmentality that compel them to strive for self-improvement and self-development.[16] In her work on migrant domestic workers in China, Yan Hairong argues that the discourse of *suzhi* operates as a mode of neoliberal governmentality. She shows how labor migration to provide urban homes with domestic workers is organized by recruiters not only as a means for migrant women to earn money, but also to improve their *suzhi*. Moreover, through domestic work rural women are supposed to gain "suzhi education" that will transform their "backward" rural consciousness.[17]

As illustrated by the above examples, migrant workers in China must contend with modes of disciplinary power *and* governmentality, yet as my research makes clear the former is not only to be found in institutions like factories. In China's low-level service sector, both workplace disciplines and self-responsibilizing discourses, or modes of subjection and subjectification, coexist, as do efforts to completely deny subjectivity. To set the context for the remainder of this chapter, below I discuss the salient characteristics of this labor assemblage, which I separate for analytical reasons only: authoritarian managerial styles as well as disciplinary regimes that incorporate appeals to self-development, which are simultaneously cross-cut by gendered hierarchies and stratification. With their emphasis on cultivating a certain type of worker—one who, on the one hand, is disciplined and has internalized a self-regulatory gaze, and on the other hand, self-manages and strives for self-development—these modes of power, as well as attempts at overt domination, at their core are intended to transform rural "peasants" into "civilized" workers and as such have implications for how mobile phones are articulated to labor processes and politics.

### Authoritarian Managerial Styles

Migrants in general are discursively constructed as a weak or "vulnerable social group" (*ruoshi qunti*), yet cultural traditions that instruct rural women to be submissive, "dutiful daughters" as well as institutionalized gender discrimination and perceptions of rural "backwardness" align to perpetuate a myth of migrant women as "passive" and "compliant." This discursive context then limits the job options available to young migrant women and positions them in the workplace within "parent-child" relationships governed by patriarchal modes of authority and control.[18] This situation is not unique to China, but the *hukou* system has institutionalized Chinese rural women's marginalization.

Authoritarian control over domestic workers and factory workers in China has been well documented.[19] What has been less explored is how migrants in various lines of low-level service work also must contend with such managerial styles. Mr. Wang, the restaurant boss mentioned at the beginning of this chapter, was not exceptional in the way he treated his workers. For example, in late May 2007 I was introduced to Ms. Xu, a Beijing woman who owned a data-processing company. She was a "self-made" woman, who in the mid-1990s had "jumped into the sea of business" (*xiahai*, in the parlance of the time) and had become quite successful, handling both domestic and international clients. Her company occupied the basement of a tall housing tower, and the employees were all migrants, mostly young rural women. They worked ten to twelve hours a day in a dimly lit area, sitting at computers and inputting data from everything from bank statements to marketing surveys. At night, the male employees retired to a nearby apartment building while the young women slept in a room adjacent to their workspace. This small room had several bunk beds and a few shelves for personal belongings. On one visit with a colleague, a discussion arose as to whether the employees would perform a task that went beyond their job responsibilities. "Sure, no problem," said Ms. Xu. She then added matter-of-factly, "They do whatever I tell them to do. There's no need to ask them. I say it and they do it. That's how it is."[20]

At first I was caught off guard by Ms. Xu's words, but her attitude was quite typical of many employers of migrant workers. In her mind, she was treating them well—supplying them with a job, housing, and food—and therefore had the right to expect their submission and obedience. Like Ms. Xu and Mr. Wang, employers in a range of contexts operate as if they own their workers, attempting to strip them of any individual agency and exerting an inordinate amount of influence over their lives. This is evident not only in demands that they participate in activities that fall outside their regular work obligations. For example, it is common in restaurants that new employees give their employers a deposit (*yajin*, usually 100 to 500 yuan, depending on the size of the restaurant) out of their first paycheck. If an employee wants to quit and receive this deposit back, he or she must first receive a good evaluation, or approval (*pizhun*), from the boss. Such evaluations are usually arbitrary and the whole system allows employers to keep all or most of a departing employee's deposit. Employers in many types of jobs also demand employees' identification cards (*shenfen zheng*). This practice, which is technically illegal, leaves workers extremely vulnerable to the whims of their employers.

*Disciplinary Regimes and Appeals to Self-Development*

In addition to authoritarian managerial styles, all of the women involved in this research—whatever their occupation—had to submit to various rules, trainings, and routines that were intended both to maximize their efficiency in the workplace *and* cultivate their *suzhi*. However, the amount of what I call "regulated drudgery," by which I mean monotonous work that requires minimal skill yet is nonetheless often highly monitored, and the extent of an accompanying internalized gaze, as well as more subtle appeals to self-transformation, varied significantly by job and specific location. For example, at some restaurants, beauty salons, and shops a common practice by management is to line up all of the employees outside on the sidewalk in front of the entrance in pseudo-military formation for a drill or a "pep talk" before the beginning of business hours (see figure 8). Imported from American enterprise culture in the 1980s, such talks can range from encouraging workers to do their best, to berating employees who committed some sort of mistake during the prior work shift. These sessions can also include shouting slogans, dancing, singing, or running up and down the block. The public nature of such activities is clearly a technique intended to produce a "practiced and subjected" worker, yet one who also *desires* self-development. It also has a performative effect in that through repetition, a disciplined, competent, hard-working staff is constituted and made visible to potential customers.

Employees (male and female), especially those who work in restaurants, also frequently have to attend mandatory training or "teamwork" sessions in the afternoon between shifts. Trainings are designed to teach employees proper etiquette in dealing with customers, including language and mannerisms. For wait staff as well as vendors in the large marketplaces, there is also an emphasis on proper posture and behavior (e.g., one should not clip one's nails in one's clothing stall). Teamwork sessions aim to build camaraderie among employees and loyalty to the worksite. In all of these, achieving the

Fig. 8. Employees at a beauty salon line up outside during their daily pep talk.

goals of a successful enterprise is collapsed with the cultivation of the enterprising self.

Again, cultivation coexists with regimentation. For example, in some marketplaces, employees can be required to stand for hours on end, to maintain an erect posture (crossing arms or leaning against the wall is forbidden, though often ignored, as in figure 9), and to try to attract customers by saying the "right" words. This means the women are not supposed to wait for someone to approach and express interest in their goods. Instead, they must call out incessantly to passersby (e.g., "Do you want to buy a bag? What kind of bag? I have Gucci, Louis Vuitton, Coach . . . ") in the hope that someone will stop and become engaged in a bargaining session.

Bosses often stand to the side or employ a male relative to make sure that employees adhere to this exhausting, disciplinary regime. As one woman, Huang Hui An, remarked, "We do all the work; the boss just hangs around

Fig. 9. Inside a large
marketplace in Beijing.

reading the newspaper and drinking tea, watching to make sure we haggle
with customers and don't steal any money."[21] It should be noted, however,
that, in contrast to the large marketplaces, in some small shops owners are
rarely around, and the young women who worked there had a fairly large
degree of autonomy regarding how they spent their time when there were no
customers present and when there were no tasks to do.

*Gendered Job Hierarchies and Stratification*

Chandra Talpade Mohanty has argued that in much of the developing
world the logic of the global economy depends on an image of a "marginalized woman worker" and a notion of "women's work" that natural-
izes certain hierarchies and ideologically constructs low-skilled, low-wage
jobs "in terms of notions of appropriate femininity, domesticity, (hetero)

Fig. 10. Young women wearing *qipao* greet customers in a restaurant.

sexuality, and racial and cultural stereotypes."[22] In chapter 2, I described the gendered hierarchy in the beauty salons and the gender-differentiated jobs. These distinctions also exist to varying degrees in restaurants and marketplaces, where both overt policies and unspoken assumptions serve to uphold "appropriate" norms of masculinity and femininity. In many Beijing restaurants, for example, men cook the food and women are the majority of servers, which hearkens back to a traditional custom whereby in public eating establishments women could only make "flour" items like noodles or dumplings while males prepared dishes of meat and vegetables (i.e., the "real" food).[23] Moreover, in all but the smallest or most inexpensive restaurants, it is customary to have at least two young attractive women stand at the door to greet customers as they enter. Although males may hold such jobs, women predominate.[24] In most restaurants, women, much more so than their male counterparts, must adhere to strict regulations regarding their appearance and decorum. Their uniforms usually consist of sheer blouses and short skirts or a *qipao*, and they are expected to be young and good looking, as they eat "the rice bowl of youth" (see figure 10).[25] Certain establishments even maintain height and weight standards, which exist especially to please male customers.[26]

In China, marketization has created a masculine business culture where deals are made and favors exchanged through banqueting at restaurants, and these banquets involve large amounts of food and alcohol and are frequently followed by visits to karaoke bars (where hostesses are often also prostitutes).[27] In this domain, women as business partners are rare, but female service staff occupy a position that is at once subservient yet crucial: their presence enables the smooth functioning of social relations that then leads to promises being made and deals being sealed. A young, attractive, attentive female waitress is an integral link in the masculine chain of talk, toasts, and transactions,[28] and she is expected to be patient and demure, even when patrons are drunk or rude. In an interview with Ji Hua, a woman who worked at a restaurant that I visited many times, she once told me, "When the male patrons are drinking they tell a lot of dirty stories and say a lot of bad words. I hate to listen to them, but there is nothing I can do since I have to stand nearby to wait on them."[29] Surely the male customers Ji Hua speaks of are aware that their language and behavior might embarrass her, but they disregard this fact since they view her as merely a *dagongmei*, or working little sister.

As with the beauty salons and restaurants, gendered power relations and divisions of labor are quite apparent in both small shops and large marketplaces in Beijing, where most of the employees are migrants. In the marketplaces, older men and women are generally running their own businesses while younger men are usually the sons or sons-in-law of the owners of the stalls where they work. Their job is not only to sell products but also to keep an eye on employees. The young women with whom they work often address these young men using fictive kin terms such as "older brother" (*dage*), thereby situating their unequal power relations within a traditional, patriarchal family ideology.[30] Such familial structures are also invoked when women live with their employers, who may or may not be relatives.

## Mobile Phones and Labor

With such modes of authority, discipline, self-optimization, and stratification, what are the possibilities for migrant women to use mobile phones for empowerment—economic or otherwise—in the workplace? Inside and outside China, a growing body of scholarship has focused on the relationship between mobile phones, income generation, and job seeking, yet the findings are inconclusive. For example, for certain types of micro-entrepreneurs, in particular Indian fishermen, the use of a mobile phone has helped reduce travel time and has enabled access to up-to-the-minute information regarding prices and demand, thereby helping to boost income.[31] In other contexts, however, the use of mobile phones by micro-entrepreneurs has shown mixed results and at times has exacerbated unequal access to information and capital.[32] In China, Jack Linchuan Qiu found that although migrant workers believed their mobile phones were crucial for job hunting, none had ever been contacted via the phone by a potential employer, and most were likely to gather employment information through interpersonal networks.[33] Patrick Law and Yinni Peng argue that mobile phones enable migrant workers to find better jobs and negotiate for higher pay, yet Raymond Ngan and Stephen Ma found that while migrant workers successfully used mobile phones to send and receive information about better working conditions, there was not a significant correlation between mobile phone ownership and a higher salary.[34]

In general, the research inside and outside of China highlights how particular types of employment and structural impediments related to socioeconomic status are crucial factors in considering the outcomes of mobile telephony among marginalized groups. However, for the most part gender has not been a significant part of the analysis. Yet feminist scholars of gender and technology have shown that the two are mutually constitutive; that is, just as social constructions of gender shape access to, attitudes toward, and uses of technology, technologies in turn are "gendered" through the discursive context in which they are appropriated.[35] Moreover, it is not only gender, but also the intersections of gender, class, and other axes of identity that play a productive role in how mobile phones are articulated to labor politics among marginalized groups.

*Mobile Phones, Job Seeking, and Social Mobility*

Most socio-culturally oriented research on the use of mobile phones among poorer groups has highlighted how social networks are intricately linked to economic survival.[36] The research on China cited above also shows how building one's relational (*guanxi*) network is of crucial importance for rural-to-urban migrants for finding employment. In China there is the perception, if not the reality, that it is often who you know, not what you know, that matters when it comes to securing a job.[37] For this reason, in addition to one's own qualifications and skills, the quality of one's social (or network) capital has important implications for the types of jobs to which a person might aspire and for whether and how easily one is able to move up the social and employment hierarchy. As I argued in chapter 3, mobile phones certainly enable migrant women to expand their social networks and increase their strong and weak ties. However, phones do not necessarily help them to establish connections with those in higher social strata than themselves due to the customary manner in which *guanxi* networks are built and the rigid class-based and place-based distinctions that characterize contemporary Chinese society.

Still, *guanxi* networks and kinship ties are extremely important for rural-to-urban migrants for job hunting, perhaps even more so than for urban residents, because of the structural barriers that migrants face in the city. Aside from legal and social discrimination, they must also be wary of unscrupulous and even violent labor practices that especially target migrant workers. There is abundant documentation of Chinese migrant workers being physically abused, having wages withheld, and being subject to numerous job hazards, including having to work with dangerous equipment and toxic chemicals. Female migrants face further perils, for example at labor markets designed to facilitate the placement of newly arrived migrants into suitable jobs. These labor markets often become the site for predatory traffickers who lure unsuspecting migrant women with promises of jobs and then sell them as prostitutes or as wives for poor peasants who cannot afford a proper dowry.[38] Not surprisingly, then, all of the migrant women I knew said that for their own protection they would never respond to a classified ad for a job or an anonymous job posting. This was seen as simply too risky. Instead, though the government has set up websites and mobile labor markets for workers, I was told numerous times that it is always best to go through a known entity such as a friend or relative in order to avoid being cheated.

Despite these limitations, many women with whom I spoke did not seem to think it was difficult to find a new job. For example, Pan Xiao Jun, who had worked at a beauty salon for the first eight months I knew her, suddenly quit her job one day. Her reasons were that the hours were too long and the pay too low. When I asked her how she would find another job, she shrugged her shoulders and said, "I have my own way of doing things and I always have. I quit my job even though others might not dare. I'm not worried about finding a new job because I am young and I know they need people like me in these jobs."[39] When asked if she thought her mobile phone could help her in any way to find a job, she said she might use it to contact friends but not to contact a stranger. Her answer reveals that certainly the mobile phone could be used for the task of finding a job, but only if a relationship is already in place. Thus, the mobile phone is not the key; instead, the social networks that rural-to-urban migrants have always relied upon to facilitate their employment in the city, long before the arrival of cell phones, are most important. The phone could just as easily be a landline for this purpose, although of course a mobile phone makes communication significantly more convenient.

Though it might be easy for a migrant woman to find employment, the jobs available to most migrant women are rather limited and stratified by gender, class, place, and age, as noted earlier. It is extremely difficult for a young migrant woman to move up the job hierarchy precisely because of her status as a young migrant woman. Pan Xiao Jun's breezy confidence, expressed in the quote above, about her ability to find another job should therefore be taken with a measure of skepticism. She certainly *could* find another job, probably without too much trouble, through relying on friends and word of mouth. Whether this would be a *better* job is another matter, particularly given the line of work she was in. In fact, shortly before I left Beijing, Pan Xiao Jun had returned to the original salon where she had been employed. Even the migrant women I knew who had attended various computer courses and other types of training with few exceptions were not able to convert these skills into better employment, except in the case of Zhuang Jie, whom I discuss below. This does not mean these women might not attain better jobs in the future, but for the time being they tended to remain in the same jobs they had had prior to the training or to be in a similar line of work. For the most part, technology use was not a means for economic mobility in the labor sphere, even when migrant women were "enterprising selves" and had "developed themselves" by improving their skill set. What Linda Martín Alcoff calls their positionality in various networks of power and ideology coalesced with and was constitutive of immobility.[40]

*Mobile Phones and Income Generation*

Once a woman found a job, could a mobile phone help her increase her income? In my fieldwork, the answer to this question was extremely context dependent. Only a few of my informants were more than twenty-four years old, and those who were older were also more likely to be married and to be micro-entrepreneurs, two details that are not incidental. As married adults, they had very different concerns, socially and economically, and therefore different uses for their phones than most of the other participants I knew. For example, Wang Anmei, an apple vendor, and Li Li, who sold jewelry, both had moved to Beijing with their husbands to set up their businesses. In separate interviews, each woman related how she and her husband devoted all of their time and energy to the business. Because they did not have landlines or computers either at their homes or in the large marketplaces where they worked, a mobile phone helped them to follow up on orders, expand the business outside the marketplace, and find up-to-date price information. They both said owning a mobile phone helped them increase their income. However, as I have argued elsewhere, a mobile phone did not sweep in and create the conditions for such success.⁴¹ With their business partners/husbands, these women had financial, entrepreneurial, and domestic strategies to which the mobile phone was articulated. Because they were autonomous owners of a small business, they could take advantage of the mobile phone's unique attribute—its mobility—to more effectively conduct their business. They were not wealthy by any means, and it is important to note that the bulk of their income still came from selling their wares at the markets. But the mobile phone allowed them a new means of connecting with customers and increasing their productivity.

In contrast, most women in my study were younger, unmarried, and were not micro-entrepreneurs. In their workplaces, characterized by the modes of power and stratification discussed earlier, they were thus operating from a very different position socially, occupationally, and financially. Even most of those employed in marketplaces similar to those of Wang Anmei and Li Li did not believe their phone could help raise their income, and they did not necessarily use it to increase their customer contacts. Compared to the micro-entrepreneurs, their differing ability, and even desire, to use a phone for economic enhancement was produced as much by their age, marital status, and occupation as by their gendered, classed, and placed (e.g., their rural origin) subjectivity. Most women valued their mobile phones more for entertainment and sociality—instant messaging, playing games, or listening to music—or for its articulation to identity rather than for work productivity.⁴² Many also expressed an almost fatalistic view of their lack of agency in work choice, such as Zhao Ning, who, when asked about her job, said,

"If I like my job, or don't like my job, it's all the same."[43] Like many others at the markets, she also stated emphatically that a mobile phone could not help increase income. Likewise, women who worked as wait staff saw no way for a cell phone to help them earn more money. Even those who were assistants in beauty salons, where they had repeat customers, did not feel a mobile phone helped them generate income, in contrast to the male stylists who freely gave out their mobile phone numbers in order to build up a client base. The women's subordinate position in the restaurants and the salons rendered them relatively powerless in this regard, whether they had mobile phones or not.

Thus, one's gendered identity, degree of social capital, and autonomy in decision making and scheduling can influence how useful a mobile phone can be for generating income. Furthermore, the perception of the qualities of the phone itself is crucial. If the phone is predominantly used for sociality and is a literal "technology of the self," as it is articulated to producing and problematizing the self, as discussed previously, then its role in economic productivity tends to be minimalized. In addition to these factors, cultural norms regarding kinship ties and familial obligations are also important. For this reason, I found that in a few cases (only in the marketplaces) some women who were not micro-entrepreneurs still said a mobile phone was important for generating income, in particular its use for gathering information on prices and supply and for following up with customers. These women were not much different from the other young women I met during my fieldwork except in one regard—all were working for a relative with whom they also lived. In this situation, helping to increase the profits of the relative who employed them was understood as something important and a necessary duty. Given the bonds between family members, the reciprocal obligations that inhere in Chinese family relationships, and the long-standing tradition in China of family-run businesses, this socio-techno practice is perhaps not surprising. The difference between working for a relative versus a stranger was clearly explained by Luo Judi, who said, "It is always better to work for a relative. They treat you better."[44] Again, we see technology used in certain ways as it is articulated to already existing relationships. Zhao Ning and those like her were "working for the man," so to speak, and thus felt no obligation to go beyond what was required of their jobs, even though they were under "pressure" to sell. On the other hand, those who were employed by relatives had a much different sense of obligation, which their mobile phones helped them fulfill, even though they didn't necessarily benefit financially.

*Mobile Phones and Surveillance*

When considering labor politics, it is crucial to understand not only whether people can use technology to better their material circumstances, but also how they can be affected by the technology use of others, particularly their employers. At the organizational level, there is already evidence that mobile phones can be deployed for surveillance and for further normalizing mechanisms of monitoring and control. Based on research on factories in southern China, for example, Qiu describes an intra-organizational system in which employers supply various types of mobile phones to employees who are distributed throughout the factory hierarchy. Employers pay part of the managers' phone bills and then demand that they leave their phones on continuously, yet factory workers are prohibited from carrying their handsets onto the factory floor.[45] In either case, the system functions as a means for managers to monitor employees' work and communications through a "wireless leash."[46] Around the globe, there has also been research on white-collar "mobile workers," whose cell phones allow management greater ability to supervise workers' productivity away from the office and make such workers potentially available outside of regular work hours.[47]

In focusing on cell phones and surveillance specifically related to work, aside from institutionalized modes of technological monitoring and white-collar workers, whose mobile phone is one more device in their wired, mobile lifestyle, an important issue is how economically and socially marginalized populations become targets of employer surveillance in more incidental, mundane ways. In the case of migrant workers owning mobile phones, employers now have a means of keeping tabs on employees that they never had before given that in the past most migrant workers did not have landlines.

In my fieldwork, mobile phone surveillance took many forms. In what follows, I first discuss one extended case followed by two briefer examples in order to reveal how mobile-related surveillance and the modes of power and gendered hierarchies highlighted earlier were mutually constituted.

### THE BOUTIQUE ASSISTANT

Wu Daiyu was twenty years old and from a small village in Hebei province. Both of her parents were farmers and she grew up extremely poor, the oldest of four children. When she was a teenager, her father had invested in a local enterprise, but when a business partner ran off with all of the money, he was left with nothing. Wu Daiyu then dropped out of middle school and worked in a local factory to help support her family. When I met her, she had been employed for about a year at a tiny boutique that largely catered to a foreign clientele and that was owned by a Beijing woman who called herself Linda. Wu Daiyu worked every day without a day off, earning 1,000 yuan per month (about US $130), half of which she sent home. She lived in a single room on the outskirts of Beijing and had an hour-long bus commute to and from her job.

Wu Daiyu bought her first mobile phone a month after she arrived in Beijing with the money she had saved from her factory job (she had given the rest of her salary to her parents). One day we had the following conversation:

CW: When you first bought a mobile phone, what kind was it?
WDY: It was a Chinese-made clamshell phone with a music player.
CW: How much did it cost?
WDY: About 800 yuan [about US $104]. I bought it because I really like to listen to music.
CW: Is it the same phone you have now?
WDY: No, it was stolen one month after I bought it. I cried the whole day after that happened. I even dreamed about it. It was in my dreams a few times. I could see it.
CW: You must have been really upset.
WDY: Yeah. I was so sad.
CW: When did you get your current phone?
WDY: I saved up my money and bought another one a few months later, but it was cheaper, about 600 yuan [about US $78], and it doesn't have a music player, which is a pity.
CW: Why didn't you buy one with a music player?
WDY: Because I was eager to buy a new phone. When I had a mobile phone I called my family once a week, but without a phone that was really hard to do with my work schedule. So I just bought a cheap one. Now I even call them twice a week [her family got a landline in 1999].[48]

I quote at length from my conversation with Wu Daiyu because her story reinforces several points I have made in previous chapters—the sacrifice that goes into purchasing a phone, its significance for maintaining links with others, its role as an entertainment device for women who usually do not have a separate digital music player and may or may not own a television set, and the devastation felt when a phone is stolen (which happens frequently). Wu Daiyu's mobile phone was a medium for communication, a symbol of her ability to manage her own resources and still display her affection and filial duty to her family, and a device that allowed her to enjoy the music that she loved. As with other women I knew, it was also articulated to her self-transformation in the city. However, after Wu Daiyu gave her mobile number to Linda, the phone took on a new role that she had never anticipated: it became something that brought her a lot of anguish. I discovered this one day when I dropped in to the boutique and noticed that Wu Daiyu looked very distraught. She then told me that in the last month Linda had been calling her on her mobile phone late at night to accuse her of stealing clothing from the shop. As Wu Daiyu explained:

> Last week at about 10:00 p.m. I was just getting home. My mobile phone rang and it was Linda. She said she couldn't find some blouses that had just arrived and she accused me of taking them. I told her they were in the back of the shop, but she wouldn't listen to me. I was so upset. I told her I would go back to the shop and show her, to prove my innocence. The buses had stopped running so I was preparing to take a taxi. I was out on the street crying because I felt so bad that she would treat me that way and because I could not afford a cab. Just as I was about to flag one down, Linda called me again and said she had found the clothing. It was where I had said it was. Then she apologized.[49]

Wu Daiyu was visibly distressed when she told me this story, and she said it was not the only time Linda had called her on her cell phone to level such accusations. However, each time Linda accused Wu Daiyu of theft, in the end it turned out that Linda either had misplaced something or had not bothered to look where Wu Daiyu suggested. Wu Daiyu said she desperately wanted to quit her job but was concerned that time spent looking for a new job was money she couldn't afford to lose. "It's really hard to take," she repeated to me. "I really can't take it."

The example of Linda and Wu Daiyu illustrates how mobile phones are articulated to already existing power relations and how socio-techno practices create new opportunities for the subordinated to be further manipulated by those in authority. Unlike the "mobile workers" whose cell phones are often supplied and paid for by their employers, Wu Daiyu's personal phone, for which she had sacrificed and shed tears, was usurped by Linda as a tool of discipline and control in a very mundane yet sinister manner. In other words, on the pretense of missing clothing, Linda used the phone as a sort of mini-virtual Panopticon to instill a self-regulatory gaze in Wu Daiyu. Furthermore, what could be termed Linda's "cellular harassment" is specific to the social construction of Wu Daiyu as a migrant worker, a subject position that is rendered subordinate, devalued, and dehumanized, especially when the signifier "female" is attached to it. In fact, given China's gender norms it is difficult to imagine Linda treating a male migrant worker in this particular manner. Linda's access to Wu Daiyu's mobile phone number was clearly an attempt to curb Wu Daiyu's sense of autonomy vis-à-vis her job and to remind her of her identity as a *dagongmei.*

Eventually Wu Daiyu devised her own countertactic to Linda's harassment. Before leaving the shop each night, she reminded Linda where any new items were and checked to make sure everything was in place. If Linda was gone, she performed this ritual with a text message, which seemed at least temporarily to defuse Linda's behavior. The last time I saw Wu Daiyu in 2007 she had actually moved in to the tiny partition in the back of the store. While such constant, close proximity in a space of enclosure certainly could have emboldened Linda's efforts to mold Wu Daiyu into a docile body, it saved Wu Daiyu rent money, a long bus commute, and the possibility of being accused of stealing, for there was no place for her to hide anything she could have possibly stolen.

### A MAINTENANCE WORKER

Although Wu Daiyu's story reveals overt efforts at discipline by an employer, other modes of surveillance and control arise because a mobile phone is so easily co-opted for work-related purposes that differ from the owner's original intentions. For example, Zhuang Jie was a young woman from Hubei province who had been in Beijing for four years. During this time she had worked very hard to "develop herself" by attending computer training courses at a branch of the Beijing library, enrolling in English-language classes, and finally entering night school at a university to receive the equivalent of a vocational degree. When I met her she was employed as a low-level supervisor, overseeing a maintenance staff of seventeen young women at a small company in Beijing. In addition to supervising them, she had to ensure that these women, with whom she shared a dormitory, were in bed by their 10:00 p.m. curfew and up and at work every morning by 8:00 a.m. She also handled some administrative duties.

Zhuang Jie had a very basic phone that she had bought to keep in touch with friends, family, and former coworkers. However, she found that over time her mobile phone primarily served work purposes, with a daily stream of text messages and voice calls to and from supervisors and colleagues.[50] The women she supervised sent her messages or called her to ask questions or relay information such as the following:

1. When will we receive our summer uniforms?
2. Where is the key to the stockroom?
3. Can you help me get more pay?
4. I'm going to be late.

Supervisors called or sent messages such as the following:

1. Go meet the delivery truck at the gate.
2. Please change Xiao Sun's position. She is not doing a good job.
3. You need to get your team members' employee numbers for their insurance forms.

In all cases, Zhuang Jie had to respond to these calls and messages as part of her job. If she was away from her office or if the office phone wasn't working (which seemed to occur frequently), she was obligated to use her mobile. Though she could receive calls for free, she had to pay to make phone calls. She also had to pay for text messages, which, while inexpensive individually, could still generate a high cost due to sheer volume. Such costs might seem trivial to those who are more well off in China, but Zhuang Jie had limited economic resources.

It is important to stress that Zhuang Jie should not be considered a "mobile worker"—she was employed within a small compound and moved about between two or three buildings, and she did not have the education, skills, and job tasks typically associated with "telework." Furthermore, like Wu Daiyu, her cell phone was not supplied by her employer and her employer did not pay for any part of her phone usage. However, her particular relationship to her employer required that because she had a mobile phone, she also had to allow her superiors to supervise her and make demands of her via her phone. In the same way, Zhuang Jie's relationship to her colleagues—to whom she was a supervisor but also a peer—created conditions whereby they could monopolize her time and monitor her via her mobile phone. With the office phone frequently broken—and no incentive for management to have it fixed—Zhuang Jie used her phone in this manner with those she supervised as well, for example, through initiating work-related text-message exchanges with certain women in her charge.

Zhuang Jie's relationships to her superiors and subordinates as these were mediated through her cell phone thus bring to mind Qiu's "wireless leash." The networks of power relations in which Zhuang Jie was situated in her workplace meant that a cell phone might decrease her autonomy even as it increased her efficiency. Still, it is important to point out that while her mobile phone was implicated in her identity as a subordinate worker, it was also an important part of her identity as a low-level supervisor, a position she was very proud to have obtained through her efforts at self-development. In this regard, Zhuang Jie was one of very few women I knew who had achieved some small degree of career mobility. Nonetheless, as much as Zhuang Jie said she valued her phone because it enabled her to stay in touch with friends and family, she was the only woman with whom I spoke who said she would be relieved—it would "save her some worry" (*bijiao shengxin*)—if she didn't have a phone because at work it had become a means for colleagues and bosses to constantly get in touch. However, she could not get rid of her phone even if she wanted to. Her colleagues enjoyed her constant availability and her employer expected her always to be on call.

SILENCE AS SURVEILLANCE

The last example of mobile phones and surveillance actually concerns a young woman without a mobile phone. The point of this narrative is to illustrate that as much as a mobile phone can be used as a medium for monitoring and control, prohibiting ownership of or confiscating a phone can serve the same purpose. In China, as usage of the Internet and mobile phones has increased extremely rapidly, there has been a corresponding moral panic regarding what are perceived to be the ill effects of these technologies. They have thus been blamed for disseminating dangerous rumors, fostering unhealthy habits like gaming addiction, and encouraging sexual immorality through enabling illicit affairs and access to pornography. These concerns about the detrimental effects of new media technologies are not unique to China, but they have generated considerable attention in a socio-cultural context where, until quite recently, mediated information was tightly controlled and an underdeveloped telecommunications infrastructure meant that many people's ability to communicate privately on the telephone was rather limited. When fears about mobile phones are linked to patriarchal modes of employee control, the ability of the mobile phone to *subvert* other modes of surveillance is what then causes anxiety for employers.

For example, Guo Yaping was nineteen and worked in her older cousin's tiny shop in an alley in one of the traditional neighborhoods in the center of Beijing. Guo Yaping had been in Beijing for about a year, and she and her cousin worked at the shop every day for about twelve hours a day. She also lived with her cousin and her cousin's husband. She said she had no friends in Beijing, which wasn't surprising given the extremely restricted social world in which she lived. Although Guo Yaping's cousin had a cell phone, she would not allow Guo Yaping to own one. When asked why she restricted Guo Yaping, her cousin said, "She is too young, and anyway, she is still learning [about the shop] and a mobile phone would distract her." She then added, "One mobile phone is enough for two people."[51]

Although Guo Yaping was an adult, in the course of our conversation her cousin referred to her as a naïve child, and she clearly assumed a parental role in Guo Yaping's life even though she herself was probably not over thirty.[52] While Guo Yaping's cousin could keep an eye on her and monitor her quite easily in the small space of the shop and the home, a mobile phone would undermine this authority and grant Guo Yaping a degree of autonomy that her cousin was not willing to let her have. Her cousin also forbade her to go to Internet cafés, saying they were dangerous places not appropriate for a young girl. In constructing Guo Yaping's identity as that of a "child" or a "naïve girl," her cousin effectively limited Guo Yaping's possibilities for individual agency and autonomy in a number of realms.

Guo Yaping's narrative is not extraordinary. I encountered other young women, such as Li Xiulan, whom I mentioned in the introduction, who were working for a relative, such as an uncle, and who were not allowed to have a phone even when a male cousin of the same age had one. However, Guo Yaping's story differs from what has been found in many western countries regarding mobile phones in parent-child relationships. In much of the literature, while a mobile phone is said to be a device that allows teens a degree of freedom, parents say they feel better about their children's safety because of the cell phone; the mobile thus provides "safe autonomy."[53] Guo Yaping's cousin—the parental figure in her life—obviously saw a mobile phone not as something offering safety or security, but as a *threat* to the young woman's safety as well as to her ability to be monitored. In other words, a mobile phone was feared for potentially allowing too much autonomy to young women whom gendered power relations discursively produce as in need of protection by an older, wiser authority figure. To Guo Yaping's cousin, the thought that someone in her charge—particularly a female— could engage in conversations with potentially *anyone* by using a mobile phone was not a comforting feeling. Rather than using a mobile phone as a monitoring device, her cousin banned cell phones altogether as a more expedient means of monitoring. In this way, a notion of young migrant women— *dagongmei*—as passive, childlike, and vulnerable was reified.

*Mobile Resistance*

My discussion thus far of migrant women's labor relations—where the intersections of their gender, class, place, and age render them relatively immobile in the labor sphere and subject to disempowering modes of mobile surveillance—should not be taken to mean that migrant women are passive subjects, determined by the state, the market, and their employers. As Foucault has argued, power relationships—as opposed to complete domination— imply that the one over whom power is exercised must be a subject who is free to act (as opposed to a slave), and the course of such action is always multiple, contingent, and often contradictory.[54] To Foucault, the fluidity of power relations also implies resistance. As he states, "At the very heart of the power relationship, and constantly provoking it, are the recalcitrance of the will and the intransigence of freedom."[55]

What forms of socio-techno resistance do migrant women in the low-level service sector engage in via their mobile phones? Before answering this question, it's worth first considering collective labor resistance by migrant workers in China in recent years, such as the strikes where workers demanded higher wages and better working conditions at various transnational corporations, including Foxconn and Honda, in the spring and summer of 2010. These workers effectively used mobile phones and the Internet to transmit information (text and images) and to organize themselves. Pun Ngai and Huilin Lu argue that such collective resistance is indicative of the second generation of migrant workers, who are more individualistic, more concerned with personal development, and less inclined to submit to harsh working conditions for the sake of economic gain. They also believe that these workers' perception of themselves as "*mingong*, a specific class position" is key to their experience.[56] They thus contend that these male and female *mingong* differ substantially from the first generation of migrant factory workers, who were mostly young women who "appropriated their own laboring body as a weapon through everyday workplace resistance."[57]

While it is true that the second generation of migrant workers differs from their forbearers in many respects, it is not only gender, class consciousness, and generation that are the primary determining factors for their modes of mobile-enabled resistance. In fact, some strikes have been organized in factories where most workers are female, and it is also important to note that the strikes have been primarily at foreign-owned, not domestic, factories.[58] Moreover, China's labor shortage of recent years, which has forced employers to raise wages and improve work conditions, has seemed to have had the most impact thus far on unskilled industrial and construction work and has affected other areas more than Beijing.

A crucial factor that must be emphasized, then, is *context*. This particular context is constituted by a certain region and a large workforce that shares the experience of life in the "dormitory labor regime."[59] Moreover, the sheer number of workers means that when they "vote with their feet" by either leaving their jobs or going on strike, the impact will be felt by management, the media will have a focal point for a story, and the affordances of text messaging and Internet worker forums can be fully exploited. In contrast, the women in my fieldwork all worked at small enterprises—often they had one or two colleagues; in the beauty salons they might have had twelve or so, and in the restaurants, at most, they might have had fourteen or fifteen coworkers or, on rare occasions, twenty. Some of them did chose to "vote with their feet," as with Pan Xiao Jun discussed earlier. However, for the most part the resistance that emerged via the phone was not collective or spectacular. Instead, its expression was individual and articulated to the body, through either unauthorized possession or usage, as I discuss below. Like the first generation of female factory workers, these young women also appropriated their own laboring bodies; in contrast, the "weapon" was a mobile phone deployed in ways that were mainly symbolic yet still meaningful. In this regard, their mobile resistance was what de Certeau calls a "tactic," used by the marginalized or those without their own space to resist those in power through "isolated actions" that take "advantage of 'opportunities.' "[60]

### UNAUTHORIZED POSSESSION
In all of the workplaces where I have conducted fieldwork, the ubiquity of cell phones means that at nearly every worksite there are explicit rules as well as tacit protocols regarding mobile phone usage. Depending on the context, employers may see mobile phones as a threat to their authority, like Guo Yaping's cousin, and employees are thus banned from bringing their phones to work altogether. This prohibition was most stringently enforced in restaurants, where if employees are caught with a phone, it is confiscated and returned either at the end of the work day or in some cases a week later, with the employee's pay docked as well. Such punishment happens not if an employee is caught *using* a phone but merely if she is discovered with one in her possession on the job. With a work environment built according to norms of patriarchal authority and control, a boss or manager serves as a parental figure and the employees, particularly the women, are constructed as childlike subjects. However, many young migrant women attempt to subvert such authority through resistance that is subtle and that is about possession rather than usage. Such "possession as resistance" is exemplified in the following conversation I had with Luo Li Kun:

cw: Do you bring your mobile phone to work despite the ban?

llk: Yes, sometimes. I want to know if I receive a message.

cw: How do you conceal your phone from others?

llk: Depending on which uniform I am wearing, I can put my phone in my pocket and no one can tell it is there but me.

cw: Do you use your phone much at work?

llk: No—once in a while, but not usually. I like to feel that I have it.

cw: Are you afraid you'll get caught?

llk: No, I'm not afraid, but it's possible.[61]

Through Luo Li Kun's words, it is clear that the mere fact of carrying a mobile phone—a very personal item—is an act of resistance against arbitrary rules that operate to regulate her behavior and strip her of her agency. To

her, just to feel her mobile phone against her body holds symbolic meaning. In de Certeau's terms, this is a "tactic," or an isolated action exercised by
someone clearly at the margins in order to take advantage of the "cracks that
particular conjunctions open in the surveillance of the proprietary powers."[62]
But such tactics are not without their risks. If Luo Li Kun's employer were to
catch her with her phone, she would have to pay 50 yuan (about US $6.50,
one-twelfth of her monthly income). Considering that all of her friends aside
from her boyfriend are still in her hometown and her mobile phone is her
primary means of keeping in touch with them, the possibility of having it
confiscated for up to a week is a risk that surpasses even the potential financial consequences.

I met other women who engaged in similar symbolic protests against
disciplinary bosses. Some women were bolder than Luo Li Kun, and they
made it clear that carrying their phone was meant to be an act of defiance.
For example, Tan Fenfang, who was a cashier at a restaurant, took advantage
of her fixed position and the large counter where she was stationed to use
her mobile phone off and on throughout her shift. Her employer had fined
her in the past for using her phone, but this punishment had not deterred
her. As she said, "These bosses can't control everything."[63] Unlike Luo Li Kun
and Tan Fenfang, however, others have internalized the boss's gaze and are
afraid to use their phones even when unsupervised, lest they get caught, their
phones confiscated, and their pay reduced.

In contrast to the restaurants, marketplaces have different rules regarding how their workers can spend their time during slow periods. Some allow
employees to read, knit, or use their mobile phones when there are no customers present. Others permit reading but ban mobile phones outright.
However, these prohibitions affect men and women at the markets differently. The "older brothers" mentioned earlier usually pay no heed to these
rules. It is commonly acknowledged that as a son or relative of the boss, they
have privileges denied to mere workers. Like their peers in the beauty salons,
they also always have state-of-the-art devices: name brand smartphones with
multiple functionality. Many of these young men were quite eager to show
me their phones, the games they played, the websites they surfed, and so on.
Though the women I knew at the markets tended not to be as brash in their
resistance to the rules regarding mobile phone use, in the most regimented
market atmosphere, where they can be under nearly constant surveillance,
it is no wonder that a mobile phone becomes linked to acts of resistance

to reclaim space and time. Thus, I often witnessed that when a boss was momentarily away or preoccupied, one of the first things many women did was check their phones. As Huang Hui An told me, "I can't use my phone when my boss is around, even when there are no customers, but when he's not looking I still will send or read messages."[64]

### IGNORING OTHERS

James Katz has called attention to the way the public use of mobile phones is a type of "dance" in which all involved "must engage in a bit of choreography" in order to be "in sync."[65] By this Katz means that the mobile phone user, his or her co-present interlocutor prior to the incoming call, or strangers within earshot all must undertake a great deal of "tacit … but indirect coordination" to navigate public space together.[66] While this type of choreography certainly takes place in China as elsewhere, in the marketplaces I often observed the opposite as well—the mobile phone used as a direct way of remaining "out of sync" with those nearby. Cell phones equipped with games, music, or QQ can become a means for migrant women to ignore customers who do not appear likely to buy something. As mentioned earlier, employees in the marketplaces are supposed to be more than attentive to customers—they are pressured by employers to practically harass passersby in order to strike up a round of bargaining. With a mobile phone, however, some migrant women actively resist such job requirements. In doing so, they not only refuse standards of social etiquette but also gender norms that cast them as passive, compliant female bodies. In a similar manner, mobile phones are also used to block out the unwanted banter of other colleagues. Among individual users, or shared among two or three people, a mobile phone can clearly be used as a socio-techno means of exclusion and erecting barriers. But beyond staking out terrain and reclaiming space, in the marketplaces migrant women (and men) use mobile phones for the most mundane of reasons: to relieve the sheer boredom of standing day in and day out in the same cramped stall doing the same repetitive job.

Whether in a restaurant or a market, clearly mobile phones do not break down the regimens of power and control that circulate in and through migrant women's lives, and they may work even to maintain these. However, because of the very fluid nature of such power, cell phones are used by migrant women to engage in their own tactics for exercising individual agency, no matter how constrained. In this regard, their resistance is characteristic of the kind that Pun documented earlier among female factory workers: for example, occasionally slowing down the production line during a rush order when they felt overworked or listening to a radio playing pop music in defiance of company rules.[67] If she desires, a young migrant woman can exert a mini-rebellion with her mobile phone on several fronts—against a rigid and arbitrary rule, against a present but unwanted customer, against her boss who is relying on her labor for his or her own gain, and, at a more existential level, against the material conditions of her life. A mobile phone at work, whether it is used or not, can produce a sense of self in a space where notions of individuality and personal autonomy are often suppressed. They therefore are implements for de Certeau's tactics—those methods that "use, manipulate, and divert" the spaces produced by the strategies of those in authority.[68] Such tactics may be empowering emotionally, but obviously they do not alter the structural constraints that migrant women face in the labor sphere.

## Conclusion

An examination of the way mobile phones are articulated within the labor sphere of young migrant women working in the low-level service sector in Beijing reveals a complex array of socio-techno practices produced by gender, class, age, and place. In this chapter, I have shown how young migrant women's mobile phone assemblage is characterized by diverse modes of power and agency that circulate in and through the work lives of young migrant women precisely because they are young migrant women. While workplace disciplines are enacted to try to mold docile workers, appeals to self-development also align with the *suzhi* discourse in China to produce these young women's worker subjectivity. The jobs that young migrant women have, and the degree of regimentation, training, and regulation to which they must submit, as well as the gendered discourses that surround them, are all technologies of power to which mobile phones are articulated.

For these women—who are ordinary workers—possession of a phone does not necessarily lead to a better job, though it might help facilitate lateral job movement when one's social networks are mobilized. The use of the phone also does not necessarily generate higher income. For most women, the phone is seen as a device for sociality, entertainment, and identity construction, not as a tool for work productivity. Exceptions occur among female micro-entrepreneurs who incorporate mobile phones into exist-ing social and business networks and among young women whose sense of familial duty motivates them to use their phones in ways that might generate greater income for their employer who was also a relative.

In contrast to these rather positive outcomes, some employers' use of mobile phones for surveillance and harassment clearly reveals the phone as a new mode of control. At the same time, for some migrant women, a mobile phone can also be used for largely symbolic tactics of resistance, and this might give a migrant woman a feeling of temporary, fleeting empowerment despite not changing or challenging the deeply embedded structural impedi-ments and patriarchal cultural norms that negatively affect her. In the labor sphere, young migrant women's mobile phone assemblage is thus deterrito-rialized and reterritorialized through flows of disciplinary power, efforts at authoritarian control, and appeals to self-development and cultivation.

Conclusion

*The Mobile Assemblage and Social Change in China*

Underlying this book are two profound transformations—one taking place within a country and one spanning the globe—that are indicative of the forces that constitute our current era. In China, the phenomena of globalization, urbanization, migration, and marketization have radically altered many people's ways of being and understanding themselves in the world. At the same time, the extensive diffusion of mobile telephony worldwide has ushered in new modes of individual and collective identity, sociality, and agency. Grounded in a notion of communication as transmission and ritual, this study has offered a long-term ethnographic exploration of the cultural, social, aesthetic, and economic aspects of the mobile phone use of young rural-to-urban migrant women working in the low-level service sector in Beijing.

Particularly among youth and young adult populations across various cultures, the mobile phone has been configured as a crucial tool for self-presentation, for distinguishing and maintaining group solidarity and boundaries, for signifying style, and for undermining parental and school authority. However, in the bulk of the research these mobile, global, digital youth are all fairly well educated (or in the process of becoming so), relatively well off, and predominantly located in developed countries. On the other hand, until recently much scholarly inquiry into mobile phone use among low-income populations or in developing countries has tended to foreground economic outcomes while paying little attention to social aspects, even though it has become apparent that these two are often hard to separate. Moreover, while some studies have highlighted gender or class or age, very few have considered the constitutive nature of technology, power, and subjectivity.

To address these gaps and to add to the growing body of research on mobile communication, this study explored how young rural-to-urban migrant women use mobile phones within very constrained and limiting circumstances in the city. Through examining how the mobile phone is articulated to social constructions of gender-, class-, place-, and age-based identities, I have mapped young migrant women's socio-techno practices, or the myriad engagements, investments, emotions, habits, and discourses that constitute young migrant women's mobile phone assemblage. This dynamic assemblage is constitutive of migrant women's subjectivity in the city, shaped as it is by technologies of power and of the self. Examining such flows and processes in a particular location among a specific group of people enables deeply contextualized knowledge that should also provide greater insight into broader social formations and power relations.

## The Mobile Phone as a Technology of the Self

Young migrant women's engagement with mobile phones must be understood within China's current quest for modernity and development. Within modernities, various power relations and positionalities produce both complementary and contradictory understandings and practices of being modern in the world. China's opening and reform path of the last few decades, which has emphasized linkages with global capitalism and neoliberal market policies that have favored eastern coastal regions, as well as the institutional barriers enacted through the *hukou* policy, have created a vast gap in living standards and life opportunities between urban and rural residents. The result is the positioning of the geographical terrain of the countryside and its residents as devoid of culture and mired in stagnation and tradition. Within this neoliberal milieu, the urban then becomes the source of progress, and by extension the location for "modern" consumer practices, lifestyles, and resources. Young rural women—configured as backward and of "low quality"—bear the burden of improving themselves by becoming self-enterprising citizens through, for example, labor migration and through engaging in transformative practices aimed at self-development.

In this context, I have shown how a mobile phone can be viewed as a literal and figurative technology of the self as it is articulated to practices, flows, signs, discourses, and emotional and financial investments that constitute subjectivity. Particularly during the time of the initial fieldwork, a mobile phone served as a form of symbolic capital, signifying young migrant women's entry, however constrained, into urban modernity. In the same way, mobile phones are constitutive of a modern discourse in which the possession of technology and technological competence are linked to ideologies of knowledge, development, and "quality" (*suzhi*). For this reason, mobile phones are not only a form of symbolic capital but also cultural capital in the sense that they require users to have certain skills, literacies, and etiquette. A lack of proficiency in any of these will potentially subject a user to disciplining by friends or coworkers, and it will also reinforce marginalization. On the other hand, though purchase, possession, and use of a mobile phone offer a means of at least partially shedding one's "rural flavor," for most *dagongmei* this hybrid rural-urban self is liminal and can never be complete—as each of my informants assured me.

As part of a globalized modernity, mobile phones are also articulated to dominant notions of gender that have arisen in parallel with the growth of China's consumer society. Just as marketization has tended to relegate women to certain occupations, it has also placed renewed emphasis on the sexualization and commodification of women's bodies. Ubiquitous discourses of essentialized gender emphasize women's "natural" traits, such as grace and gentleness, and promote certain notions of inner and outer beauty. In my fieldwork, as a technology of the self, a mobile phone was often articulated to these gendered discourses through the way it was supposed to look (pretty), the manner in which it was spoken about, and the method in which it was used. Camera phones emerged in particular as technologies of gender as they were deployed for modes of self-fashioning that aligned with notions of urban femininity.

The ways that the mobile phone is articulated to young migrant women's desire for self-development and self-improvement reveal how the party-state's modernization goals have become deeply internalized in the minds and bodies of China's citizens. Nonetheless, as I have argued throughout this book, in certain contexts, in particular in the workplace, migrant women can be subject as well to modes of disciplinary power. Mobile phones are indeed technologies of the self, yet they can also serve as the means through which a panoptic gaze attempts to discipline and mold docile workers.

## Mobile Communication, Immobile Mobility, and Necessary Convergence

All of the young women involved in my study had journeyed hundreds of kilometers from home to work in Beijing, but in the city their lives were marked by economic and social marginalization and a circumscribed social world. In this book I have elaborated on the notion of immobile mobility as a way both to capture this paradox and to denote a socio-techno means of surpassing spatial, temporal, physical, and structural boundaries. Numerous socio-techno practices articulated to mobile phones—in social relationships, in camera-phone use, and in the workplace—reveal how the phone enabled such immobile mobility. Because most migrant women do not have easy access to a landline and until recently few had a personal computer, cell phones provide them with an important means for expanding their social networks, most often through ways that are in accordance with *guanxi* principles. For example, most women denote the names in their mobile phones almost always through some form of shared (*tong*) relationship to themselves—a colleague, person from the same hometown or province, a classmate, and so on. Such social networking practices mean, however, that for the most part those in their contact lists are like them (e.g., "not Beijing people").

Equally important to the expanded social networks enabled by the mobile phone is the way migrant women use mobile communication to enrich their social networks. Given the constraints on women's time, the circumscribed social world they occupy in the city, and the far distances that often separate them from those with whom they are emotionally close, the ability to surpass these spatial, temporal, and structural barriers through the immobile mobility provided by the cell phone is extremely important. Thus, the mobile phone is not only a supportive communication device, but also an expansive communication technology used to keep in touch with friends, both near and far, who are both geographically unreachable. Immobile mobility enabled by cell phones is not just a means for engaging in "meaningless" exchange of short text messages, jokes, or chat; it is a significant way for women to ease the sometimes devastating loneliness and isolation they experience in the city.

Emotional needs are also met through the way the mobile phone allows young migrant women to explore their sexual identity and to develop intimate relationships. Such mobile-facilitated relationships are often pursued in accordance with existing cultural norms, or through a blending of the technological (the mobile phone) and the traditional (intermediaries were widely used). In a few cases, young migrant women are breaking down barriers by, for example, dating Beijing men. The long-term nature of all of these relationships, many maintained almost strictly through the phone, again exemplifies the cell phone as an expansive communication technology that is used to transform selves and articulate emotions and desires. These social aspects of immobile mobility, or how the phone is used for expanded and enriched social networks and relationships, are perhaps the clearest manifestation of the use of the mobile phone for communication as transmission and ritual.

Still, aside from the exception of dating Beijing men, the friendships, companionship, community, and belonging maintained through the phone were revealed, for the most part, to be in line with *guanxi* principles, as mentioned above, meaning few women had friends with an urban *hukou*, though their mobile phone contacts may have included an employer or a staff member from a non-governmental organization. Thus, mobile phones do not necessarily enable young migrant women to transcend their own social strata, and certain mobile practices can reify their position as Others in the city. As I argued in chapter 3, this conclusion should not be surprising, for immobile mobility should not be conflated with social mobility.

In addition to social mobility, an important question is whether mobile phones can be successfully deployed for economic mobility. The evidence from this study indicates that unless a woman is a micro-entrepreneur, a mobile phone does not greatly enhance economic outcomes because of migrant women's positionality in the labor force. In other words, mobile phones are certainly useful for connecting with friends or colleagues who can facilitate job searches, yet a *different* job does not necessarily mean higher income or more potential for advancement. Strikes among factory workers (often facilitated partly through new media technology use), demographic changes, a new labor law, economic restructuring, and larger social transformations in recent years have led to better conditions for migrant workers in general. However, this research found that migrant women employed in small enterprises—restaurants, markets and shops, and beauty salons—tend to remain relatively immobile in the workforce regardless of whether they have mobile phones or have made an effort to improve their technological skills. Moreover, employers' use of mobile phones for surveillance and harassment of young migrant women at times can lead to their further marginalization. In still other instances, employers (who are relatives) enact a form of surveillance through prohibiting ownership altogether. In this way, they can maintain their authority and prevent the autonomy that they fear the cell phone would offer.

Although workplace rules and disciplines certainly vary, many women are employed in jobs that give them very little autonomy while at the workplace. When a phone is prohibited as a means of workplace control and efficiency, some women still bring their phones to work as a form of resistance. Such symbolic resistance certainly does not change the power relations of the workplace; also, if she is caught, a woman could jeopardize her income and even her job, while her boss, of course, has nothing to lose. Nonetheless, a mobile phone could be said to provide a means of psychological empowerment as it is articulated to overt modes of power and authority. Despite such constraints, some women definitely use their phones to plan for the future by, for example, archiving professional achievements with the phone's camera or by gathering a network of strong and weak ties that might be useful for a hoped-for future business either in Beijing or back home in the countryside.

Such archiving via the phone, along with certain imaging practices, entertainment uses such as gaming or listening to music, and the social networking discussed above, exemplify what I have called "necessary convergence." That is, in contrast to middle- and upper-class technology users with digital cameras, desktop computers, and multiple ways to access the Internet, young migrant women converge all of these uses onto one delivery technology, the mobile phone. Such necessary convergence is a result of constrained economic resources and limited access to new media technologies. It thus contrasts with what I term "selective convergence," such as someone using a smartphone to read email for the sake of convenience or efficiency when he or she owns a personal computer. Necessary convergence reveals the ingenuity and creativity that can arise under very limited circumstances. As it enables users to overcome certain constraints, it is another means of achieving immobile mobility. However, as much as necessary convergence can be celebrated for at least partly alleviating digital inequality, its own limits become apparent if we consider, for example, that many migrant women said that, given the option, they would prefer to use a computer to go online, store photos, type documents, and so forth.

The practices, habits, investments, and discourses just discussed show the multiple logics of mobile phones and immobile mobility. Immobile mobility allows for overcoming myriad constraints, yet it can never erase these completely. At the same time, immobile mobility is not something fixed; rather, as constitutive of young migrant women's mobile phone assemblage, immobile mobility reveals how practices and processes materialize, are deterritorialized and reterritorialized, and in the process create and constrain certain possibilities and potentialities.

The Significance of the Mobile Assemblage

As Wise notes, every assemblage is made up of certain qualities, or "affects and effectivity"; thus, when mapping an assemblage it is crucial to think not only about "what [the assemblage] is, but what it can do."[1] In this book I have sought to understand how a specific discursive context—China in the new millennium—produces particular power relations and constructions of gender, class, place, and age, which in turn constitute young migrant women's mobile phone assemblage. What does a very localized study of a particular group of women tell us about larger societal transformations and about the role of mobile communication within these? How does this research add to our knowledge about the intersections of subjectivity, technology, and power? There are several key contributions that this study makes, and in combination they refuse simplistic binaries of inclusion versus exclusion, emancipation versus subjugation, and agency versus control in understandings of technology and society.

First, within processes of migration, particularly in the context of widescale urbanization, uneven technology diffusion, rapid societal transformation, and extremely disparate access to social and economic resources among different segments of the population, the connectivity and necessary convergence provided through the mobile phone cannot be underestimated. This critical access is extremely significant, given the temporal, spatial, and institutional constraints placed on groups such as young migrant women. Connectivity means communication, which lies at the heart of the social world, and such connectivity allows migrants—often isolated, often discriminated against—an anchoring and inclusion in networks of sociality and modes of self-transformation that are crucial to their well-being in the city.

In this regard, the sheer convenience of the cell phone is not a trivial matter. For most migrant women, the mobile phone is not just one more communication device added to a fixed-line phone or a computer with Internet access. It is their primary, if not only, means of keeping in touch with others. Certainly prior to the arrival of the mobile phone, migrant workers remained in contact with family and very close friends by using public phones, writing letters, beeping with pagers, and so forth. However, the transformation in ease and frequency of access facilitated via the mobile phone might be hard to fathom for those of us who have been surrounded by ubiquitous telephony our entire lives, and, for the last decade or two, pervasive computing and Internet access. For migrant women, and most likely for other populations with similarly constrained material circumstances, the mobile phone thus serves as a counter-domination tactic against such limiting and limited life conditions.

Second, this research suggests that a notion of the mobile phone as an assemblage made up of the articulation of myriad socio-techno practices grounded in the material conditions of everyday life forecloses deterministic arguments regarding technology and society. A growing body of research has posited the existence of universal understandings and practices associated with cell phones and young people. While noting certain similarities, other studies have cautioned that mobile phone usage must be understood as it arises within a given socio-cultural context. As I have argued throughout this book, mobile communication expresses a particular discursive context and gives rise to a particular assemblage as it is articulated to myriad practices, representations, and feelings that are also productive of this context. Thus, to say that for migrant women the mobile phone is part of forming a "modern" identity means that the cell phone is articulated to a sense of selfhood associated with urban life and not the countryside. In another context, such an articulation might not occur; likewise, to say that a mobile phone is "cool" or "fashionable" does not mean the same thing as saying it is "modern."

Though young migrant women might use mobile phones in ways that are similar to how young people across the globe use them—for social networking, dating, and performing acts of identity—a notion of socio-techno practices also enables deeper insight into how such uses signal the emergence of larger socio-cultural transformations. For example, when migrant women independently use mobile phones to forge romantic relationships long before face-to-face contact occurs, they are not only pursuing their individual desires or using the text function of the phone to overcome shyness. They are also challenging long-standing cultural norms in the countryside that are rooted in notions of patriarchy and filial piety. Their personal engagement with technology thus has broader social implications, as I will discuss in more detail below.

A focus on socio-techno practices also enables us to see how identity, sociality, and technology are intricately connected. Identity is not a solely individual project; rather, people shape themselves in relation to others in various ways, in this case through mobile phones. Thus, mobile phones are integrated into current social practices—such as *guanxi*—that dictate appropriate notions of relationship building and sociability. At the same time, a cell phone opens up new possibilities for the enactment of social practices. Alternate spaces give rise to transformations, rather than ruptures, as evidenced in the way migrant women use mobile phones to find *wangyou*, or net friends. Still, socio-techno practices may be articulated to new modes of exclusion when, for example, certain users are not proficient in competencies and rules that arise in relation to technology.

Third, and closely related to the above point, this study sheds light on the constitutive nature of gender, technology, and power. For example, unlike several previous feminist critiques of technology, what this study reveals is that it is not that women are left out in relations of technology. Young migrant women certainly participate in China's "mobile revolution," and this participation is important not only for their inclusion in sociality but also as a way for them to understand and affirm their gender identity. The manner in which this gender identity is expressed—particularly through emphasis on the feminine appearance of the phone—shows that technology also has a disciplining function. As a mobile phone is embedded in notions of dominant femininity, it serves to reproduce and create new disciplinary practices of femininity that align with essentialized notions of gender.

While young women participate in mobile telephony in equal numbers to young men, at the same time, unequal material conditions of men and women—the result of structural impediments and social constructions of gender—mean that certain women's access to and usage of technology are more constrained. If we read this as resulting only from economic factors, we miss the larger way in which power operates to create a discursive context that produces not only gendered practices but also gendered understandings of technology use. These gendered discourses, which intersect with constructions of age, class, and place, circulate at the most mundane level to perpetuate asymmetries in men's and women's relationships with technology.

Given that mobile phones can help to reify class, place, and gender differences and exclusions, does this mean a mobile phone is just another consumer item, the desire for which operates to subsume capitalism's extraction of migrant women's surplus labor while promising superficial transformative possibilities? In several studies of migrants in different cultures, scholars point to migrant workers' participation in exploitative labor as evidence that they are deceived (or duped) into laboring only to use the fruits of their work to perpetuate the very system that exploits them. Of course, cell phones do encourage the capitalist consumption that would be impossible without the labor of the "docile body" of the migrant worker. However, this argument is both problematic and simplistic. It presents once again the scholar with the "view from nowhere" (in Susan Bordo's words), whose own labor somehow does not reproduce a less-than-perfect system and whose own consumption practices do not enable the very relations of global capital they are critiquing. Moreover, it neglects consideration of how modes of neoliberal governmentality perpetuate a notion of self and market, the disarticulation of which is nearly impossible in our current historical moment. It also ignores the multiple articulations of the mobile phone assemblage.

Thus, a fourth contribution this study makes is that rather than configuring mobile phones as one more ruse of capital, we should grasp how for marginalized groups, mobile phones are articulated to multiple forms of agency amid myriad constraints. Mobile phones offer a means for people to construct the self, maintain connections, make autonomous decisions regarding love and intimacy, engage in play, and resist inequitable conditions. In other words, the mobile phone is articulated to multiple types of personal meaning making and transformation, and it brings many forms of *pleasure*.

My discussion so far has focused primarily on personal and individual dimensions of migrant women's use of mobile communication while only hinting at broader societal implications. However, a final contribution of this research is to provide further insight into the connection between technology use and social change in China in two areas: women's autonomy and migrant workers' collective empowerment.

Just as with the issue of whether migration itself enables greater autonomy for Chinese rural women, the question of the relationship between mobile communication and women's autonomy does not have a singular answer since autonomy is rarely all or nothing; rather, there are degrees of autonomy. Clearly, mobile phones do not by their mere existence fundamentally alter the structural and material conditions that serve both to enable and constrain possibilities for autonomy. However, young migrant women's autonomy in dating decisions, which are facilitated via the mobile phone, is a significant challenge to rural traditions regarding young women's role in the family and, by extension, in the larger society. Though rural marital practices can vary according to region, in many cases young women's choices in marriage can be extremely constrained. As ever larger numbers of migrant women are using mobile phones to establish and maintain intimate relationships in the city, and as more and more women are staying longer or permanently in the city, there is reason to believe these relationships will last. Thus, while this use of mobile phones will not destroy patriarchy in the larger society, it certainly can challenge and weaken its grip.

The existence in China's cities of increasing numbers of not only female but also male migrants also has implications for collective empowerment. Migrants' very presence in cities has troubled the binaries of urban and rural that are entrenched in Chinese culture. The second generation of migrant workers, of which all of my informants are a part, has been shown as a whole to be less willing to put up with the terrible conditions in the city that their parents had faced. In particular, the refusal of those who work in factories to accept poor pay and substandard conditions has led to improvements in pay for many workers, not just factory workers, yet so has a more conciliatory stance by the government as well as demographic shifts that have resulted in a labor shortage that is quite acute especially in industrial work, as mentioned earlier. Although my research on the ground found that cell phone resistance in the workplace was largely symbolic, migrant women's use of mobile phones to challenge their subordinate positions has long-term implications. Generally speaking, in the city young migrant women in the low-level service sector are in positions of weakness vis-à-vis their employers and the overall society, yet this does not mean that in the future my informants or others like them will not utilize new media technologies to join a larger social movement. In the more immediate term, their use of mobile phones to build up contacts for future employment and business opportunities is one way women are attempting to empower themselves. In doing so, they are potentially transforming the position of rural women in the larger society.

I have sought to add to the body of scholarship that insists that practices and understandings of technology must be studied not only among a certain age group or gender, but as these practices are intricately connected to and arise within a particular discursive context. In this way, we can see similarities in technology use across cultures and also extract the fine nuances and diverse shades of meaning that technologies have for different groups, thereby creating a richer, "thicker" understanding of technology, culture, and social change. At the same time, a limitation of my study is that most of the informants were women, as with much of the ethnographic scholarship on migrant workers in China. This focus on female migrant workers could be attributed to several factors—the neglect of gender in earlier migration scholarship, the fact that the bulk of the research has been conducted by feminist ethnographers, and the desire to give voice to a segment seen as the most marginalized of a subaltern group. Though a small number of young men were included in this study for comparative purposes, future research that includes male and female migrant workers while still keeping gender as an analytical focus will provide deeper insights into technology, migration, and social transformation in China.

To conclude, though mobile phones and migration both are about mobility, which embodies movement, flow, and dynamism, studying the mobility of people and technology necessitates studying conditions of immobility. Immobile mobility is about overcoming spatial, temporal, structural, and institutional barriers. At the same time, structures, institutions, discourses, and practices are not static. Young migrant women's mobile phone assemblage is part of a larger societal assemblage that continues to shift and transform. These shifting dynamics should give hope that new possibilities for social change in China will emerge even as others will be foreclosed.

An ethnographic inquiry is designed to generate new knowledge that ideally results in the creation of a lens through which people can view certain phenomena or see things in a new way. Rather than verifying theory, it aims to build theory that is persuasive and convincing. A very brief overview of the research methodology of this study was discussed in the introduction, but here I provide more detail on the participants, choice of research sites, the individuals and organizations that helped facilitate the research, and the types of interactions I had with my informants.

As noted earlier, the research began with a short exploratory trip to Beijing in the summer of 2005. Most of the data were gathered during ten months of fieldwork from the fall of 2006 through the summer of 2007. From 2008 to 2011 I made follow-up trips to Beijing as well as visits to the Chinese countryside in Anhui and Shandong. In this way, I was able to document continuities as well as shifting formations in migrant women's mobile phone assemblage. I also had the opportunity to meet new people while remaining in touch with a small number of women I met during the initial fieldwork.

The participants in the study were primarily young migrant women, as well as a small number of migrant men, who ranged in age from sixteen to twenty-seven years old, although most were between eighteen and twenty-three. The majority had migrated to Beijing after finishing at least some junior middle school, though a few had graduated from a vocational high school while some had not completed primary school. Most participants came from rural villages. Some came from small towns, and these participants were more likely to have had more formal schooling. The young migrant women and men involved in this research came from provinces as varied as Heilongjiang, Jilin, Liaoning, Inner Mongolia, Sichuan, Ningxia, Shaanxi, Jiangsu, and Guangdong, though most were from Anhui, Hubei, Hebei, Henan, Shandong, and Gansu.

The choice of restaurants, marketplaces, and beauty salons as the primary sites for the research was guided by three main considerations. First, the majority of prior ethnographic research involving female migrants in China has been conducted among workers in southern factories or with domestic workers, usually in Beijing. Most studies examining the mobile phone use of migrant workers (male and female) have also been carried out among factory workers in the south (using interviews and focus groups). In order to add to, but not duplicate, this body of knowledge I chose work sites that employ a large number of migrants yet have remained relatively unexamined. Another factor, and one that is more important methodologically, is that a major goal of this study was to see how mobile phones were integrated into the daily lives of migrant women. The very public nature of these sites meant that I could observe mobile phone use in everyday contexts. A final reason is that such sites allowed for ease of access and the ability to interact in a somewhat "natural" fashion, which would not have been possible among workers in factories or in people's private homes.

Aside from restaurants, marketplaces, and beauty salons, a number of more "official" locations were important for making connections and building friendships with migrant women. One of these was the Beijing Cultural Development Center for Rural Women (Beijing Nongjianü Wenhua Fazhan Zhongxin), which has several programs for both rural and migrant women and also oversees the Migrant Women's Club (Dagongmei zhi Jia) and the Practical Skills Training Center for Rural Women (PSTCRW) (Nongjianü Shiyong Jineng Peixun Xuexiao). The Migrant Women's Club was established in 1996 by urban intellectuals to provide a "home away from home" for migrant women in Beijing. The club offers various types of training, support services, and social networking opportunities for a large number of migrant women (and men) in Beijing. However, because it is fairly well known in China and abroad, it tends to be a bit overrun by foreign scholars and activists who use the club as a resource for meeting migrant women and conducting research. Many long-term members have occasionally expressed resentment about this situation, and understandably so, and for this reason I attended very few of the club's activities. However, two of its staff members were nonetheless very supportive of my research and introduced me to select club members, invited me to club activities, and took me to migrant markets and schools in Beijing.

The PSTCRW provides a variety of free short-term courses in subjects such as computer training, hairstyling, and waitressing, along with free room and board as well as job placement for rural women who are selected mostly from impoverished villages in provinces outside Beijing. During the fall of 2006 I went to the school every week and interacted with a group of thirty-two young women who were enrolled in a three-month computer course at the school. I was able to follow their progress from the time of their arrival, through their training and graduation, and then, with half of them, their job placement in Beijing. This allowed me to gain a better understanding of their transition from rural to urban life and to see how they went from being non-users of technology (due to lack of resources) to gaining technological skills, becoming *dagongmei*, and, in many cases, purchasing their first mobile phones.

A final organization that was very important in the course of my fieldwork was the Culture and Communication Center for Facilitators (Xiezuozhe Wenhua Chuanbo Zhongxin). Usually known simply as Facilitator (Xiezuozhe), it was established in 2003 to serve the migrant population in Beijing.[1] Like the Migrant Women's Club it provides rural-to-urban migrants with a variety of resources and training courses, and it is also a place for members to go in the evenings to eat dinner and socialize. I frequently participated in the center's Sunday afternoon activities (which were usually training sessions on topics ranging from labor laws to medical benefits), and I attended monthly birthday parties and holiday gatherings. To give back, I volunteered to teach Friday evening English courses.

The ethnography relied on extensive participant observation and casual interactions with migrant men and women at their places of employment and sometimes at their residences. During the extended fieldwork period I created a rotating schedule of visiting various restaurants, marketplaces, and beauty salons each day. On subsequent research trips I visited these same sites, though often the employees had changed. Each site required a slightly different approach to gathering data due to the variety of work environments in terms of job requirements, regimens, and schedules. Much of my interaction with the women and men employed at these sites was initially centered around mobile phone use, and most informants were more than willing to show me the contents of their phones—text messages, pictures, names in their address books, and, during later trips, QQ groups, and so on. However, we also talked about everything from work to relationships to television shows to future goals.

In Beijing I visited a variety of beauty salons—from bare-bones sites to upscale locations—but most of the salons where I spent a significant amount of time offered relatively inexpensive services to a range of customers who were mainly Chinese. They were midsized establishments, usually with six to ten employees, and in some cases with a few more (usually with more women than men), all of whom were young and from rural areas. The salons were perhaps the easiest place to observe and have conversations due to the fact that when women were not busy, most spent their time relatively freely, chatting online and off, sending text messages, thumbing through magazines, or doing each other's hair. During my long fieldwork period, I frequented five salons on a regular basis and had frequent hair washes and shoulder massages, which provided a good way to talk as well as to compensate the women for their time. In these salons I became a regular client, a participant observer, an informal English tutor, and, with a few women, a friend.

Compared to the beauty salons, restaurants were more difficult environments in which to gather rich ethnographic data. I could not go "behind the scenes" and observe interactions that went on in the kitchen, and I could not linger at a table for an extended period of time. With one exception I was not allowed to observe training sessions or other types of employee-employer meetings. My most extensive participant observation occurred at three restaurants where I had connections via Chinese friends. During the extended fieldwork period, I visited two of these restaurants about once a week, usually during lunch or dinner, and sometimes during the afternoon lull, though not as frequently then because employees usually took a nap at that time. Because the third restaurant was quite a distance from my home, I went there every two to three weeks to talk to the wait staff I knew and occasionally to chat with the boss as well.

Beijing has a diverse array of shopping venues spread throughout the city, including several huge marketplaces located in vast structures with four or five floors, each jammed with row upon row of stalls occupied by vendors hawking everything from small electronics to designer purses and watches to name-brand athletic shoes and clothing (all of it fake). I visited various types of shopping venues and spoke with many employees on several occasions, but I spent extended time at three small clothing stores and in three different large marketplaces. In the migrant enclaves that sit on the outskirts of the city there are also markets, many of them outdoors. These markets are vastly different from the other markets in terms of the goods that are sold and due to the fact that all of the customers as well as the vendors are migrants. I occasionally went to one of these migrant markets to chat with two different women who had been introduced to me through a staff member of the Migrant Women's Club.

In addition to participant observation, I conducted more than seventy-eight semistructured interviews in Chinese with rural-to-urban migrant women as well as twenty-one interviews with male migrants. These interviewees included some of the participants mentioned at the various sites above, women I met through different NGOs such as the Migrant Women's Club and Facilitator, and thirty-two young women enrolled at the PSTCRW. Some interviews were done during women's work hours and thus were interrupted or cut short, but over half of these interviews were in depth and lasted over an hour. Often an interview led to a more long-term relationship and sometimes vice versa. In addition to interviewing migrant workers, I also interviewed three employers; two staff members at the NGOs mentioned above; and the director, director of education, and two computer instructors at the PSTCRW. Interview questions covered basic demographic and employment information, traditional media use, and mobile phone and Internet usage. When possible, interviews were recorded and then transcribed; when it was not possible to tape record, I took extensive notes during the interview.

At the end of the initial fieldwork, mobile phone diaries were also collected from seven female and two male migrants whom I knew fairly well. The purpose was for them to document their mobile phone use for four days over a one-week period. The format of the diaries was adapted from the work of Mizuko Ito.[2] Participants were instructed to record the date, time, context, and content of all voice calls, text messages, mobile Internet use, camera use, file downloading or sending, and game playing during an entire day. They were also asked to document whether there were any problems with the intended use of their phone (such as poor reception). Once the diaries were collected, translated, and analyzed, follow-up interviews were conducted to generate deeper insights into what emerged as key moments of communication and certain trends in usage.

# NOTES

NOTES TO INTRODUCTION

1. To protect the privacy of participants, all names of people and places of employment are pseudonyms.

2. At the time of my initial fieldwork in 2006 and 2007, the exchange rate between the dollar and the yuan was about $1.00 = ¥7.7. Although the rate has since changed, I use this rate throughout the manuscript when calculating dollars unless otherwise indicated.

3. Interview in Beijing, April 19, 2007. SIM, or Subscriber Identity Module, cards are used in GSM (Global System for Mobile Communication) mobile phones. They have a unique ID and function like a memory chip, storing phone numbers, text messages, and other data. They can be switched in and out of GSM mobile phones quite easily.

4. The figure on teledensity in 1980 comes from Lee, "Telecommunications and Development: An Introduction," 16. According to China's Ministry of Industry and Information Technology (2011), by the end of November 2011 China had about 975 million mobile phone subscribers, representing a penetration rate of about 74 percent. At the end of 2011, there were 513 million Internet users in China, for a penetration rate of 38.3 percent, according to the China Internet Network Information Center's (CNNIC) "Hulianwangluo" [29th statistical report].

5. Foucault, "Technologies of the Self," 18.

6. This idea is taken from Stuart Hall's notion in "Introduction: Who Needs Identity?" (4) that identity must be viewed as "a process of becoming rather than being," not a clasping at "roots but a coming-to-terms-with our routes."

7. Carey, *Communication as Culture*, 15. Shortly after I returned to the United States from my fieldwork in 2007, Sarah Banet-Weiser suggested Carey's definition of communication as a way to understand mobile phone use. I am grateful for this insight.

8. Ibid., 18.

9. Ibid., 23.

10. There are edited volumes such as Ito, Okabe, and Matsuda's *Personal, Portable, Pedestrian* (on Japan) and Pertierra and colleagues' *Txt-ing Selves* (on the Philippines). An exception is Horst and Miller's *The Cell Phone*, which is an ethnographic exploration of mobile phone use among low-income Jamaicans. Cohen,

Lemish, and Schejter's *The Wonder Phone* is about mobile phone use in Israel, but it is not an ethnography.

11. Most research on female migrants has been conducted among domestic workers or factory workers. See, for example, Jacka, *Rural Women*; Gaetano and Jacka, *On the Move*; Pun, *Made in China*; Sun, *Maid in China*; Yan, *New Masters*; and Tan, "Jiating Celue" [Family strategy] and "Nüxing Liudong" [Female migrants]. Patrick Law and his team at Hong Kong Polytechnic University have conducted much of the research on mobile phone use by southern factory workers.

12. Exceptions include Tiantian Zheng's *Red Lights,* an ethnography of sex workers in Dalian. A small portion of the service workers who are the subject of Amy Hanser's *Service Encounters* were migrants.

13. My definition of socio-techno practices aligns with previous research on the telephone, the Internet, and the mobile phone in which these technologies are seen not as sweeping in and changing people's lives but rather as being integrated into prior communication practices and ways of life. See, for example, Fischer, *America Calling,* and Horst and Miller, *Cell Phone.* See also Wallis, "(Im)mobile Mobility," 64.

14. In *Modernity at Large* (33), Arjun Appadurai designates ethnoscapes, mediascapes, technoscapes, financescapes, and ideoscapes, which deterritorialize culture, space, place, and time, as constitutive of mass migration and the pervasiveness of electronic media.

15. A talk presented at the Annenberg Research Network on International Communication in April 2005 by Sebastian Ureta on the spatial immobility of low-income families in Chile first started my thinking about this term. I do not recall him using the term "immobile mobility," yet later I learned that he had in fact presented a different paper elsewhere with this term in the title. However, our uses differ. See Ureta, "Evanescent Connection" and "Immobile Mobility." My definition of immobile mobility here is adapted from Wallis, "(Im)mobile Mobility," 64.

16. See, for example, Fortunati, "Mobile Phone." On low-income families in Chile, see Ureta, "Immobile Mobility." With the widespread diffusion of smartphones, more and more people in the United States, especially among a younger demographic, are also less likely to have landlines in their homes. See http://news.cnet.com/8301-13506_3-20004885-17.html?part=rss&subj=news&tag=2547-1_3-0-20.

17. Prensky, "Digital Natives."

18. Jenkins, *Convergence Culture*, 2–3.

19. Jenkins's arguments are grounded in a western context, and he acknowledges that his description of convergence culture is based on a relatively privileged group that is "disproportionately white, male, middle class, and college educated" (*Convergence Culture*, 23). See also Palfrey and Gassner, *Born Digital.*

20. In *Convergence Culture* (3, 15) Jenkins states his emphasis is on the cultural dimensions of convergence and that he is less concerned with the significance of "delivery technologies," or the tools that are used to access media content (like a cassette deck) because these often become obsolete over time and are replaced by newer

ones. He calls the dream of certain technophiles that one device will be used to consume all media content the "black box fallacy." That it is false, he argues, is proven by the plethora of gadgets (television, DVR, game console, etc.) that consume space in his living room. On this debate see also Ian Bogost's review of *Convergence Culture*: http://www.bogost.com/writing/review_of_convergence_culture.shtml.

21. My point is not to dismiss historical changes over time that render certain delivery technologies, such as the Victrola, eight-track tape players, and cassette tapes, obsolete. I agree that the "black box fallacy" is a fallacy from a technological invention standpoint. My point here is to consider how one "black box" does often suffice for those who use technology within very limited material circumstances.

22. From a Cheskin Research report cited by Jenkins in *Convergence Culture*, 15.

23. In his study of the Chinese Internet, *Power of the Internet* (21), Yang Guobin notes that there "is always something new" when studying the online realm, yet he argues that although technological, social, or political changes occur daily, this should not be taken to mean "that what happened yesterday is meaningless for today, for every little development in the past becomes a part of the present." He therefore states that he offers a "living record."

24. Foucault, "Governmentality," 102–103; see also "Subject and Power," 341. On Foucault's move from disciplinary power to governmentality, see Gordon, "Governmental Rationality," 4.

25. Foucault, "Governmentality," 87.

26. Jeffreys and Sigley, "Governmentality, Governance and China," 3.

27. Aihwa Ong is probably most associated with this argument. See her *Neoliberalism as Exception*.

28. Jeffreys and Sigley, "Governmentality, Governance and China," 5. The notion of facilitative and authoritarian dimensions comes from Mitchell Dean, cited in Jeffreys and Sigley.

29. Rose, "Governing the Enterprising Self," 144.

30. Foucault, "Technologies of the Self," 18.

31. Ibid., 19.

32. Ong and Zhang, "Introduction," 2.

33. For example, prior to the 2008 Summer Olympics, campaigns in Beijing were aimed at everything from eradicating spitting in public to monthly "queuing" days that encouraged people to stand in orderly lines while waiting for public transportation.

34. Yan, *New Masters*, 125.

35. Foucault, "Subject and Power," 327. On subjectification, see Rabinow, "Introduction."

36. Foucault, *Care of the Self*, 50.

37. In "Governmentality" (102), Foucault argues against seeing disciplinary society as replaced by a society of government. Aihwa Ong has also made this point, and though I agree with her basic argument, I disagree with her application. I take this issue up in more detail in chapter 5.

38. On power and women's bodies, see Bartky, "Foucault, Femininity," 65. See also Bordo, *Unbearable Weight*, 27.

39. Perhaps most representative of this approach, in "Introduction" (6), Mizuko Ito notes that such studies "posit that technologies are both constructive of and constructed by historical, social, and cultural contexts, and they argue against the analytic separation of the social and technical."

40. Rich Ling uses domestication theory in his pathbreaking work, *The Mobile Connection*, but he calls it "more of a method or an approach" than a theory (32). He draws on other theorists, including Erving Goffman and Joshua Meyrowitz. Horst and Miller, in their excellent *The Cell Phone*, one of the first books to look at the mobile phone in the developing world, also use domestication theory. In *Mobile Media in the Asia-Pacific*, Hjorth uses domestication theory along with Judith Butler's theory of gender performativity. For an overview of the tenets of domestication theory and how these have and could be applied to studies of mobile telephony, see Haddon, "Domestication and Mobile Telephony."

41. Goggin, *Cell Phone Culture*, 6–10.

42. Du Gay et al., *Doing Cultural Studies*, 3.

43. Actor-network theory was originally formulated by Bruno Latour.

44. Goggin, *Cell Phone Culture*, 11. On this criticism of ANT from a feminist perspective, see Cockburn, "Circuit of Technology," and Wajcman, *Technofeminism*.

45. See, for example, DeLanda, *New Philosophy of Society*; Ong, *Neoliberalism as Exception*; Grosz, *Volatile Bodies*; Slack and Wise, *Culture + Technology*; Murphie and Potts, *Culture and Technology*; and Savat and Poster, *Deleuze and New Technology*.

46. Slack and Wise, *Culture + Technology*, 97.

47. Hall and Grossberg, "On Postmodernism and Articulation," 141.

48. Hall, cited in Slack, "Theory and Method," 115.

49. Slack, "Theory and Method," 125.

50. Slack and Wise, *Culture + Technology*, 113.

51. In *A Thousand Plateaus* (88–90), Deleuze and Guattari state that an assemblage is made up of two axes. The horizontal axis contains two segments: *content* (bodies [both human and non-human], actions, and passions and their intermingling) and *expression* (of acts, words, statements, and signs). They call the first the *machinic assemblage* and the second the *collective assemblage of enunciation*. As DeLanda notes in *New Philosophy of Society* (12), it is not always possible to separate these elements because "a given component may play a mixture of material and expressive roles by exercising different sets of capacities." Thus, like many who have appropriated these terms, I only use the word "assemblage."

52. Wise, "Assemblage," 78.

53. Ibid., 77.

54. Deleuze and Guattari, *Thousand Plateaus*, 88.

55. On understanding a mobile phone as an assemblage, see Wise, "Assemblage," 81–84.

56. Grosz, *Volatile Bodies*, 166. In *Chaosophy* (41), Guattari also calls the concept of assemblage a "tool."

57. Ong, *Neoliberalism as Exception*, 17.

58. Slack and Wise, *Culture + Technology*, 130.

59. See, for example, Ito, "New Set of Rules," and Katz and Aakhus, *Perpetual Contact*. Rich Ling had been examining mobile phone use in Norway since the late 1990s. See also Brown, Green, and Harper, *Wireless World*.

60. Exceptions include Pertierra and colleagues' *Txt-ing Selves* on mobile phone use in the Philippines and Jonathan Donner's work among micro-entrepreneurs in Africa. See, for example, "What Mobile Phones Mean."

61. In the following brief overview, I focus on studies that have taken a sociological, anthropological, or cultural approach rather than an information communication technology for development (ICT4D) approach because the former body of research more closely aligns with my own.

62. See especially Ling and Yttri, "Hyper-Coordination." See also Ling, *Mobile Connection*, chapter 4; Ito, "Mobile Phones, Japanese Youth"; Castells et al., *Mobile Communication and Society*, chapter 5; and the edited volumes by Ling and Pederson, *Mobile Communications*, and by Ling and Campbell, *Reconstruction of Space and Time*.

63. Ito and Okabe, "Technosocial Situations," 264-266; Turkle, "Always On," 121.

64. On gifting and ritual use of the phone, see Johnsen, "Social Context," and Taylor and Harper, "Gift of *Gab*?" Among certain low-income populations, however, these social uses aren't always distinguishable from economic ones. In *Cell Phone*, Horst and Miller coin the term "link up" to describe how the use of the mobile phone by low-income Jamaicans blurs the distinction between social and economic uses. On such blurring, see also Donner, "Blurring Livelihoods."

65. On fashion, see Fortunati, "Italy: Stereotypes"; Ling, *Mobile Connection*, 85; and Katz and Sugiyama, "Mobile Phones as Fashion Statements." On the phone and identity, see Lobet-Maris, "Mobile Phone Tribes"; Green, "Outwardly Mobile"; Oksman and Rautiainen, "Extension of the Hand"; and Stald, "Mobile Identity." On identity and digital media more generally, see Buckingham, *Youth, Identity and Digital Media*, and Ito et al., *Hanging Out*. Much of the early research on mobile telephony drew on Erving Goffman's vast body of work, especially his notions of interaction ritual and frontstage-backstage, to theorize how the mobile phone is used for self-presentation and the performance of identity. See, for example, Geser, "Towards a Sociological Theory." See also Ling, *Mobile Connection*, especially pp. 105-106 and chapter 6. An early mobile phone conference with the theme "Front Stage—Back Stage" in Grimstad, Norway, in June 2003 later became the basis for Ling and Pedersen's edited volume, *Mobile Communications*.

66. Plant, "On the Mobile," 12-14; Oksman and Rautiainen, "Extension of the Hand," 107; and Oksman and Rautiainen, " 'Perhaps It's a Body Part,' " 297. On gendered preferences, see Skog, "Mobiles and the Norwegian Teen." In *Wonder Phone* (163-167), Cohen, Lemish, and Schejter note that discourses about mobile phones

by men and women contradict their actual uses, which reveal much greater similarity. In *Mobile Communication* (51), Castells and colleagues discuss how in certain Asian countries, particularly Japan, a culture of cute (*kawaii*) has developed around girls' decorating of their mobile phones.

67. Hjorth, *Mobile Media*.
68. Exceptions include Bell, "Age of the Thumb"; Fortunati et al., "Beijing Calling"; Guo and Wu, "Dancing Thumbs"; and Wang, *Brand New China*, chapter 6.
69. On transnational migrants' use of mobile phones and other forms of new media, see the special issue of *Global Networks* edited by Panagakos and Horst on "Return to Cyberia." See also Burrell and Anderson, " 'I Have Great Desires' "; Horst and Miller, *Cell Phone*; and Thompson, "Mobile Phones." On China's rural-to-urban migrants, mobile phones, and translocal ties, see Cartier, Castells, and Qiu, "Information Have-less"; Law and Peng, "Use of Mobile Phones"; and Wei and Qian, "Mobile Hearth."
70. See, for example, Lin and Tong, "Mobile Cultures"; Luo and Peng, "Guanyu Zhongguo Nanbu Nongmingong" [On migrant workers in southern China]; Ma and Cheng, "'Naked' Bodies"; and Wallis, "Traditional Meets the Technological."
71. Chu and Yang, "Mobile Phones and New Migrant Workers," 232. See also Yang and Chu, "Shouji" [Mobile phone], and Law and Peng, "Use of Mobile Phones."
72. In "Use of Mobile Phones" (250), Law and Peng note that migrants use phones to find jobs but that owning a phone is not connected to gaining a higher income. See also Yang, "Preliminary Study."
73. In *Working-Class Network Society*, Qiu uses the term "information have-less" to move beyond the false binary of haves and have-nots within debates about the "digital divide."
74. The important works in this area are too numerous to cite here, but those that are especially noteworthy include Balsamo, *Technologies of the Gendered Body*; Cockburn and Ormrod, *Gender and Technology*; Mazzarella, *Girl Wide Web*; and Wajcman, *Feminism Confronts Technology* and *Technofeminism*. See as well Lerman, Oldenziel, and Mohun, *Gender and Technology*.
75. Fortunati, "Gender and the Mobile Phone," 23–25.
76. In *Mobile Media*, Hjorth includes studies of mobile users in Tokyo, Seoul, Hong Kong, and Melbourne.
77. While this is true of Hjorth's work cited above, this critique is not meant to diminish her contribution. In the popular media, *Wired* magazine's "Japanese Schoolgirl Watch" is representative of such a stereotype.
78. On how gender, class, race, and ethnicity have shaped technology, and access to technology, in the United States, see, for example, Gray, *Video Playtime*; Marvin, *When Old Technologies Were New*; Nakamura, *Cybertypes* and *Digitizing Race*; Spigel, *Make Room for TV*; and chapter 4 in Watkins, *Young and the Digital*, to name just a few.
79. Migrant workers make up only one part of the "have-less" that Qiu analyzes, and though he devotes considerable attention to class, he pays much less attention to gender.

80. A similar lacuna is evident in the area of what could be broadly labeled as "youth studies," where even recent edited volumes, which take a more global approach and consider issues such as class, include research on immigrant youth in western contexts but not in Asia. See, for example, Skelton and Valentine, *Cool Places*, and Dolby and Rizvi's *Youth Moves*. An exception is Maira and Soep's *Youthscapes* and Amit-Talai and Wulff's *Youth Cultures*, which has one chapter on youth in Kathmandu. Likewise, volumes on Asian youth almost never include rural-to-urban migrants. See, for example, Rodrigues and Smaill, *Youth, Media and Culture in the Asia Pacific Region*. An exception is Donald, Dirndorfer Anderson, and Spry, *Youth, Society and Mobile Media in Asia*, in which I contributed a chapter.
81. Bucholtz, "Youth and Cultural Practice," 526; Cole and Durham, "Introduction," 5, 8.
82. The youth in nearly all of the research on mobile telephony that initially inspired this study were high school and college students, in other words, in the UN-designated age range for youth. The research design of this study (with all but two participants single and most aged seventeen to twenty-three, with a few a year or two younger or older) was motivated by a desire to find out how young people living in very different material and structural conditions from the youth in these prior studies used mobile phones.
83. Maira and Soep, "Introduction," in *Youthscapes*, xviii, xv. See also Bucholtz, "Youth and Cultural Practice," 528, and Smaill, "Asia Pacific Modernities," 7.
84. Prensky, "Digital Natives."
85. Wang, *Brand New China*, 77–102 and chapter 6.
86. These terms come from *Hanging Out*, Ito and colleagues' rich ethnographic exploration of youth digital media practices.
87. Goggin notes this gap as well (see *Cell Phone Culture*, 5) and attributes it to a lack of a cultural perspective.
88. See, for example, Ito, "Mobile Phones, Japanese Youth," and Ling and Yttri, "Control, Emancipation, and Status."
89. The works are too numerous to list. See, for example, Constable, *Maid to Order*; Hondagneu-Sotelo, *Gendered Transitions* and *Doméstica*; and Parreñas, *Force of Domesticity*. For a focus on gender and migration, see Donato et al., "A Glass Half Full?" and Salzinger, *Genders in Production*.
90. On intersectionality as a response to the primary focus on gender in second-wave U.S. feminism, see Collins, *Black Feminist Thought*, and Crenshaw, "Mapping the Margins."
91. In *Made in China*, Pun remarks on the "triple oppressions of the Chinese dagongmei by global capitalism, state socialism, and familial patriarchy that work hand in hand to produce particular labor exploitations along lines of class, gender, and rural-urban disparity" (4).
92. Pun, *Made in China*, 111.
93. Lee, *Gender and the South China Miracle*, 109.
94. Spielberg, "Myth," 113.

95. Lee, *Gender and the South China Miracle*, 128.
96. Jacka, *Rural Women*, 44. Such sentiments were also confirmed in my own research.
97. Yan, *New Masters*, 37.
98. Bucholtz, "Youth and Cultural Practice," 532. This construction of the young women in this study as "youth" is not only apparent in discourses of *dagongmei*, but also in how they defined themselves as well as the way that others—colleagues, employers, academics, staff from non-governmental organizations—referred to them. In my interactions with numerous people in China during the course of my research, young migrant women were often called "children." University students were sometimes referred to in this way as well.
99. The "precariat" combines the words "precarious" and "proletariat" and originated in Japan to describe a new class of part-time contract workers. For an academic view of the precariat, see Ross, *Nice Work*.
100. Pun, *Made in China*, 12.
101. Ibid., 11.
102. Yan, "Spectralization of the Rural," 586.
103. Geertz, "Thick Description," 7.
104. Critiques of ethnography include its implication in imperialist projects; its use of "scientific" methods to try to render a distant culture transparent and fully knowable; and its belief that observations by a "qualified author" (read: white, western male) grounded in positivist principles could guarantee explanation of "exotic" peoples. See Clifford, "On Ethnographic Authority."
105. Clifford, "Introduction," 9.
106. By feminist ethnography I do not mean that the supposedly female qualities of empathy and intuition and women's propensity to focus on the interpersonal and experiential become the basis for a methodology that is able to avoid the unequal power relations, exploitation, and false objectivity associated with traditional research methods. For a summary and critique of this viewpoint, see Stacey, "Can There Be a Feminist Ethnography?"
107. Scott, "Experience," 24. I am indebted to this insight into how to reconcile ethnographic feminist research with Scott's critique of feminists' reliance on experience to Banet-Weiser in *The Most Beautiful Girl*, 13-18. Although Banet-Weiser's subject is American beauty pageant contestants, a topic about as far removed from Chinese migrant women as could be imagined, her discussion of feminist methodology applied to ethnography is extremely insightful and helpful. See also Jacka, *Rural Women*, 10-20.
108. Gray, *Research Practice*, 25.
109. Wendy A. Weiss, cited in Murphy and Kraidy, "International Communication," 315.
110. Bettie, *Women without Class*, 23.
111. Cited in ibid.
112. See, for example, Lotz, "Assessing Qualitative Television Audience Research." See also Visweswaran, *Fictions of Feminist Ethnography*.

NOTES TO CHAPTER 1

1. "Western Digital," or "WD" means *waidi*. "Phoenix Man" refers to young men born into poor families in the countryside, but who, through their educational attainments, succeed in the city, sometimes even marrying urban women. See http://baike.baidu.com/view/1217646.html.

2. For the graphic, translations in English of Tianya posts, and subsequent reactions on the KDS forum, see http://www.chinasmack.com/2008/pictures/tianya-posters-angry-with-shanghainese-on-kds.html. The discussion that follows is based on these translations as well as the original KDS and Tianya posts in Chinese.

3. Social networking sites such as Kaixin001, which caters to a predominantly young adult urban demographic, are another locale for such debates. For examples of discussions about *waidiren* in Beijing that emerged on Kaixin001 and then were posted elsewhere, see http://bbs.city.tianya.cn/tianyacity/content/39/1/962565.shtml and http://bbs.yahoo.cn/read.php?tid=670298. I am thankful to Xi Cui for bringing these to my attention.

4. The Great Proletarian Cultural Revolution was launched by Mao Zedong in 1966 as an effort to reconsolidate power and to purge the Party of what he called "bourgeois" and "rightist elements." It resulted in wide-scale political and social chaos, and, in many cases, violent struggles between various Red Guard factions. Numerous people were publicly humiliated, beaten, and jailed, and it is estimated that tens of thousands of people were killed. Although several western scholars demarcate the Cultural Revolution as lasting from 1966 to 1969, the post-Mao Chinese leadership marked the official end with the death of Chairman Mao and subsequent trial of the Gang of Four in 1976. This discursive construction of the "ten years of chaos" allowed the new leadership to establish a clean break with the past and declare itself the legitimate leaders of a new era.

5. Khan and Riskin note in *Inequality and Poverty* (3) that in the 1980s China's average annual GDP growth rate was 10.2 percent, compared to just 5.5 percent during the 1970s; in the first half of the 1990s it was 12.8 percent. In the last several years this number has continued to hover in the double digits, falling somewhat during the global economic recession in 2008 and 2009. In 2010, China overtook Japan as the world's second largest economy.

6. Potter and Potter, *China's Peasants*, 296.

7. The *baojia* system is discussed in Wang, *Organizing through Division*, 34–35. Unless otherwise noted, the information in the following discussion is based on Zhao, "Rural-to-Urban Migration." A detailed account of the beginnings of the *hukou* system under Mao can be found in Cheng and Selden, "Origins and Consequences," as well as in Wang, *Organizing through Division*. For an account of the *hukou* prior to and after the reforms and how the *hukou* relates to migrant women, see Jacka and Gaetano, "Introduction," 14–20.

8. As Knight and Song note in *Rural-Urban Divide* (8), savings from agriculture supported urban industrialization, following a "price scissors" policy.

9. The two major exceptions include the disastrous "Great Leap Forward" of 1958-1960, when Mao's campaign to transform China rapidly from an agrarian to an industrialized society brought many farmers to urban centers to take jobs in factories as part of the push for industrialization. When this campaign ended in failure, these temporary workers were sent back to the countryside. It is estimated that, as a result of Great Leap policies, over thirty million people died of starvation, primarily in rural areas. For an account of the Great Leap in relation to *hukou* policy, see Cheng and Selden, "Origins and Consequences." The second exception was during the Cultural Revolution, when, beginning in 1968, in order to quell some of the chaos caused by zealous Red Guards, Mao sent urban youth to the countryside to "learn" from poor peasants. As Potter and Potter point out in *China's Peasants* (303), rather than create greater understanding between rural and urban residents, this policy exacerbated resentment and prejudice between the two groups.

10. Solinger, *Contesting Citizenship*, 9.

11. Zhang, "Spatiality and Urban Citizenship," 315.

12. Potter and Potter, *China's Peasants*, 300. As many have noted, while China's Communist revolution was indeed a peasant revolution, Mao seemed to agree at least partially with Friedrich Engels, who distrusted peasants as too conservative and thus unable to have proper revolutionary consciousness.

13. For an extended discussion on the growth of the urban-rural divide and "the peasant question" in early 20th-century China, see Jacka, *Rural Women*, 33-37.

14. Cohen, "Cultural and Political Inventions," 154-155.

15. Ibid., 154 (emphasis in original).

16. Potter and Potter, *China's Peasants*, 304.

17. Ibid., 307-310.

18. Ho, "Rural Non-agricultural Development," 360.

19. Khan and Riskin, *Inequality and Poverty*, 4.

20. Li, "Labor Migration," 305.

21. Khan and Riskin, *Inequality and Poverty*, 5.

22. French, "In Chinese Boomtown."

23. Khan and Riskin, *Inequality and Poverty*, 8.

24. Huang, *Capitalism with Chinese Characteristics*, chapter 2. Huang thus argues that more economic liberalization and market reform are needed to enable rural areas to realize once again their entrepreneurial potential. For a critique of Huang's argument, see Andreas, "A Shanghai Model?"

25. Khan and Riskin, *Inequality and Poverty*, 4.

26. Ibid., 49.

27. Lei, "Bringing the City Back In," 311. Every year since 2004, the government's No. 1 Document has focused on rural areas. See http://politics.people.com.cn/GB/1026/10893985.html.

28. Khan and Riskin, "China's Household Income," 358.

29. Xinhua, "Backgrounder."

30. See http://finance.sina.com.cn/g/20100923/06448698190.shtml. A Gini coefficient over 0.4 is supposed to be a warning sign of a dangerous level of inequality.
31. Fan, "Migration and Gender," 425.
32. Tan, "Leaving Home," 248.
33. China Population and Development Research Center, "Zhongguo Liudong Renkou" [China's floating population].
34. Xinhua, "Beijing's Population."
35. In China, internal migration is distinguished between temporary, non-*hukou* migration, which is called "floating" (hence, the "floating population") and permanent (official) *hukou* migration (*qianyi*). The percentage of official migrants is relatively small.
36. As Mallee notes in "Migration, Hukou and Resistance" (139), in the 1980s, migrants were thought of as a group of rural escapees "walking blind" (*mangliu*) in the city, though this notion of "blind migration" is not common now.
37. Khan and Riskin, "China's Household Income," 375. These authors also note the income disparity among the migrant population, in particular between those who are entrepreneurs and those who are laborers.
38. See, for example, Wang, "Nongmingong" [Peasant workers]. On the spatial separation of migrants, see Zhang, *Strangers in the City*. See also Fan and Taubmann, "Migrant Enclaves."
39. "Laodong Baozhangbu Diaocha" [Ministry of Labor and Social Security report].
40. There have been numerous discussions about these problems both in the academic and popular press. For a recent survey, see Li, "Nongmingong Liudong Guochengzhong de Xuqiu yu Zhangai" [Demands and barriers in the flow of migrant workers].
41. Zhang, *Strangers in the City*, especially chapter 7.
42. Zhao, "Rural-to-Urban Migration," 25. On migrant workers and unfair fees, see also "Qingli Shi Nongmingong Jiaofei" [Clear up fees on peasant workers], http://news.sina.com.cn/c/2007-02-27/153411299577s.shtml.
43. Wang, *Organizing through Division*, 191. The Sun Zhigang case has had extensive coverage in academic and popular outlets in both Chinese and English. See, for example, Zhao, *Communication in China*, chapter 5. On the role of new media technologies in the case, see Yu, "From Active Audience."
44. Wang, "Renovating the Great Floodgate," 345. During the Beijing Olympics, migrant workers who weren't necessary to the "successful" functioning of the games were also rounded up and sent home.
45. State Council, "Guowuyuan."
46. "Beijingshi Zhengfu" [Beijing municipal government].
47. I taught an English class in a migrant elementary school in Beijing in 2007 and the contrast between the poor classroom conditions there compared to schools for urban residents was extremely striking.
48. Wang, *Organizing through Division*, 187.
49. Wang, "Renovating the Great Floodgate," 342.

50. According to Wang in *Organizing through Division* (189), at the time, only one person who applied was qualified to obtain this *hukou*.

51. Wang, "Renovating the Great Floodgate," 350–351. See also Chan and Buckingham, "Is China Abolishing the *Hukou* System?" Both Wang and Chan and Buckingham note that, in many ways, the elimination of the agricultural/non-agricultural distinction has hurt peasant farmers because with the loss of their agricultural *hukou* they have also lost certain benefits as well as the rights to their land and have thus become prime targets for land grabs by corrupt officials.

52. Tan, "Nüxing Liudong" [Female migrants], 246.

53. On May 31, 2010, the central government's website issued a notice that contained eleven key areas for reform. The seventh area, advocating the coordination of urban and rural reform, included a statement on deepening the reform of the *hukou* system by relaxing settlement requirements in medium-sized and small cities and in small towns. See http://www.gov.cn/zwgk/2010-05/31/content_1617026. htm. On June 6, 2010, the Xinhua News Agency published the *Medium to Long-term National Human Resource Development Plan (2010–2020)*, which included a statement on gradually establishing a unified *hukou*. See http://news.xinhuanet. com/politics/2010-06/06/c_12188202.htm. The Twelfth Five-Year Plan, formally adopted in March 2011, like the Eleventh Five-Year Plan, included language on *hukou* reform. See Eurasia Group, *China's Rebalancing Act*.

54. Knight and Song, *Rural-Urban Divide*, 13.

55. On the "sealed management" policy, see http://chinadigitaltimes.net/2010/07/ the-truth-behind-beijings-sealing-the-village-management/.

56. Wang, *Organizing through Division*, 26. Chan and Buckingham also note in "Is China Abolishing the *Hukou* System?" (605) that now the divide is based on local versus outsider (rural-to-urban migrants) rather than agricultural versus non-agricultural *hukou*.

57. For a macro-level analysis of how place of origin influences migration patterns and outcomes in China, see Solinger, *Contesting Citizenship*.

58. Fan, *China on the Move*, 76; Duan, Zhang, and Lu, "Zhongguo Nüxing Liudong Renkou Zhuangkang" [State of migrant women], 12.

59. Fan, *China on the Move*, 78.

60. Gaetano, "Filial Daughters," 52.

61. Tan, "Nüxing Liudong" [Female migrants], 240. On transnational migration, see, for example, Ehrenreich and Hochschild, *Global Woman*; Hondagneu-Sotelo, *Doméstica*; Parreñas, *Force of Domesticity*; and Salzinger, *Genders in Production*. In China, married rural women, unlike single female migrants, are more likely to become small entrepreneurs in the city, often with their spouses. Some also work on construction sites alongside their husbands, making about 50 to 80 percent of what males make because they are less able to do heavy physical labor.

62. Solinger, *Contesting Citizenship*, 202. As Gaetano notes in "Filial Daughters" (55), maids are positioned at the bottom of the social hierarchy because in China serving others is seen traditionally as undignified. In *Made in China*, Pun also

discusses how in China's southern factories a person's regional and ethnic back-ground "embodies a sense of spatial inequality far more subtle than the rural-urban disparity" (121).

63. Song, "Role of Women"; Tan, "Nüxing Liudong" [Female migrants], 242. On the perceived docility of Filipina maids in Hong Kong and of factory workers in Mexico's *maquiladoras*, see Constable, *Maid to Order*, and Salzinger, *Genders in Production*, respectively. In recent years, protesters demanding higher wages and better working conditions in China's southern factories have been just as likely to be male as female, thus challenging a notion of female docility.

64. Song, "Role of Women," 78; Wang, "Gendered Migration," 237. For a recent survey, see Xia, "Liudong Renkou Gongzi Shouru Yinxiang Yinsuzhong de Xingbie Chayi" [Sexual difference in factors affecting the wage earnings of the floating population].

65. Pun and Smith, "Putting the Transnational Labor Process."

66. Tan, "Nüxing Liudong" [Female migrants], 241.

67. Fan, "Out to the City," 187; Beynon, "Dilemmas of the Heart," 133.

68. Duan, Zhang, and Lu, "Zhongguo Nüxing Liudong Renkou Zhuangkang" [State of migrant women], 17.

69. On second-generation migrant workers, see Wang, "An Investigation." See also Chu and Yang, "Mobile Phones and New Migrant Workers," 226-227. Even in an earlier phase of migration, women were more likely to migrate for self-develop-ment rather than survival. See Cai, "Qianyi Juece" [Migration decision making]. For discussions of many of the themes in this paragraph, see Gaetano and Jacka, *On the Move*; Jacka, *Rural Women*; Lee, *Gender and the South China Miracle*; and Tan, "Jiating Celue" [Family strategy].

70. See, for example, Song, "Role of Women," and Beynon, "Dilemmas of the Heart."

71. Beynon, "Dilemmas of the Heart," 138 (emphasis in original).

72. Gaetano, "Filial Daughters," 72.

73. See, for example, Xie, "Most Migrant Workers."

74. Beynon, "Dilemmas of the Heart," 135. On future business, see Fan, "Out to the City," 196-197.

75. Fan, "Out to the City," 196-197.

76. Murphy, *How Migrant Labor Is Changing*, 173. See also Connelly, Roberts, Xie, and Zheng, "Waichu Dagong dui Nongcun Funü Diwei de Yingxiang" [The impact of migration on the position of rural women].

77. Pessar and Mahler, "Transnational Migration," 815. See also Hondagneu-Sotelo, *Gendered Transitions*; Oishi, *Women in Motion*; Parreñas, *Force of Domesticity*; and Salzinger, *Genders in Production*.

78. Hondagneu-Sotelo, *Gendered Transitions*, 191.

79. While this phrase does capture vast swaths of the Chinese countryside, it doesn't necessarily represent all villages, such as those in eastern coastal regions that are considered relatively well-off.

80. Yan "Spectralization of the Rural," 579.

81. Kipnis, "*Suzhi*," 304. See also Jacka, *Rural Women*, 41–42. A special issue of *positions,* vol. 17, no. 3, is devoted to *suzhi.*
82. Kipnis, "*Suzhi*," 298.
83. Ibid. As Kipnis notes (301), "education for quality" is not the same as "quality education" or the quality of education, which is translated as *jiaoyu zhiliang.*
84. Yan, *New Masters*, 114, 118.
85. Rose, "Governing the Enterprising Self." On neoliberal governmentality and *suzhi* in China, besides Yan Hairong's work, see the special issue of *positions* vol. 17, no. 3, Jeffreys, *China's Governmentalities,* and Anagnost, "Corporeal Politics."
86. See, for example, Wang, "Quanguo Zhigong Suzhi Lantu Huijiu" [National blueprint of workers' *suzhi* laid out].
87. On government plans, see Chen, "Suzhi Tisheng" [Higher quality], and "Shandong dui 'Shiyiwu' Qijian Nongmingong Suzhi Jiaoyu Tichu Mingque Mubiao" [Shandong clarifies goals of *suzhi* education for migrant workers during the "Eleventh Five Year Plan"]. On *suzhi* and domestic worker recruitment, see Sun, *Maid in China,* and Yan, *New Masters.*
88. See, for example, Lei, "Rural Taste." For a conservative academic approach to young rural women, see Wang, "Nongcun Nüxing Qingnian" [Rural female youth].
89. Sun, "Indoctrinization, Fetishization."
90. Song, "Role of Women," 85.
91. Tan Shen, personal correspondence, Beijing, July 20, 2005.
92. Lu, "To Be Relatively Comfortable," 124.
93. Davis, "Introduction," 1.
94. Asian Development Bank, "Reducing Inequalities in China."
95. Yan, "Politics of Consumerism," 163.
96. Ibid., 164.
97. Ibid., 167.
98. Davis, "Introduction," 11.
99. Ibid. Constraints have remained in several areas, including reproduction through the one-child policy.
100. I was in Beijing for the openings of the first McDonald's and Pizza Hut in 1990. These events generated much interest among everyday Chinese because these establishments were something new and "modern." Kentucky Fried Chicken opened in Beijing in 1987.
101. Davis, "Introduction," 12–13.
102. Nearly every Chinese adult who is middle-aged or older can recite some form of the "three big items" over the decades. These examples come from Yan, "Politics of Consumerism," 170.
103. On definitions and debates regarding consumer citizenship, see Banet-Weiser, *Kids Rule!* chapter 1. See also Canclini, *Citizens and Consumers.*
104. Invoking consumer citizenship is not meant to minimize other forms of political expression in China, whether protests by rural farmers against land grabs by

corrupt officials or the nationalism expressed by many Chinese citizens when they feel China's rights as a nation have been violated or when they perceive China to have lost face as a result of actions by other nations. In such cases, however, the fact that eventually the Chinese government steps in to quell unrest or nationalistic fervor shows the limits for Chinese in expressing their political citizenship.

105. See, for example, Davis, *Consumer Revolution*.

106. Ong and Zhang, "Introduction," 13.

107. Lu, "To Be Relatively Comfortable," 125.

108. Ibid.

109. See, for example, Li et al., *Shehui Chongtu* [Social conflict]; Lu, *Dangdai Zhong-guo* [Contemporary China]; and Li, *Nongminggong yu Zhongguo Shehui Fenceng* [Urban migrant workers and social stratification in China]. On Chinese youth and social stratification, see Rosen, "State of Youth."

110. Anagnost, " From 'Class' to 'Social Strata,' " 501-502.

111. Ibid., 504.

112. Building a harmonious society was formally enshrined as Party doctrine in October 2006.

113. See, for example, "New Socialist Countryside."

114. Riley, "Gender Equality," 79.

115. See, for example, Robinson, "Of Women." See also Jacka, "Back to the Wok." On the shifting gender discourse in China from the Mao era to now and its implications for women's employment, see Tong, "Mainstream Discourse." On myriad issues confronting Chinese women in the 1990s, see also Li, Zhu, and Dong, *Pingdeng yu Fazhan* [Equality and development].

116. Zhang, "Mediating Time," 94.

117. Ibid.

118. Although a labor law implemented in 2008 was supposed to do away with such employment discrimination, it is still widespread. On the implementation of the law in relation to Chinese women, see the special issue of *Funü Yanjiu Luncong* (*Collection of women's studies*), 2009, 2.

119. Ling, "Sex Machine," 280.

120. Tan, "Nüxing Liudong" [Female migrants], 242.

121. For a discussion of the influence of traditional gender discourse during the pre-reform era and the intersection of traditional, state, and market gender discourses in contemporary China, see Wu, "From State Discourse."

122. On the "postponement" of women's liberation and equality, see Stacey, *Patriarchy and Socialist Revolution*, and Wolf, *Revolution Postponed*. For a critique of their position, see Anagnost, "Transformations of Gender."

123. Yang, "From Gender Erasure," 41.

124. Hooper, " 'Flower Vase,' " 170.

125. For a more detailed account of the Iron Girls, see Honig and Hershatter, *Personal Voices*, 23-26.

126. Evans, "Past, Perfect or Imperfect"; Honig and Hershatter, *Personal Voices*; Hooper, " 'Flower Vase.' "
127. Wang, " 'Nüxing Yizhi' " [On the difference between "feminine consciousness"].
128. Honig and Hershatter, *Personal Voices*, 25.
129. For a detailed examination of continuity in gendered discourses between the pre-Mao, Mao, and post-Mao eras, see Evans, *Women and Sexuality*.
130. See, for example, Bu, *Meijie Yu Xingbie* [Media and gender]. One of the most popular television shows of 2010 in China was *Feicheng Wurao* [If you are the one], a reality-type dating show in which most of the female contestants were young and beautiful and made clear their expectations that their potential suitor should be wealthy.
131. Evans, "Marketing Femininity," 221.
132. Evans, "Fashions and Feminine Consumption," 173.
133. Zhao, *Communication in China*, especially chapter 2; Sun, *Maid in China*, especially chapter 2.
134. He, "History of Telecommunications," 69.
135. Ibid., 69, 73.
136. Ibid., 75.
137. Xu and Liang, "Policy and Regulations," 128.
138. Mueller and Tan, *China in the Information Age*, 26.
139. This figure is based on a September 2010 conversion rate of 6.7 yuan to US $1.
140. He, "History of Telecommunications," 82.
141. Harwit, "China's Telecommunications Industry," 185.
142. Lee, "Uneven Development," 115. As many have argued, such uneven diffusion was not accidental but was in line with the government's focus on telecommunications as a force for economic development. As Zhao and Schiller argue in "Dances with Wolves?" (144), "The telecommunication needs of 'foreign invested enterprises' located in major cities and the coastal region, actually dominated telecommunications system development priorities."
143. Liang and Yang, "Networks," 17.
144. He, "History of Telecommunications," 82.
145. Qiu, *Working-Class Network Society*, 54.
146. For an extended analysis on the interrelations among China's telecommunications development, its integration with global capitalism, and the reconfiguration of working-class labor, see Qiu, *Working-Class Network Society*, and Hong, *Labor*.
147. Mueller and Tan, *China in the Information Age*, 13.
148. Ibid.
149. Lu and Wong, *China's Telecommunications Market*, 2, cited in Zhao, " 'Universal Service,' " 109. Zhao offers a compelling account of how marketization and neoliberal economic policies led to "uneven development by design."
150. Xu and Liang, "Policy and Regulations," 129. Unless noted, the discussion of China Unicom comes from Xu and Liang (128–131). For a detailed description and analysis of the establishment of China Unicom, see Mueller and Tan, *China in the*

*Information Age*, chapter 3. For an overview of the growth of mobile phones in China, see Qiu, *Working-Class Network Society*, 53-60.

151. Loo, "Telecommunications Reforms," 705.
152. Ibid.
153. Guoxin handled wireless paging, China Satellite was established for satellite communications, and China Netcom focused on Internet service. See Wan, "Sector Reform," 172. Guoxin was later absorbed into China Unicom.
154. Ibid., 173.
155. Loo, "Telecommunications Reforms," 707.
156. China Telecom and China Unicom were granted licenses for CDMA2000 and WCDMA, respectively, which were both global 3G standards. China Mobile was granted a license for China's homegrown 3G technology, TD-SCDMA.
157. Lynch, "Nature and Consequences," 182.
158. China Ministry of Information Industry, "2007 Nian Quanguo Tongxinye" [National Telecommunications Industry].
159. Zhao, " 'Universal Service,' " 109.
160. Ibid., 115.
161. Ibid.
162. International Telecommunication Union, "Measuring the Information Society," 1.
163. Lynch, "Nature and Consequences," 183.
164. China Ministry of Information Industry (http://www.mii.gov.cn).
165. China Ministry of Industry and Information Technology, "*Tongxinye fazhan*" (Telecommunications industry development)
166. Li and Wang, "China's Telecommunications Universal Service," 7.
167. Nystedt, "China Mobile."
168. McEwen, "People's Republic of Wireless."
169. In "Information Have-less," Cartier, Castells, and Qiu designate prepaid phone cards, text messaging, and Little Smart as less expensive forms of ICTs used by the information have-less (as opposed to "have-nots"). See also Qiu, *Working-Class Network Society*, especially chapter 3. It should be noted that text messaging and prepaid phone cards are widely used by many in China, not only by the "have-less." Also, Little Smart (*Xiaolingtong*), which is a less expensive mobile phone with limited geographic mobility (and often poor reception quality) experienced phenomenal growth between 1999 and 2006, when its use began to decline. See Qiu, "Accidental Accomplishment." During my fieldwork in 2006-2007 in Beijing, very few migrant workers I knew used Little Smart, reflecting the increasing affordability of standard mobile phones, the substandard quality of Little Smart service, and the stigma of Little Smart as "a poor man's ICT." In 2009, the MIIT announced that Little Smart would be retired in 2011 in order to allow more frequency space for 3G networks. Though they did not use Little Smart, many migrants I knew had brandless, or *shanzhai*, phones. On *shanzhai* phones, see Wallis and Qiu, "*Shanzhaiji*."
170. Phillips, "Mobile Internet."

171. This could change because China Unicom has become the exclusive operator for the iPhone in China, and China Mobile has been forced to use the TD-SCDMA (home-grown) 3G standard.
172. http://www.chinamobile.com/gotone/profile/intro/.
173. Ibid.
174. Ibid. On its "spirit" page, GoTone has short bios of several people (Chinese and Western) who represent the "I Can" spirit (optimistic, successful, tenacious), including Kathryn Bigelow and J. D. Salinger. See http://10086.cn/gotone/profile/spirit/.
175. This is somewhat akin to area codes in parts of the United States, as in Los Angeles, where a 310 area code, which signifies a Westside residence, carries more prestige than an 818 area code, which is used for phone numbers in the San Fernando Valley. More recently, the growth in mobile subscriptions and plans and the arrival of 3G, which has brought new prefixes, has meant a blurring of plans and prefixes in China.
176. "Chinese Expected to Send 17 Billion."
177. CNNIC, "Hulianwangluo" [29th statistical report].
178. Author interviews with Kongzhong and Sina employees, Beijing, August 2008.

NOTES TO CHAPTER 2

1. For more on the Beijing Cultural Development Center for Rural Women, see the appendix.
2. One televised public service ad was a cartoon depicting two Chinese people who are asked directions by foreign tourists. One gives the wrong directions out of spite and the other does so to avoid admitting he doesn't know the answer, which would entail a loss of face. The message was that these were both inappropriate responses. This ad was just one of numerous mediated messages and exercises intended to prepare Beijing residents to deal with tourists in a "civilized" manner. In February 2007, for example, Beijing instituted monthly "queuing" days, complete with uniformed workers placed at bus and subway stops to make sure people properly waited in line.
3. For a discussion on modernity and tradition, see Gaonkar, "On Alternative Modernities."
4. See, for example, Jacka, *Rural Women*, especially chapter 2; Gaetano, "Filial Daughters"; Yan, *New Masters*; and Tan, "Nüxing Liudong" [Female migrants].
5. Interview in Beijing, November 13, 2006.
6. Interview with Zhao Yanlin, Beijing, November 27, 2006.
7. Mobile telephony has spread rapidly to rural areas since I conducted extended fieldwork in 2006 and 2007. In follow-up research during 2009 in remote parts of Anhui province, for example, I saw China Mobile's logo and ads spray painted on the stone and brick walls of many villages, as mentioned in chapter 1. Through interviews there, however, it became clear that purchasing a phone was still beyond the means of most local teenagers and young adults.

8. Castells, *Rise of the Network Society*, chapters 6 and 7.

9. In *The Location of Culture*, Homi Bhabha theorizes what he calls an "interstitial passage between fixed identifications [that] opens up the possibility of a cultural hybridity that entertains difference without an assumed imposed hierarchy" (5). This "third space" is supposed to create the possibility for agency, particularly for the subaltern, who is reinscribed into a location where contestation is possible.

10. Interview in Beijing, December 7, 2006.

11. Modernity has various meanings depending on the context in which it is used. Here I am distinguishing modernity from modernization, meaning projects for economic development, industrialization, and so on. For an insightful discussion on such issues, see Felski, *Gender of Modernity*, 12-13.

12. Gaonkar, "On Alternative Modernities," 2. For another account of a migrant woman's journey to the city as it relates to modernity, see Gaetano, "Off the Farm," 1-8. My discussion here is indebted to some of her insights.

13. Appadurai, *Modernity at Large*, 33.

14. In the first chapter of *The Consequences of Modernity*, Giddens discusses the "consequences of modernity," including discontinuities, dislocation of space and time, the disembedding of social relations from local contexts, and new modes of trust and risk.

15. In *The Consequences of Modernity*, Giddens asserts that the consequences of modernity are becoming "more radicalized and universalized than before" (3). Marshall Berman, in his exposé on modernity, *All That Is Solid Melts into Air*, asserts that the forces of modernity cut across "all boundaries of geography and ethnicity, of class and nationality, of religion and ideology" (15).

16. Hodgson, "Introduction," 9. See also Felski, *Gender of Modernity*, 2.

17. Yang, "Introduction," 18-19.

18. Though I will discuss this idea later in the chapter, it is worth noting here that during my conversation with Xiao Luo she mentioned that she did not use the Internet. When I asked her why not, she said that although her boyfriend regularly went to Internet cafés, he did not allow her to go. He told her that such cafés were "dangerous" and not a proper place for a young woman, and she took him at his word.

19. See, for example, Chakrabarty, "Postcoloniality"; Goldstein, "Introduction"; McClintock, *Imperial Leather*; and Rofel, *Other Modernities*. Such a notion also draws attention to the way that the teleology of modernity has aligned with Enlightenment discourses of progress and rationality that have served to justify colonialism, imperialism, slavery, and the othering of non-western cultures and people.

20. Hodgson, "Introduction," 7.

21. Rofel, *Other Modernities*, 9.

22. Ibid., 9-10.

23. On the role of the imagination in conceptualizations of modernity, see Appadurai, *Modernity at Large*, 3, 31.

24. Yan, *New Masters*, 132.

25. For a discussion of how ethnic minorities in China are similarly positioned, see Schein, "Performing Modernity."

26. Rofel, *Other Modernities*, 12.

27. Hodgson, "Introduction," 7.

28. Bordo, *Unbearable Weight*, 16.

29. Yan, "Spectralization of the Rural," 578.

30. Several scholars have made this point. See, for example, Jacka, *Rural Women*, 31; and Sun, "*Suzhi* on the Move," 618-619. On the body as a sign system or discourse to be read, see Balsamo, *Technologies of the Gendered Body*; Bordo, *Unbearable Weight*; and Suleiman, *Female Body in Western Culture*, among others.

31. Bartky, "Foucault, Femininity," 65.

32. Ibid., 71. In *Unbearable Weight* (27), Susan Bordo adds that such dominant forms of gendered selfhood and subjectivity are not maintained primarily through coercion (though they certainly can be) but rather through one's own self-surveillance and adherence to gender norms.

33. Rofel, *Desiring China*, 118.

34. De Lauretis, *Technologies of Gender*.

35. Zhu, "Shenti Zhiben" [Body capital].

36. Interview in Beijing, December 2, 2006.

37. See, for example, Lei, "Rural Taste."

38. The only exceptions were the thirty-two young women enrolled in the computer training course, simply because they were not working and had no income. As soon as they got jobs, they all purchased cell phones. I did meet four working women who were non-users of cell phones. Two of them were not allowed to have phones, including Li Xiulan discussed in the introduction and another woman I will introduce in chapter 5. The other two said they had no friends and rarely ventured far from their workplace so they did not need a phone. They were clear exceptions to the norm.

39. It is noteworthy that one of these young women was married and one was living with her boyfriend.

40. Second-hand phones are a common part of the low-end handset ecology in China and can be purchased for around 50 yuan (around US $6.50 during the initial fieldwork). They are often of questionable quality and origin (e.g., many have been stolen and then pawned). *Shanzhai*, or "copy-cat," phones are produced in southern China and are relatively inexpensive. They can have their own brand or mimic a foreign brand. Newer *shanzhai* phones are loaded with functions. See Wallis and Qiu, *Shanzhaiji*.

41. See, for example, Law and Peng, "Use of Mobile Phones," 247; and Chu and Yang, "Mobile Phones and New Migrant Workers," 225. In the popular media, see Li, "Mobiles Better Migrant Workers' Lives."

42. Chu and Yang, "Mobile Phones and New Migrant Workers," 232; Qiu, *Working-Class Network Society*, 69.

43. Bourdieu, *Distinction*, 57; in "The Ideological Genesis of Needs," Baudrillard argues that in postmodernity objects of consumption operate within the logic of signification, taking on meanings as signs that bear little relationship to their functional purpose. Such signs relate to each other in opposition and serve to differentiate individuals from one another as well as to confer status.
44. The "Veblen effect" refers to Thorstein Veblen's writing on "conspicuous consumption." In using this term, Arjun Appadurai cites Neil McKendrick. See *Modernity at Large*, 66.
45. See, for example, Appadurai, "Introduction"; Slater, *Consumer Culture and Modernity*; and Miller et al., *Shopping, Place and Identity*.
46. As of July 2010, the last period of fieldwork before this manuscript was submitted for publication, although many young rural women I met had purchased mobile phones before migrating, still many did not, especially those who had come from more impoverished areas.
47. Interview in Beijing, October 30, 2006.
48. Slater, *Consumer Culture and Modernity*, 3.
49. Ibid.
50. See, for example, Ling, *Mobile Connection*, and Stald, "Mobile Identity."
51. Pertierra et al., *Txt-ing Selves*.
52. Interview in Beijing, March 14, 2007.
53. Mohanty, *Feminism without Borders*, 142.
54. Yan, "Neoliberal Governmentality," 494.
55. In *New Masters*, Yan Hairong has linked governmentality to the *suzhi* discourse by showing the interconnections among poverty-relief campaigns, migration, and migrant women's cultivation of *suzhi*. She focuses on migrant women recruited as *baomu*, or nannies, for urbanites and how this work discipline is framed as providing the women an opportunity to cultivate *suzhi*.
56. Schein, "Performing Modernity," 364 (emphasis in original).
57. Butler, *Gender Trouble*, 23.
58. Interview in Beijing, February 5, 2007.
59. Featherstone, "Postmodernism," 270. See, for example, Hjorth, *Mobile Media*.
60. Balsamo, *Technologies of the Gendered Body*. Although Balsamo is primarily concerned with how biotechnologies such as cosmetic surgery and weight lifting reconfigure the material female body, I borrow her broader argument regarding the relationship between gender and technology.
61. See, for example, Pun, "Subsumption or Consumption?" and Yan, *New Masters*, chapter 4.
62. The discussion that follows is relevant to basic cell phones. High-end mobile phones also allow for a character input method in which a stylus is used to write the character directly on the screen, as with certain smartphones in the United States and elsewhere. During my initial fieldwork none of the migrant women I knew had such a phone, and on subsequent research trips, even women who had this capability on their phones did not use it.

63. See, for example, Ito, "Mobile Phones, Japanese Youth," 145, and Kasesniemi and Rautiainen, "Mobile Culture," 186.
64. The stratification among different groups of migrants has been noted by many. As Dorothy Solinger states in *Contesting Citizenship*, "Henan women looked down on Anhuinese and Sichuanese women for becoming *baomu* (nursemaids), and Sichuanese disparaged those Henanese and Anhui people who gathered trash; Anhui scrap-pickers were generally despised by all" (202).
65. Interview in Beijing, April 25, 2007.
66. It is rare for young women who are illiterate to migrate to a large city. I observed this same practice among middle-aged illiterate women in the countryside in Shandong province.
67. In "Mobile Cultures," Lin and Tong also argue that text messaging promotes new forms of literacy.
68. Wallis, "(Im)mobile Mobility."
69. Urban residents send prewritten messages as well, especially during holidays such as Spring Festival. In my experience, however, these were more likely to be humorous or, if sincere, were less likely to use ornamental language.
70. Such a critique recalls how housewives who watch soap operas have been constructed.
71. Cartier et al., "Information Have-less," 21.
72. Lei, "Rural Taste."
73. The quoted material in the subheading of this section is the title of Rita Felski's book, which sought to put gender into analyses of modernity.
74. See, for example, Banks, *Hair Matters*, and Kang, *Managed Hand*.
75. This policy was widespread in Beijing but not necessarily in other parts of China. Women are not admitted to most hairstyling schools in Beijing either.
76. During a follow-up research trip in 2011 I noticed that some salons had started to employ males only, with the rationale that even these types of jobs (especially massage) were too difficult for women. Most salons still had male and female employees, however.
77. Interview in Beijing, February 23, 2007.
78. Interview in Beijing, December 12, 2006.
79. Interview with Xiao Xuan, Beijing, December 8, 2006.
80. Interview in Beijing, February 23, 2007.
81. Cockburn, "Circuit of Technology," 39.
82. Ibid., 40, 41 (emphasis in original).
83. Balsamo, *Technologies of the Gendered Body*.
84. Interview in Beijing, February 23, 2007.
85. Felski, *Gender of Modernity*, 1.
86. See also Cohen et al., *Wonder Phone*.
87. Cockburn, "Circuit of Technology."
88. Rofel, *Other Modernities*, 17.

NOTES TO CHAPTER 3

1. Many migrant women I knew had to deal with poor reception because of base-ment housing as well. See also Sun, *Maid in China*, 111.

2. King, "Kuan-hsi and Network Building," 65. See also Hamilton and Wang, "Intro-duction," 25.

3. Fei, *From the Soil*, 62-63.

4. Cited in Yang, *Gifts, Favors, and Banquets*, 295.

5. See, for example, Hwang, "Face and Favor"; Yang, *Gifts, Favors, and Banquets*; and Yan, *Flow of Gifts*. See also Yan, *Individualization of Chinese Society*. Conducting research among migrant workers in China's southern factories, Chu and Yang also use this concept in "Mobile Phones and New Migrant Workers," 231.

6. Hamilton and Wang, "Introduction," 21.

7. Fei, *From the Soil*, 70.

8. King, "Kuan-hsi and Network Building," 73.

9. Ibid., 66, 67.

10. Yan, *Flow of Gifts*, 74.

11. Gold et al., "Introduction to the Study of *Guanxi*," 6.

12. See Gold et al., *Social Connections in China*. See also Yang, *Gifts, Favors, and Banquets*.

13. Kipnis, *Producing Guanxi*, 8. See also Yan, *Flow of Gifts*, 227-228.

14. Yan, *Flow of Gifts*, 99-100.

15. Yang, *Gifts, Favors, and Banquets*, 76.

16. Yan, *Flow of Gifts*, 101-102, 226-227. See also Wilson, "Face, Norms, and Instrumentality."

17. Bourdieu, "Forms of Capital," 248.

18. The relevance of Bourdieu's notion of social capital to Chinese society is revealed in a 2007 survey among Chinese youth that found that nearly 46 percent of respondents agreed that "friends were a kind of capital." Zhang, cited in Rosen, "Chinese Youth," fn. 7, 174.

19. Bourdieu, "Forms of Capital," 249.

20. Both Yan, *Flow of Gifts*, and Yang, *Gifts, Favors, and Banquets*, make this point.

21. Gold et al., "Introduction to the Study of *Guanxi*," 8. See also Yan, *Flow of Gifts*, 80.

22. Kipnis, *Producing Guanxi*, 23.

23. Ibid., 24. See also, Wilson, "Face, Norms, and Instrumentality," 166. As Mayfair Mei-hui Yang notes in *Gifts, Favors, and Banquets*, in discussions of *guanxi*, the affective component is usually translated as *renqing*, meaning "proper human feelings," but also referring to the cultivation and internalization of proper codes of conduct that govern modes of social interaction and "the bond of reciprocity and mutual aid between two people, based on emotional attachment or the sense of obligation and indebtedness" (68, 111). On the other hand, *ganqing* (feeling)

emphasizes affect and emotions, and as such this term is used in connection to *guanxi* only by scholars discussing its more expressive, non-instrumental forms as found with close friendships and familial relationships.

24. For example, in a 1998 survey of female cell phone users in the United States, the top reason given for owning a mobile phone was "communications in an emergency" (cited in Robbins and Turner, "United States: Popular, Pragmatic and Problematic," 84). See also Castells et al., *Mobile Communication and Society*, 45.
25. Interview in Beijing, February 5, 2007.
26. Interview in Beijing, April 15, 2007.
27. Wang, "Nongmingong de 'Banchengshihua' " [Peasant workers' "semi-urbaniza-tion"], 41.
28. Interview in Beijing, February 5, 2007.
29. Law and Peng, "Use of Mobile Phones," 251.
30. Ibid. Previous fieldwork in southern factories, however, has noted strong divisions along ethnic and regional lines among workers. See note 62 in chapter 1 and Lee, *Gender and the South China Miracle*.
31. These findings are similar to those of Peng, "Internet Use of Migrant Workers," 50-51.
32. Yang, *Gifts, Favors, and Banquets*, 111.
33. Hwang, "Face and Favor," 963.
34. The importance placed on invoking destiny in establishing relationships was borne out several times in my interactions with my informants. We did not share bonds of locale, school, work, or experience, but once we had forged a relation-ship many women insisted it was destiny that we had met.
35. Wellman et al., "Does the Internet Increase, Decrease, or Supplement Social Capital?" 437.
36. Alcoff, *Visible Identities*, 148.
37. Interview in Beijing, March 29, 2007.
38. Ling, *Mobile Connection*, 111.
39. Ibid.
40. See, for example, Ito, "Personal Portable Pedestrian." See also Katz and Aakhus, *Perpetual Contact*. Of course, youth separated from good friends due to university attendance also must negotiate distances via mobile phones, but their access to other communication technologies and modes of travel along with their chances to make new friends in their new locations far surpass that of the women in this study.
41. Yoon, "Retraditionalizing the Mobile," 330-331.
42. Chu and Yang also comment that text messages help migrants counter "cultural insulation." See "Mobile Phones and New Migrant Workers," 230.
43. Interview with Xiao Chen in Beijing, March, 14, 2007.
44. Ling and Yttri "Hyper-coordination," 140. On digital gift giving, see Johnsen, "Social Context," 167, and Taylor and Harper, "Gift of *Gab*?" 267.

45. Interview in Beijing, July 2, 2010. Calling is still used for more personal issues that require deep conversation and where it is felt that texting or instant messaging is too tiresome. Most women are very shrewd about finding the best prepaid calling plans that allow for free incoming calls, or they utilize special numbers that lock in cheap calling rates if they are inputted before the number that one is calling. In either case, both economics and norms of reciprocity determine who initiates or receives a call.

46. Zhao, *Communication in China*, 88–89; Sun, *Maid in China*, especially chapter 2.

47. Bu Wei, personal correspondence, February 5, 2007.

48. Vincent, "Emotional Attachment," 40. See also Vincent and Fortunati, *Electronic Emotion*.

49. Interview in Beijing, July 2, 2010.

50. Interview in Beijing, July 1, 2010.

51. See, for example, Koch et al., "Beauty Is in the Eye."

52. Lukoff, "China's Top Four." On a similar divide between Facebook and MySpace, see boyd, "White Flight?"

53. Phillips, "Mobile Internet." In "Access + Digital Literacy," Allison Clark has also noted how the celebratory tone regarding the finding that African Americans are the most active users of the mobile Internet misses the fact that mobile phone use does not enable one to be competitive in the global economy: "you can't research, write nor print a paper from a mobile device" (http://hastac.org/blogs/allison-clark/access-digital-literacy-new-civil-rights-part-2-it-what-it).

54. I am keenly aware of the heteronormativity in the following discussion, but open gay and lesbian relationships can only be found in large urban areas like Shanghai and Beijing, and gay marriage is not part of contemporary Chinese discourse, in the Foucaultian sense.

55. See Judd, *Gender and Power*, 181. See also Davis and Harrell, "Introduction," 10.

56. For example, Kipnis in *Producing Guanxi* (137) states that in rural areas parents play a large role in "free love" marriages. Yan, however, in *Flow of Gifts* (40) notes the increasing prevalence of "personal choice" and mutual affection in young couples' marital decisions in the village he studied. See also Yan, "Courtship, Love and Premarital Sex," and *Private Life under Socialism*.

57. Johnson, "Family Strategies and Economic Transformation," 118.

58. Riley, "Interwoven Lives," 794, 798. During my fieldwork I knew a few women who went home to marry someone their parents had found for them. These weren't "blind marriages," however, as they had a choice in the matter.

59. Xu, "Social Origins of Historical Changes," 45. See also Whyte, "Changes in Mate Choice," 184–185.

60. Pan et al., *Dangdai Zhongguoren* [Contemporary China], 163.

61. Friedman, "Spoken Pleasures"; Jacka, *Rural Women*; Yan, *Flow of Gifts* and *Private Life*.

62. Pan, "Transformations in the Primary Life Cycle," 22–23, 35. See also Farrer, "Sexual Citizenship." In the popular press, see Beech, "Sex and the Single Chinese."

63. Davis and Harrell, "Introduction," 10. In *Chen Village* (10), Chan, Madsen, and Unger found that some village parents view early marriages as a sign of a prosperous family, because less well-off families need to delay the marriage of their offspring in order to accumulate finances for the marriage costs. Some villagers surmised, however, that the reason for the early marriages was an increase in pregnancies out of wedlock. See also Sui, "Reconstituting Dowry and Brideprice," 181.
64. Interview in Beijing, April 15, 2007.
65. Zheng, "Waichu Jingli dui Nongcun Funü Chuhun Nianling de Yingxiang" [Migration and age at first marriage of rural women].
66. Research Team, "Impact of Migration," 33.
67. These patterns vary by province and depend on a number of factors, including traditional views about female morality and chastity.
68. Fan, "Out to the City," 179; Tan, "Leaving Home," 251.
69. Tan, "Leaving Home," 252. Xie Lihua, the founder of the Beijing Cultural Development Center for Rural Women, called the increasing number of rural women remaining in Beijing well into their late twenties and early thirties a growing social crisis. Cited in Jacka, *Rural Women,* 154.
70. Beynon, "Dilemmas of the Heart," 142; Luo et al., "Migration Experiences of Young Women," 237.
71. In "Use of Mobile Phones," Law and Peng note that such practices were common among factory workers in southern China, as do Lin and Tong in "Mobile Cultures," implying that perhaps there are regional differences or different cultures of practice. Pertierra found this practice to be quite common in the Philippines as well. See "Mobile Phones, Identity and Discursive Intimacy," 35–36.
72. Wallis, "Traditional Meets the Technological," 62; Ma and Cheng, " 'Naked' Bodies," 314.
73. This practice has especially emerged since 2008 and 2009.
74. The first two narratives are also in Wallis, "Traditional Meets the Technological."
75. Interview in Beijing, April 24, 2007.
76. Ibid.
77. On texting and intimacy among migrant workers, see also Chu and Yang, "Mobile Phones and New Migrant Workers," 229.
78. See, for example, Ellwood-Clayton, "Virtual Strangers," and Prøitz, "Intimacy Fiction."
79. Katz and Aakhus, *Perpetual Contact*; Vincent, "Living with Mobile Phones," 164.
80. See, for example, Weilenmann and Larsson, "Local Use and Sharing."
81. Interview in Beijing, December 12, 2006.
82. In 2009, the government formerly ordered the *Xiaolingtong* to be phased out to make way for further development of China's domestic 3G standard, TD-SCDMA. See Wang, "China's Wireless Service."
83. In the pre-reform and early reform eras, Xiao Zhao's army experience would have ensured more career mobility in the future, but this is not necessarily the case now. I am thankful to an anonymous reviewer for this clarification.

84. See, for example, Beynon, "Dilemmas of the Heart"; Luo et al., "Migration Experiences of Young Women."
85. Beynon, "Dilemmas of the Heart," 143; Gaetano, "Filial Daughters," 288.
86. See, for example, Yan, *New Masters*, 246-247.
87. Jacka, *Rural Women*, 87-91, 93.
88. Yan, "McDonald's in Beijing."
89. Gergen, "Self and Community," 111.

NOTES TO CHAPTER 4

1. See, for example, Hjorth, "Snapshots"; Lee, "Women's Creation"; Oksman, "Mobile Visuality"; and Van House and Davis, "Social Life."
2. Gye, "Picture This," 279.
3. In "Women's Creation," Lee's study involved thirteen Korean undergraduates, two high school students, and two designated as "other." In "Camera Phone," Martin's participants were French undergraduates. In "Snapshots," Hjorth's study involved thirty-four Korean university students. In "Uses of Personal Networked Digital Imaging," Van House and colleagues reported on thirteen graduate student users in the United States. Exceptions include Okabe and Ito's "Everyday Contexts," which had two high school students, eight college students, two housewives in their forties, and three professionals aged twenty-nine to thirty-four, and Oksman's "Mobile Visuality," whose participants ranged in age from thirteen to sixty-five (no other demographic data are provided). For his study in Beijing, "A World through the Camera Phone Lens," Bo interviewed sixteen middle-class urban residents, ranging in age from twenty-two to fifty.
4. By "everyday" use, I am distinguishing the women here from participants in a range of projects in which camera phones have been distributed to low-income or immigrant populations so that they can engage in digital storytelling. See, for example, PhotoVoice (http://www.photovoice.org/whatwedo/info/favourite_session_by_gary_waite/) and Mobile Voices (http://vozmob.net/).
5. On Kodak cameras and the democratization of images, see Slater, "Consuming Kodak." See also Tagg, *Burden of Representation*, 54-56.
6. Gye, "Picture This," 279.
7. Numerous scholars have noted the transitory nature of camera-phone images due to their poor quality, including Hjorth, "Snapshots," 233; Lee, "Women's Creation"; Okabe and Ito, "Everyday Contexts," 99; and Riviére, "Mobile Camera Phones," 176. The preference for digital cameras to document special or important occasions has been found by Kindberg et al., "How and Why"; Martin, "Camera Phones," 9; Okabe and Ito, "Everyday Contexts," 99; and Van House and Davis, "Social Life." Newer smartphones with superior imaging quality may change this situation.
8. Appadurai, *Modernity at Large*, 31.
9. The analytic categories of "technosocial situations" of camera-phone use they developed were personal archiving, intimate visual co-presence, and peer-to-peer

news. These were an attempt to move beyond approaches that view technological practices as emergent strictly through personal interaction or that seek to generate abstract categories that can transcend specific social and cultural contexts. See Okabe and Ito, "Everyday Contexts."

10. Kember, "Shadow of the Object," 206.

11. The interest in art photography in China has grown in tandem with the West's fascination with China's contemporary art scene. For an overview, see Pollack, "Chinese Photography." For a collection of contemporary art photography with a selected bibliography, see Lütgens and Van Tuyl, *The Chinese: Photography and Video from China*. For the history of early photography in China, see Ma et al., *Zhongguo Sheying Shi* [History of photography in China]. For a rare discussion of personal images, as these compare to state images, in 1970s China, see Huang, "Locating Family Portraits."

12. Jenner, *China*, 187.

13. Interviews with Beijing residents, August 2008.

14. Even in the mid-1990s, camera ownership was highly stratified based on region. According to Davis, "Introduction" (4), although in 1995 in Beijing 87 percent of households had cameras, even in Shanghai this figure fell to 52 percent, and the national average was 31 percent.

15. In this sense, these arrangements are somewhat similar to the Glamour Shots studios that cropped up in the United States in the late 1980s and that continue to serve a clientele of mostly young and middle-aged women. See http://www.glamourshots.com/.

16. According to Ding in "Survey," the eighth most profitable industry in China in 2008 was wedding photography.

17. For a fascinating account of photography in late 19th-century and early 20th-century China, see Pang, "Photography, Performance."

18. Mitchell, *Picture Theory*, 11.

19. While the latter might be expected in light of the very constrained economic circumstances these women faced, low multimedia message service (MMS) usage has been found in research looking at everyday mobile phone use in a variety of contexts and among a variety of groups. See, for example, Ling, "Trust, Cohesion and Social Networks," and Martin, "Camera Phones," 10. Exceptions have been found among groups in an experimental setting: that is, they have been supplied with camera phones and their expenditures are covered by the researchers. See, for example, Ling and Julsrud, "Grounded Genres." See also Koskinen, *Mobile Multimedia in Action*. Other exceptions include groups supplied with camera phones and MMS service as part of an action-based research project such as Mobile Voices (see note 4 above).

20. During the initial research period, there was no Chinese equivalent of Flickr, and women did not participate in any sort of social networking site that would have allowed them to upload photos to the web. On return visits in 2009 and 2010, many women were accessing the Internet, mostly QQ, on their phones and some

were uploading images to QQ's Qzone. Most only allowed friends to view images they had uploaded.

21. Sontag, *On Photography*, 3.
22. Oksman and Rautiainen, "Extension of the Hand." In Okabe and Ito's "Everyday Contexts," they report that one participant stated, "The camera phone is my eye" (90).
23. Van House and Davis, "Social Life."
24. Okabe and Ito, "Everyday Contexts," 90; Oksman, "Mobile Visuality," 110; and Riviére, "Mobile Camera Phones," 180.
25. Okabe and Ito, "Everyday Contexts," 87.
26. Oksman, "MMS and Its Early Adopters," 359.
27. Kindberg et al., "How and Why."
28. Sontag, *On Photography*, 4. See also Tagg, *Burden of Representation*, 63, and Sekula, "Body and the Archive."
29. Batchen, "Desiring Production Itself," 25.
30. Burgin, "Art, Common Sense and Photography," 41.
31. I am grateful to Jenny Chio for this insight.
32. Watney, "On the Institutions of Photography."
33. Ibid, 159.
34. See, for example, Bourdieu, *Photography*, and Spence and Holland, *Family Snaps*. For a comparison of conventional cameras and camera phones related to such themes, see Gye, "Picture This."
35. Much has been written on the connection between leisure and personal photography. See, for example, Holland, "Introduction," 4, and Chalfen, *Snapshot Versions*.
36. On camera phones and sociality, see, among others, Lee, "Women's Creation"; Martin, "Camera Phones," 9; Okabe and Ito, "Everyday Contexts," 99; and Van House and Davis, "Social Life."
37. Bourdieu, *Photography*, 31-39; Barthes, *Camera Lucida*, 79.
38. On using camera phones to memorialize events, see Kindberg et al., "How and Why." See also Van House and Davis, "Social Life."
39. On customization of mobile phones and camera phones, see Hjorth, "Postal Presence" and "Snapshots," 233. On camera phones and identity, see Okabe and Ito, "Everyday Contexts," 90, and Scifo, "Domestication of Cameraphone," 365.
40. Van House and Davis, "Social Life."
41. Beijing, August 18, 2008.
42. Bartky, "Foucault, Femininity," 65.
43. De Lauretis, *Technologies of Gender*, 9.
44. Lee, "Women's Creation."
45. Ibid.
46. One woman I met had saved up her money and paid 300 yuan (about US $39) to go to a photography studio when she was in her hometown during Spring Festival. She had then used her camera phone to snap pictures of all 240 proofs so she could keep these with her. She could only afford to have one photo enlarged and framed.

47. For an explanation of the "ethical government of the self," see Dean, *Governmentality*, 27.
48. Giddens, *Modernity and Self Identity*, 5. Giddens acknowledges that those at the margins have "differential access to forms of self-actualization and empowerment" (6).
49. This emotional aspect of mobile phones has been studied extensively by Jane Vincent. See, for example, "Emotion, My Mobile."
50. Interview in Beijing, April 4, 2007.
51. In "Everyday Contexts," Okabe and Ito stress the significance of the highly personalized viewpoint that is expressed through images stored in mobile phones. In "Snapshots of *Almost* Contact," Hjorth also notes pictures of objects, but these often had a social purpose (e.g., "the first two beers ordered on the night of celebration with friends" [233]).
52. Bourdieu, *Distinction*, 35.
53. Barthes, *Camera Lucida*, 27. See also Martin, "Camera Phone."
54. Sontag, *On Photography*, 16.
55. Baudrillard, "Simulacra and Simulations."
56. Kember, "Shadow of the Object," 202. On photography as only "partial evidence," see Winston, " 'The Camera Never Lies,' " and Tagg, *Burden of Representation*, 2.
57. Barthes, *Camera Lucida*, 77, 82. I realize I am slightly misusing Barthes since his point is mainly about the connection between memory and photography.
58. Kember, "Shadow of the Object," 211.
59. Sontag, *On Photography*, 3.
60. Campbell, *Romantic Ethic*, 89. I am grateful to Josh Heuman for this reference.
61. Interview in Beijing, May 31, 2007.
62. On reflexive ethnography, see Bird, *Audience in Everyday Life*.
63. Kindberg et al., "How and Why."
64. Ibid.
65. Since I began my fieldwork in 2006 the price of personal computers has decreased, and in the last couple of years some of the women I know have pooled their money together with a sibling or boyfriend and bought a home computer that can be shared. On the use of social networking sites, in particular QQ, see chapter 3.

NOTES TO CHAPTER 5

1. Sun Heng is a former migrant worker and the founder of the New Worker Art Troupe. He is a leader in using the arts to advocate for migrant rights.
2. They were making about 500 yuan per month, which was quite low even for a waitressing job.
3. In such cases of exploitation, or where even physical abuse takes place, women who seek legal assistance from a non-governmental organization (NGO) are a very small minority. Many migrant women are unaware of or not involved in the NGOs that serve the migrant community.

4. The law mandated labor contracts, severance pay, and a higher minimum wage, yet implementation, especially in small enterprises in the private sector (where nearly all of the women in this study worked), has been uneven and difficult to enforce. So far the law has seemed to have had the most impact on large enterprises, such as factories in southern China, where workers' pay has increased. In Beijing wages have increased in most lines of work since 2008 in order to keep up with inflation, but not necessarily as a result of the labor law.

5. I borrow (and reinterpret) the phrase from Ithiel de Sola Pool, though he used it long before the advent of the widespread use of mobile phones in everyday life. In *Technologies of Freedom* he raised concerns about the tension between government regulation and individual freedom. The liberatory view of mobile phones is embodied in James Katz's assertion in *Magic in the Air* (8): "It may be that no technology has done more to give individuals freedom than the mobile phone."

6. Winner, "Do Artifacts Have Politics?"

7. Deleuze, "Postscript," 4; Foucault, *Discipline and Punish*, 136.

8. Deleuze, "Postscript," 4.

9. Ibid., 6.

10. Hardt and Negri, *Empire*, as cited in Ong, *Neoliberalism as Exception*, 123.

11. Ong, *Neoliberalism as Exception*, 21.

12. Ibid., 124.

13. Ibid., see also all of chapter 5 of Ong.

14. Lee, *Gender and the South China Miracle*, 9, 128; Pun, *Made in China*, 116.

15. Pun, *Made in China*, chapter 3.

16. Anagnost, "Corporeal Politics," 193–194.

17. Yan, *New Masters*, 114 and 124–129. See also my earlier discussion in chapter 1.

18. See, for example, Gaetano, "Filial Daughters," and Pun, *Made in China*. Urban women and college-educated women also face gender discrimination in employment. See, for example, Lu, "Zhiye Xingbie Qishi" [Sexual discrimination in occupations].

19. See the research of Pun, C. K. Lee, and Yan Hairong discussed above as well as Sun Wanning's large body of scholarship on domestic workers, in particular *Maid in China*.

20. Beijing, May 24, 2007.

21. Interview in Beijing, April 6, 2007.

22. Mohanty, *Feminism without Borders*, 142, 143.

23. This practice is not far removed from the western construction of a chef as a masculine subject position.

24. Greeters also exist in beauty salons, but young men only hold this job when they first arrive.

25. Zhen, "Mediating Time," 94. See my discussion of this term in chapter 1.

26. The 2008 labor law banned such practice. Though height and weight standards in job advertisements are not as common as they used to be, in many establishments they remain as unspoken requirements.

27. The stories of banqueting and "eating out of the public funds" are legion and a major source of concern about official corruption because in China the line between private entrepreneurship and government bureaucracy is indeed tenuous. Those who have prospered most in the market economy in China are those who were able to parlay their Party affiliation or government position into lucrative business opportunities. See, for example, Liu, *Otherness of Self*, and Goodman, "Why China."

28. Liu, *Otherness of Self*. This type of gendered restaurant culture is pervasive regardless of whether a dining establishment is considered common or extravagant or whether the customers are male or female.

29. Interview in Beijing, December 2, 2006.

30. The use of fictive kin terms is common practice in China and was not unique to the marketplaces. It is not only young women who call older young men "older brother." A young man may address an older young woman as "big sister." Such naming is meant to show a degree of familiarity but also maintains status hierarchies.

31. On fisherman, see Abraham, "Mobile Phones and Economic Development," and Jensen, "Digital Provide."

32. See, for example, Jagun, Heeks, and Whalley, "Impact of Mobile Telephony" and Overå, "Mobile Traders and Mobile Phones." See also chapter 5 in Horst and Miller, *Cell Phone*.

33. Qiu, "Working-Class ICTs," 341. Qiu does not clarify whether such contacts were in place prior to owning a phone or were a result of social network applications used through the phone.

34. Law and Peng, "Use of Mobile Phones," 250; Ngan and Ma, "Relationship of Mobile Telephony," 58-59.

35. Cockburn, "Circuit of Technology"; Wajcman, *Technofeminism*.

36. In *Cell Phone*, especially chapter 5, Horst and Miller make this point through discussing what they call "link up." In "Blurring Livelihoods," Donner also argues that the economic benefits of mobile telephony are not always easy to disentangle from social uses and users' prior social networks.

37. See, for example, the work of Bian, including "Institutional Holes."

38. Bu and Qiu, "Report on Media Education Strategies."

39. Interview in Beijing, December 4, 2006.

40. Alcoff, *Visible Identities*, 148. See also my explanation of positionality in chapter 3.

41. See Wallis, "Mobile Phones without Guarantees."

42. Similar usages were also found by Peng, "Internet Use of Migrant Workers," 50.

43. Interview in Beijing, April 5, 2007.

44. Interview in Beijing, March 14, 2007.

45. Qiu, "Wireless Leash," 85.

46. Ibid.

47. See, for example, Kim, "Korea: Personal Meanings," and Laurier, "Region as a Socio-Technical Accomplishment." On mobile-enabled monitoring in peer and familial relationships, see Green, "Who's Watching Whom?" See also, Ling, *Mobile Connection*, 100, and Ito, "Mobile Phones, Japanese Youth," 139. On whether or not cell phones allow work to impinge on free time and family life, see Wajcman, Bittman, and Brown, "Families without Borders."

48. Interview in Beijing, March 23, 2007.

49. Interview in Beijing, April 4, 2007. A bus ticket for an hour's journey probably cost one or two Chinese yuan. A cab after 9:00 p.m. would have probably cost about 35 yuan. Migrant workers never take taxis unless it is a dire emergency.

50. In four days of mobile phone logs she recorded forty uses of her mobile phone, for an average of about ten uses per day. Only about one-quarter of these were for communication with friends or family. The rest consisted of text messages and phone calls from supervisors or colleagues. This finding contrasts markedly with those of Wajcman and colleagues in "Families without Borders" (640), who found that 89 percent of mobile calls by a range of middle-class women in Australia were for social purposes.

51. Interview in Beijing, December 4, 2006.

52. I should note that cultural norms in China dictate that an elder relative, especially an elder sibling, aunt, uncle, or cousin, should serve a parental role in the absence of the actual parents.

53. Castells et al., *Mobile Communication and Society*, 247.

54. Foucault, "Subject and Power," 340.

55. Ibid., 342.

56. Pun and Lu, "Unfinished Proletarianization," 495.

57. Ibid., 496.

58. See, for example, Watts, "Workers in China." The government is much more likely to allow strikes at foreign-owned companies because the workers' anger can be displaced onto a "foreign" entity such as Japan or Taiwan rather than the Chinese state.

59. Pun and Smith, "Putting the Transnational Labor Process," 27.

60. De Certeau, *Practice of Everyday Life*, 37.

61. Interview in Beijing, December 7, 2006.

62. De Certeau, *Practice of Everyday Life*, 37. In contrast to tactics, strategies are a calculated manipulation of a power relationship by those in a dominant position.

63. Interview in Beijing, March 21, 2007.

64. Interview in Beijing, April 6, 2007.

65. Katz, *Magic in the Air*, 58.

66. Ibid., 59.

67. Pun, *Made in China*, 92, 102.

68. De Certeau, *Practice of Everyday Life*, 30.

NOTE TO CONCLUSION

1. Wise, "Assemblage," 78 (emphasis in original).

NOTES TO APPENDIX

1. Facilitator was established by Li Tao and Li Zhen, who had formerly been employed by the Beijing Cultural Development Center. Li Tao was in charge of the Migrant Women's Club and Li Zhen was the editor in chief of *Rural Women*. They both left in 2003 under less than amicable circumstances and set up Facilitator.
2. Ito, "Mobile Phones, Japanese Youth," 132.

BIBLIOGRAPHY

Abraham, Reuben. "Mobile Phones and Economic Development: Evidence from the
    Fishing Industry in India." *Information Technologies and International Development*
    4, no. 1 (2007): 5-17.
Alcoff, Linda. *Visible Identities: Race, Gender, and the Self.* Oxford: Oxford University
    Press, 2006.
Amit-Talai, Vered, and Helena Wulff, eds. *Youth Cultures: A Cross-Cultural Perspective.*
    London: Routledge, 1995.
Anagnost, Ann. "The Corporeal Politics of Quality (*Suzhi*)." *Public Culture* 16, no. 2
    (2004): 189-208.
———. "From 'Class' to 'Social Strata': Grasping the Social Totality in Reform-Era
    China." *Third World Quarterly* 29, no. 3 (2008): 497-519.
———. "Transformations of Gender in Modern China." In *Gender and Anthropol-
    ogy: Critical Reviews for Research and Teaching*, edited by Sandra Morgan, 313-342.
    Washington, D.C.: American Anthropological Association, 1989.
Andreas, Joel. "A Shanghai Model: On Capitalism with Chinese Characteristics." *New
    Left Review* 65 (2010): 63-85.
Appadurai, Arjun. "Introduction: Commodities and the Politics of Value." In *The Social
    Life of Things: Commodities in Cultural Perspective*, edited by Arjun Appadurai,
    3-63. Cambridge: Cambridge University Press, 1986.
———. *Modernity at Large: Cultural Dimensions of Globalization.* Minneapolis: Univer-
    sity of Minnesota Press, 1996.
Asian Development Bank. "Reducing Inequalities in China Requires
    Inclusive Growth," August 9, 2007, http://www.adb.org/media/
    Articles/2007/12084-chinese-economics-growths/.
Balsamo, Anne. *Technologies of the Gendered Body.* Durham: Duke University Press,
    1996.
Banet-Weiser, Sarah. *Kids Rule! Nickelodeon and Consumer Citizenship.* Durham: Duke
    University Press, 2007.
———. *The Most Beautiful Girl in the World: Beauty Pageants and National Identity.*
    Berkeley: University of California Press, 1999.
Banks, Ingrid. *Hair Matters: Beauty, Power, and Black Women's Consciousness.* New
    York: NYU Press, 2000.
Barthes, Roland. *Camera Lucida: Reflections on Photography.* Translated by Richard
    Howard. New York: Hill and Wang, 1981.

Bartky, Sandra Lee. "Foucault, Femininity, and the Modernization of Patriarchal Power." In *Femininity and Domination: Studies in the Phenomenology of Oppression*, 48-75. New York: Routledge, 1990.

Batchen, Geoffrey. "Desiring Production Itself: Notes on the Invention of Photography." In *Cartographies: Poststructuralism and the Mapping of Bodies and Spaces*, edited by Rosalyn Diprose and Robyn Ferrell, 13-26. Sydney: Allen and Unwin, 1991.

Baudrillard, Jean. "The Ideological Genesis of Needs." In *The Consumer Society Reader*, edited by Juliet B. Schor and Douglas B. Holt, 57-80. New York: New Press, 2000.

———. "Simulacra and Simulations." In *Jean Baudrillard: Selected Writings*, edited by Mark Poster, 166-184. Stanford: Stanford University Press, 1988.

Beech, Hannah. "Sex and the Single Chinese." *Time* online, December 5, 2005, http://www.time.com/time/magazine/article/0,9171,1137697-2,00.html.

"Beijingshi Zhengfu Jiang Xinsheng'er Ke Suifu Ruhu Xieru Xin Fagui" [Beijing municipal government writes new regulation that newborn can register following father]. *Beijing Morning Post*, April 7, 2006, http://news.xinhuanet.com/legal/2006-04/07/content_4394449.htm.

Bell, Genevieve. "The Age of the Thumb: A Cultural Reading of Mobile Technologies from Asia." In *Thumb Culture: The Meaning of Mobile Phones for Society*, edited by Peter Glotz, Stefan Bertschi, and Chris Locke, 67-87. New Brunswick, N.J.: Transaction, 2005.

Berman, Marshall. *All That Is Solid Melts into Air: The Experience of Modernity*. New York: Simon and Schuster, 1982.

Bettie, Julie. *Women without Class: Girls, Race, and Identity*. Berkeley: University of California Press, 2003.

Beynon, Louise. "Dilemmas of the Heart: Rural Working Women and Their Hopes for the Future." In *On the Move: Women and Rural-to-Urban Migration in Contemporary China*, edited by Arianne M. Gaetano and Tamara Jacka, 131-150. New York: Columbia University Press, 2004.

Bhabha, Homi K. *The Location of Culture*. London: Routledge, 1994.

Bian, Yanjie. "Institutional Holes and Job Mobility Processes: *Guanxi* Mechanisms in China's Emergent Labor Markets." In *Social Connections in China: Institutions, Culture, and the Changing Nature of Guanxi*, edited by Thomas Gold, Doug Guthrie, and David L. Wank, 117-135. Cambridge: Cambridge University Press, 2002.

Bird, Elizabeth. *The Audience in Everyday Life: Living in a Media World*. New York: Routledge, 2003.

Bo, Gai. "A World through the Camera Phone Lens: A Case Study of Beijing Camera Phone Use." *Knowledge, Technology, & Policy* 22 (2009): 195-204.

Bordo, Susan. *Unbearable Weight: Feminism, Western Culture and the Body*. Berkeley: University of California Press, 1993.

Bourdieu, Pierre. *Distinction: A Social Critique of the Judgment of Taste*. Translated by Richard Nice. Cambridge: Harvard University Press, 1984.

———. "The Forms of Capital." In *Handbook of Theory and Research for the Sociology of Education*, edited by John G. Richardson, 241-258. New York: Greenwood, 1986.

———. *Photography: A Middle-Brow Art*. Stanford: Stanford University Press, 1990.

boyd, danah. "White Flight in Networked Publics? How Race and Class Shaped American Teen Engagement with Myspace and Facebook." In *Race after the Internet*, edited by Lisa Nakamura, Peter Chow-White, and Alondra Nelson, 203-222. New York: Routledge, 2012.

Brown, Barry, Nicola Green, and Richard Harper, eds. *Wireless World: Social and Interactional Aspects of the Mobile Age*. London: Springer, 2002.

Bu, Wei, ed. *Meijie yu Xingbie* [Media and gender]. Nanjing: Jiangsu People's Press, 2001.

Bu, Wei, and Jack Linchuan Qiu. "Report on Media Education Strategies for the Prevention of Trafficking in Women in Sichuan Province." Beijing: Center for Media Communication and Youth Development Studies, Institute of Journalism and Communication, Chinese Academy of Social Sciences, 2002.

Bucholtz, Mary. "Youth and Cultural Practice." *Annual Review of Anthropology* 31 (2002): 525-552.

Buckingham, David, ed. *Youth, Identity and Digital Media*. Cambridge: MIT Press, 2008.

Burgin, Victor. "Art, Common Sense and Photography." In *Visual Culture: The Reader*, edited by Jessica Evans and Stuart Hall, 41-50. London: Sage, 1999.

Burrell, Jenna, and Ken Anderson. "'I Have Great Desires to Look Beyond My World.'" *New Media & Society* 10, no. 2 (2008): 203-224.

Butler, Judith. *Gender Trouble: Feminism and the Subversion of Identity*. New York: Routledge, 1990.

Cai, Fang. "Qianyi Juece Zhong de Jiating Jiaose he Xingbie Tezhen" [The role of family and gender characteristics in migration decision making]. *Renkou Yanjiu* [Population research] 21, no. 2 (1997): 7-21.

Campbell, Colin. *The Romantic Ethic and the Spirit of Modern Consumerism*. Oxford: Blackwell, 1987.

Canclini, Nestor García. *Consumers and Citizens: Globalization and Multicultural Conflicts*. Translated by George Yudice. Minneapolis: University of Minnesota Press, 2001.

Carey, James. *Communication as Culture: Essays on Media and Society*. New York: Routledge, 1989.

Cartier, Carolyn, Manuel Castells, and Jack Linchuan Qiu. "The Information Have-less: Inequality, Mobility, and Translocal Networks in Chinese Cities." *Studies in Comparative International Development* 40, no. 2 (2005): 9-34.

Castells, Manuel. *The Rise of the Network Society*. 2nd ed. Oxford: Blackwell, 2000.

Castells, Manuel, Mireia Fernandez-Ardevol, Jack Linchuan Qiu, and Araba Sey. *Mobile Communication and Society: A Global Perspective*. Cambridge: MIT Press, 2007.

Chakrabarty, Dipesh. "Postcoloniality and the Artifice of History: Who Speaks for 'Indian' Pasts?" *Representations* 37 (1992): 1–26.

Chalfen, Richard. *Snapshot Versions of Life*. Bowling Green, Ohio: Bowling Green State University Popular Press, 1987.

Chan, Anita, Richard Madsen, and Jonathan Unger. *Chen Village under Mao and Deng: Expanded and Updated Edition*. Berkeley: University of California Press, 1992.

Chan, Kam Wing, and Will Buckingham. "Is China Abolishing the *Hukou* System?" *China Quarterly* 195 (2008): 582–606.

Chen, Xiaoyan. "Suzhi Tisheng, Chengjiu Nongmingong de Fazhan zhi Lu" [Enhance the quality of peasant workers, pave the way for their successful development]. *People's Daily* [People.com], September 26. 2007, http://acftu.people.com.cn/ GB/6314178.html.

Cheng, Tiejun, and Mark Selden. "The Origins and Social Consequences of China's *Hukou* System." *China Quarterly* 139 (1994): 644–668.

China Internet Network Information Center (CNNIC). "Di 29 Ci Zhongguo Hulian-wangluo Fazhan Zhuangkuang Tongji Baogao" [The 29th statistical report of China's Internet development], January 2012, http://www.cnnic.cn/dtygg/dtgg/201201/ W020120116337628870651.pdf.

China Ministry of Industry and Information Technology (MIIT). "Tongxinye Fazhan Shitou Lianghao" [Telecommunications industry development maintains momentum] December 2011, http://miit.gov.cn/n11293472/n11293832/n11294132/ n12858447/14405153.html.

China Ministry of Information Industry (MII). "2007 Nian Quanguo Tongxinye Fazhan Tongji Baogao" [National telecommunications industry development statistical report], February 2008, http://www.mii.gov.cn//art/2008/02/04/ art_2001_36139.html.

China Population and Development Research Center (CPDRC). "Zhongguo Liudong Renkou Yida 2.21yi, Nongcun Liushou Laoren you 4000wan" [China's floating population reaches 221 million, and there are 40 million left-behind seniors in rural areas], no date, http://www.cpdrc.org.cn/tjsj/tjsj_cy_detail.asp?id=15484.

"Chinese Expected to Send 17 Billion Text Messages during Spring Festival," February 7, 2008, http://english.sina.com/china/1/2008/0207/145269.html.

Chu, Wai-chu, and Shanhua Yang. "Mobile Phones and New Migrant Workers in a South China Village: An Initial Analysis of the Interplay between the 'Social' and the 'Technological.' " In *New Technologies in Global Societies*, edited by Pui-lam Law, Leopoldina Fortunati, and Shanhua Yang, 221–244. Singapore: World Scientific, 2006.

Clark, Allison. "Access + Digital Literacy Is the New Civil Rights Part 2: It Is What It Is," October 29, 2009, http://www.hastac.org/blogs/allison-clark/ access-digital-literacy-new-civil-rights-part-2-it-what-it.

Clifford, James. "Introduction: Partial Truths." In *Writing Culture: The Poetics and Politics of Ethnography*, edited by James Clifford and George E. Marcus, 1–26. Berkeley: University of California Press, 1986.

————. "On Ethnographic Authority." In *The Predicament of Culture: Twentieth-Century Ethnography, Literature, and Art,* edited by James Clifford, 21–54. Cambridge: Harvard University Press, 1988.

Cockburn, Cynthia. "The Circuit of Technology: Gender, Identity and Power." In *Consuming Technologies: Media and Information in Domestic Spaces,* edited by Roger Silverstone and Eric Hirsch, 32–47. London: Routledge, 1992.

Cockburn, Cynthia, and Susan Ormrod. *Gender and Technology in the Making.* London: Sage, 1993.

Cohen, Akiba A., Dafna Lemish, and Amit M. Schejter. *The Wonder Phone in the Land of Miracles: Mobile Telephony in Israel.* Cresskill, N.J.: Hampton Press, 2008.

Cohen, Myron. "Cultural and Political Inventions in Modern China: The Case of the Chinese 'Peasant.'" In *China in Transformation,* edited by Wei-ming Tu, 154–155. Cambridge: Harvard University Press, 1994.

Cole, Jennifer, and Deborah Durham. "Introduction: Globalization and the Temporalities of Children and Youth." In *Figuring the Future: Globalization and the Temporalities of Children and Youth,* edited by Jennifer Cole and Deborah Durham, 3–24. Santa Fe, N.M.: School for Advanced Research Press, 2008.

Collins, Patricia Hill. *Black Feminist Thought.* New York: Routledge, 2000.

Connelly, Rachel, Kenneth Roberts, Xie Zhenming, and Zheng Zhenzhen. "Waichu Dagong dui Nongcun Funü Diwei de Yingxiang" [The impact of migration on the position of rural women]. In *Renkou Liudong yu Nongcun Funü Fazhan* [Migration and rural women's development], edited by Zheng Zhenzhen and Xie Zhenming, 151–174. Beijing: Social Sciences Academic Press, 2004.

Constable, Nicole. *Maid to Order in Hong Kong: Stories of Migrant Workers.* 2nd ed. Ithaca: Cornell University Press, 2007.

Crenshaw, Kimberlé. "Mapping the Margins: Intersectionality, Identity Politics, and Violence against Women of Color." *Stanford Law Review* 43, no. 6 (1991): 1241–1299.

Davis, Deborah, ed. *The Consumer Revolution in Urban China.* Berkeley: University of California Press, 2000.

————. "Introduction: A Revolution in Consumption." In *The Consumer Revolution in Urban China,* edited by Deborah Davis, 1–22. Berkeley: University of California Press, 2000.

Davis, Deborah, and Stevan Harrell. "Introduction: The Impact of Post-Mao Reforms on Family Life." In *Chinese Families in the Post-Mao Era,* edited by Deborah Davis and Stevan Harrell, 1–22. Berkeley: University of California Press, 1993.

Dean, Mitchell. *Governmentality: Power and Rule in Modern Society.* Thousand Oaks: Sage, 1999.

De Certeau, Michel. *The Practice of Everyday Life.* Translated by Steven Rendall. Berkeley: University of California Press, 2002.

DeLanda, Manuel. *A New Philosophy of Society: Assemblage Theory and Social Complexity.* New York: Continuum, 2006.

De Lauretis, Teresa. *Technologies of Gender: Essays on Theory, Film, and Fiction.* Bloomington: Indiana University Press, 1987.

Deleuze, Gilles. "Postscript on the Societies of Control." *October* 59, Winter (1992): 3-7.

Deleuze, Gilles, and Félix Guattari. *A Thousand Plateaus: Capitalism and Schizophrenia.* Translated by Brian Massumi. Minneapolis: University of Minnesota Press, 1987.

Ding, Qi. "Survey: Real Estate Most Profitable Industry in China." *China Daily,* March 14, 2008, http://www.chinadaily.com.cn/bizchina/2008-03/14/content_6537584.htm.

Ding, Wei, and Tian Qian. "The Mobile Hearth: A Case Study on New Media Usage and Migrant Workers' Social Relationships." Refereed proceedings of the Australian and New Zealand Communications Association Annual Conference, Brisbane, Australia, July 8-10, 2009.

Dolby, Nadine, and Fazal Rizvi, eds. *Youth Moves: Identities and Education in Global Perspective.* New York: Routledge, 2008.

Donald, Stephanie Hemelryk, Theresa Dirndorfer Anderson, and Damien Spry, eds. *Youth, Society and Mobile Media in Asia.* New York: Routledge, 2010.

Donato, Katherine M., Donna Gabaccia, Jennifer Holdaway, Martin Manalansan, and Patricia R. Pessar. "A Glass Half Full? Gender in Migration Studies." *International Migration Review* 40, no. 1 (2006): 3-26.

Donner, Jonathan. "Blurring Livelihoods and Lives: The Social Uses of Mobile Phones and Socioeconomic Development." *Innovations* 4, no. 1 (2009): 91-101.

———. "What Mobile Phones Mean to Rwandan Entrepreneurs." In *Mobile Democracy: Essays on Society, Self and Politics,* edited by Kristof Nyiri, 393-410. Vienna: Passagen-Verlag, 2003.

Duan, Chengrong, Fei Zhang, and Xuehe Lu. "Zhongguo Nüxing Liudong Renkou Zhuangkang Yanjiu" [Research on the state of migrant women in China]. *Funü Yanjiu Luncong* [*Collection of women's studies*] 4 (2009): 11-18, 27.

du Gay, Paul, Stuart Hall, Linda Janes, Hugh Mackay, and Keith Negus. *Doing Cultural Studies: The Story of the Sony Walkman.* London: Sage, 1997.

Ehrenreich, Barbara, and Arlie R. Hochschild, eds. *Global Woman: Nannies, Maids, and Sex Workers in the New Economy.* New York: Holt, 2002.

Ellwood-Clayton, Bella. "Virtual Strangers: Young Love and Texting in the Filipino Archipelago of Cyberspace." In *Mobile Democracy: Essays on Society, Self and Politics,* edited by Kristof Nyiri, 225-235. Vienna: Passagen-Verlag, 2003.

Eurasia Group. "China's Great Rebalancing Act." New York, August 2011, http://eurasiagroup.net/item-files/China's%20Great%20Rebalancing%20Act/China%20Rebalancing.pdf

Evans, Harriet. "Fashions and Feminine Consumption." In *Consuming China: Approaches to Cultural Change in Contemporary China,* edited by Kevin Latham, Stuart Thompson and Jakob Klein, 173-189. New York: Routledge, 2006.

———. "Marketing Femininity: Images of the Modern Chinese Woman." In *China beyond the Headlines,* edited by Timothy B. Weston and Lionel M. Jensen, 210-244. Lanham, MD: Rowman and Littlefield, 2000.

———. "Past, Perfect or Imperfect: Changing Images of the Ideal Wife." In *Chinese Femininities/Chinese Masculinities,* edited by Susan Brownell and Jeffrey N. Wasserstrom, 335-360. Berkeley: University of California Press, 2002.

————. *Women and Sexuality in China: Female Sexuality and Gender since 1949*. New York: Continuum, 1997.

Fan, C. Cindy. *China on the Move: Migration, the State, and the Household*. New York: Routledge, 2008.

————. "Migration and Gender in China." In *China Review 2000*, edited by Chunming Lau and Jianfa Shen, 434-435. Hong Kong: Chinese University Press, 2000.

————. "Out to the City and Back to the Village: The Experiences and Contributions of Rural Women Migrating from Sichuan and Anhui." In *On the Move: Women and Rural-to-Urban Migration in Contemporary China*, edited by Arianne M. Gaetano and Tamara Jacka, 177-206. New York: Columbia University Press, 2004.

Fan, Jie, and Wolfgang Taubmann. "Migrant Enclaves in Large Chinese Cities." In *The New Chinese City: Globalization and Market Reform*, edited by John R. Logan, 183-197. Malden, Mass.: Blackwell, 2002.

Farrer, James. "Sexual Citizenship and the Politics of Sexual Storytelling among Chinese Youth." In *Sex and Sexuality in China*, edited by Elaine Jeffreys, 102-123. London: Routledge, 2006.

Featherstone, Mike. "Postmodernism and the Aestheticization of Everyday Life." In *Modernity and Identity*, edited by Scott Lash and Jonathan Friedman, 265-290. Oxford: Blackwell, 1992.

Fei, Xiaotong. *From the Soil: The Foundations of Chinese Society*. Translated by Gary G. Hamilton and Zheng Wang. Berkeley: University of California Press, 1992.

Felski, Rita. *The Gender of Modernity*. Cambridge: Harvard University Press, 1995.

Fischer, Claude. *America Calling: A Social History of the Telephone to 1940*. Berkeley: University of California Press, 1992.

Fortunati, Leopoldina. "Gender and the Mobile Phone." In *Mobile Technologies: From Telecommunications to Media*, edited by Gerard Goggin and Larissa Hjorth, 23-34. New York: Routledge, 2009.

————. "Italy: Stereotypes, True and False." In *Perpetual Contact: Mobile Communication, Private Talk, Public Performance*, edited by James E. Katz and Mark Aakhus, 42-62. Cambridge: Cambridge University Press, 2002.

————. "The Mobile Phone: Local and Global Dimensions." In *A Sense of Place: The Global and the Local in Mobile Communication*, edited by Kristof Nyiri, 61-70. Vienna: Passagen Verlag, 2005.

Fortunati, Leopoldina, Anna Maria Manganelli, Pui-lam Law, and Shanhua Yang. "Beijing Calling . . . Mobile Communication in Contemporary China." *Knowledge, Technology & Policy* 21, no. 1 (2008): 19-27.

Foucault, Michel. *The Care of the Self: The History of Sexuality, Vol. 3*. Translated by Robert Hurley. New York: Vintage, 1988.

————. *Discipline and Punish: The Birth of the Prison*. Translated by Alan Sheridan. 2nd ed. New York: Random House, 1995.

————. "Governmentality." In *The Foucault Effect: Studies in Governmentality*, edited by Graham Burchell, Colin Gordon, and Peter Miller, 87-104. Chicago: University of Chicago Press, 1991.

———. "The Subject and Power." In *Power: Essential Works of Foucault, 1954–1984, Volume Three*, edited by James Faubion, 326–348. New York: New Press, 2000.

———. "Technologies of the Self." In *Technologies of the Self: A Seminar with Michel Foucault*, edited by Luther H. Martin, Huck Gutman, and Patrick H. Hutton, 16–49. Amherst: University of Massachusetts Press, 1988.

French, Howard. "In Chinese Boomtown, Middle Class Pushes Back." *New York Times*, December 18, 2006, www.nytimes.com/2006/12/18/world/asia/18shenzhen.html.

Friedman, Sara L. "Spoken Pleasures and Dangerous Desires: Sexuality, Marriage, and the State in Rural Southeastern China." *East Asia: An International Quarterly* 18, no. 4 (2000): 13–39.

Gaetano, Arianne M. "Filial Daughters, Modern Women: Migrant Domestic Workers in Post-Mao Beijing." In *On the Move: Women and Rural-to-Urban Migration in Contemporary China*, edited by Arianne M. Gaetano and Tamara Jacka, 41–79. New York: Columbia University Press, 2004.

———. "Off the Farm: Rural Chinese Women's Experiences of Labor Mobility and Modernity in Post-Mao China (1984–2002)." Ph.D. dissertation, University of Southern California, 2005.

Gaetano, Arianne M., and Tamara Jacka, eds. *On the Move: Women and Rural-to-Urban Migration in Contemporary China*. New York: Columbia University Press, 2004.

Gaonkar, Dilip Parameshwar. "On Alternative Modernities." *Public Culture* 11, no. 1 (1999): 1–18.

Geertz, Clifford. "Thick Description: Toward an Interpretive Theory of Culture." In *The Interpretation of Cultures*, 3–30. New York: Basic Books, 1973.

Gergen, Kenneth J. "Self and Community in the New Floating Worlds." In *Mobile Democracy: Essays on Society, Self and Politics*, edited by Kristof Nyiri, 103–114. Vienna: Passagen-Verlag, 2003.

Geser, Hans. "Towards a Sociological Theory of the Mobile Phone," 2004, http://socio.ch/mobile/t_geser1.htm.

Giddens, Anthony. *The Consequences of Modernity*. Stanford: Stanford University Press, 1990.

———. *Modernity and Self Identity: Self and Society in the Late Modern Age*. Stanford: Stanford University Press, 1991.

Goggin, Gerard. *Cell Phone Culture: Mobile Technology in Everyday Life*. New York: Routledge, 2006.

Gold, Thomas, Doug Guthrie, and David L. Wank. "An Introduction to the Study of Guanxi." In *Social Connections in China: Institutions, Culture, and the Changing Nature of Guanxi*, edited by Thomas Gold, Doug Guthrie, and David L. Wank, 3–20. Cambridge: Cambridge University Press, 2002.

———, eds. *Social Connections in China: Institutions, Culture, and the Changing Nature of Guanxi*. Cambridge: Cambridge University Press, 2002.

Goldstein, Joshua L. "Introduction." In *Everyday Modernity in China*, edited by Madeleine Yue Dong and Joshua L. Goldstein, 3-21. Seattle: University of Washington Press, 2006.

Goodman, David S. G. "Why China Has No New Middle Class: Cadres, Managers and Entrepreneurs." In *The New Rich in China: Future Rulers, Present Lives*, edited by David S. G. Goodman, 23-37. New York: Routledge, 2008.

Gordon, Colin. "Governmental Rationality: An Introduction." In *The Foucault Effect: Studies in Governmentality*, edited by Graham Burchell, Colin Gordon, and Peter Miller, 1-51. Chicago: University of Chicago Press, 1991.

Gray, Ann. *Research Practice for Cultural Studies: Ethnographic Methods and Lived Cultures*. London: Sage, 2003.

———. *Video Playtime: The Gendering of a Leisure Technology*. London: Routledge, 1992.

Green, Nicola. "Outwardly Mobile: Young People and Mobile Technologies." In *Machines That Become Us: The Social Context of Personal Communication Technology*, edited by James E. Katz, 201-217. New Brunswick, N.J.: Transaction, 2003.

———. "Who's Watching Whom? Monitoring and Accountability in Mobile Relations." In *Wireless World: Social and Interactional Aspects of the Mobile Age*, edited by Barry Brown, Nicola Green, and Richard Harper, 32-45. London: Springer, 2002.

Grosz, Elizabeth. *Volatile Bodies: Toward a Corporeal Feminism*. Bloomington: Indiana University Press.

Guattari, Félix. *Chaosophy*. Edited by Sylvére Lotringer. New York: Semiotexte, 1995.

Guo, Zhenzhi, and Mei Wu. "Dancing Thumbs: Mobile Telephony in Contemporary China." In *China's Information and Communications Technology Revolution: Social Changes and State Responses*, edited by Xiaoling Zhang and Yongnian Zheng, 34-51. New York: Routledge, 2009.

Gye, Lisa. "Picture This: The Impact of Mobile Camera Phones on Personal Photographic Practices." *Continuum: Journal of Media and Cultural Studies* 21, no. 2 (2007): 279-288.

Haddon, Leslie. "Domestication and Mobile Telephony." In *Machines That Become Us: The Social Context of Personal Communication Technology*, edited by James E. Katz, 43-55. New Brunswick, N.J.: Transaction, 2003.

Hall, Stuart. "Introduction: Who Needs Identity?" In *Questions of Cultural Identity*, edited by Stuart Hall and Paul du Gay, 1-17. London: Sage, 1996.

Hall, Stuart, and Lawrence Grossberg. "On Postmodernism and Articulation: An Interview with Stuart Hall." In *Stuart Hall: Critical Dialogues in Cultural Studies*, edited by David Morley and Kuan-Hsing Chen, 131-159. London: Routledge, 1996.

Hamilton, Gary G., and Zheng Wang. "Introduction." In *From the Soil: The Foundations of Chinese Society: A Translation of Xiangtu Zhongguo by Fei Xiaotong*, 1-36. Berkeley: University of California Press, 1992.

Hanser, Amy. *Service Encounters: Class, Gender, and the Market for Social Distinction in Urban China*. Stanford: Stanford University Press, 2008.

Harwit, Eric. "China's Telecommunications Industry: Development Patterns and Policies." *Pacific Affairs* 71, no. 2 (1998): 175-193.

He, Zhou. "A History of Telecommunications in China: Development and Policy Implications." In *Telecommunications and Development in China*, edited by Paul S. N. Lee, 55-87. Cresskill, N.J.: Hampton Press, 1997.

Hjorth, Larissa. *Mobile Media in the Asia-Pacific: Gender and the Art of Being Mobile*. London: Routledge, 2009.

———. "Postal Presence: A Case Study of Mobile Customization and Gender in Melbourne." In *Thumb Culture: The Meaning of Mobile Phones for Society*, edited by Peter Glotz, Stefan Bertschi, and Chris Locke, 53-66. New Brunswick, N.J.: Transaction, 2005.

———. "Snapshots of *Almost* Contact: The Rise of Camera Phone Practices and a Case Study in Seoul, Korea." *Continuum: Journal of Media and Cultural Studies* 21, no. 2 (2007): 227-238.

Ho, Samuel P. S. "Rural Non-agricultural Development in Post-Reform China: Growth, Development Patterns, and Issues." *Pacific Affairs* 68, no. 3 (1995): 360-391.

Hodgson, Dorothy L. "Introduction: Of Modernity/Modernities, Gender, and Ethnography." In *Gendered Modernities: Ethnographic Perspectives*, edited by Dorothy L. Hodgson, 1-23. New York: Palgrave, 2001.

Holland, Patricia. "Introduction: History, Memory and the Family Album." In *Family Snaps: The Meanings of Domestic Photography*, edited by Jo Spence and Patricia Holland. London: Virago, 1991.

Hondagneu-Sotelo, Pierrette. *Doméstica: Immigrant Workers Cleaning and Caring in the Shadows of Affluence*. Berkeley: University of California Press, 2001.

———. *Gendered Transitions: Mexican Experiences of Immigration*. Berkeley: University of California Press, 1994.

Hong, Yu. *Labor, Class Formation, and China's Informationized Policy of Economic Development*. Lanham, Md.: Lexington, 2011.

Honig, Emily, and Gail Hershatter. *Personal Voices: Chinese Women in the 1980s*. Stanford: Stanford University Press, 1988.

Hooper, Beverley. " 'Flower Vase and Housewife': Women and Consumerism in Post-Mao China." In *Gender and Power in Affluent Asia*, edited by Krishna Sen and Maila Stivens, 167-193. London: Routledge, 1998.

Horst, Heather A., and Daniel Miller. *The Cell Phone: An Anthropology of Communication*. New York: Berg, 2006.

Huang, Nicole. "Locating Family Portraits: Everyday Images from 1970s China." *positions: east asia cultures critique* 18 (2010): 671-693.

Huang, Yasheng. *Capitalism with Chinese Characteristics: Entrepreneurship and the State*. New York: Cambridge University Press, 2008.

Hwang, Kwang-huo. "Face and Favor: The Chinese Power Game." *American Journal of Sociology* 92 (1987): 944-974.

International Telecommunication Union. "Measuring the Information Society." Geneva, 2010, http://www.itu.int/net/pressoffice/backgrounders/general/pdf/5.pdf.

Ito, Mizuko. "Introduction: Personal, Portable, Pedestrian." In *Personal, Portable, Pedestrian: Mobile Phones in Japanese Life*, edited by Mizuko Ito, Daisuke Okabe, and Misa Matsuda, 1-16. Cambridge: MIT Press, 2005.

———. "Mobile Phones, Japanese Youth, and the Re-Placement of Social Contact." In *Mobile Communications: Re-Negotiation of the Social Sphere*, edited by Rich Ling and Per E. Pedersen, 131-148. London: Springer, 2005.

———. "A New Set of Rules for a Newly Wireless Society." *Japan Media Review*, February 14, 2003, http://www.japanmediareview.com/japan/wireless/1043770650.php.

———. "Personal Portable Pedestrian: Lessons from Japanese Mobile Phone Use." Paper presented at the Mobile Communication and Social Change Conference, Seoul, South Korea, October 18-19, 2004.

Ito, Mizuko, and Daisuke Okabe. "Technosocial Situations: Emergent Structuring of Mobile E-Mail Use." In *Personal, Portable, Pedestrian: Mobile Phones in Japanese Life*, edited by Mizuko Ito, Daisuke Okabe, and Misa Matsuda, 257-273. Cambridge: MIT Press, 2005.

Ito, Mizuko, Daisuke Okabe, and Misa Matsuda, eds. *Personal, Portable, Pedestrian: Mobile Phones in Japanese Life*. Cambridge: MIT Press, 2005.

Ito, Mizuko, Sonja Baumer, Matteo Bittani, danah boyd, Rachel Cody, Becky Herr-Stephenson, Heather A. Horst, Patricia G. Lange, Dilan Mahendran, Katynka Z. Martínez, C. J. Pascoe, Dan Perkel, Laura Robinson, Christo Sims, and Lisa Tripp. *Hanging Out, Messing Around, and Geeking Out: Kids Living and Learning with New Media*. Cambridge: MIT Press, 2010.

Jacka, Tamara. "Back to the Wok: Women and Employment in Chinese Industry in the 1980s." *Australian Journal of Chinese Affairs* 24 (1990): 1-23.

———. *Rural Women in Urban China: Gender, Migration, and Social Change*. Armonk, N.Y.: M. E. Sharpe, 2005.

Jacka, Tamara, and Arianne M. Gaetano. "Introduction: Focusing on Migrant Women." In *On the Move: Women and Rural-to-Urban Migration in Contemporary China*, edited by Arianne M. Gaetano and Tamara Jacka, 1-38. New York: Columbia University Press, 2004.

Jagun, Abi, Richard Heeks, and Jason Whalley. "The Impact of Mobile Telephony on Developing Country Micro-Enterprise: A Nigerian Case Study." *Information Technologies and International Development* 4, no. 4 (2008): 47-65.

Jeffreys, Elaine, ed. *China's Governmentalities: Governing Change, Changing Government*. New York: Routledge, 2009.

Jeffreys, Elaine, and Gary Sigley. "Governmentality, Governance and China." In *China's Governmentalities: Governing Change, Changing Government*, edited by Elaine Jeffreys, 1-23. London: Routledge, 2009.

Jenkins, Henry. *Convergence Culture: Where Old and New Media Collide*. New York: NYU Press, 2006.

Jenner, W. J. F. *China: A Photohistory, 1937-1987*. London: Thames and Hudson, 1988.

Jensen, Robert. "The Digital Provide: Information (Technology), Market Performance, and Welfare in the South Indian Fisheries Sector." *Quarterly Journal of Economics* 122, no. 3 (2007): 879-924.

Johnsen, Truls Erik. "The Social Context of the Mobile Phone Use of Norwegian Teens." In *Machines That Become Us: The Social Context of Personal Communication Technology*, edited by James E. Katz, 161-169. New Brunswick, N.J.: Transaction, 2003.

Johnson, Graham E. "Family Strategies and Economic Transformation in Rural China: Some Evidence from the Pearl River Delta." In *Chinese Families in the Post-Mao Era*, edited by Deborah Davis and Stevan Harrell, 103-136. Berkeley: University of California Press, 1993.

Judd, Ellen R. *Gender and Power in Rural North China*. Stanford: Stanford University Press, 1994.

Kang, Miliann. *The Managed Hand: Race, Gender, and the Body in Beauty Service Work*. Berkeley: University of California Press, 2010.

Kasesniemi, Eija-Liisa, and Pirjo Rautiainen. "Mobile Culture of Children and Teenagers in Finland." In *Perpetual Contact: Mobile Communication, Private Talk, Public Performance*, edited by James E. Katz and Mark Aakhus, 170-192. Cambridge: Cambridge University Press, 2002.

Katz, James E. *Magic in the Air: Mobile Communication and the Transformation of Social Life*. New Brunswick, N.J.: Transaction, 2006.

Katz, James E., and Mark Aakhus, eds. *Perpetual Contact: Mobile Communication, Private Talk, Public Performance*. Cambridge: Cambridge University Press, 2002.

Katz, James E., and Satomi Sugiyama. "Mobile Phones as Fashion Statements: The Co-Creation of Mobile Communication's Public Meaning," 2005, http://www.scils. rutgers.edu/ci/cmcs/publications/articles/mobile%20phones%20as%20fashion%20 statements.pdf.

Kember, Sarah. " 'The Shadow of the Object': Photography and Realism." In *The Photography Reader*, edited by Liz Wells, 202-217. New York: Routledge, 2003.

Khan, Azizur Rahman, and Carl Riskin. "China's Household Income and Its Distribution, 1995 and 2002." *China Quarterly* 182 (2005): 356-384.

———. *Inequality and Poverty in the Age of Globalization*. Oxford: Oxford University Press, 2001.

Kim, Shin Dong. "Korea: Personal Meanings." In *Perpetual Contact: Mobile Communication, Private Talk, Public Performance*, edited by James E. Katz and Mark Aakhus, 63-79. Cambridge: Cambridge University Press, 2002.

Kindberg, Tim, Mirjana Spasojevic, Rowanne Fleck, and Abigail Sellen. "How and Why People Use Camera Phones." HP Laboratories Bristol, 2004, http://www.hpl. hp.com/techreports/2004/HPL-2004-216.pdf.

King, Ambrose Yeo-chi. "Kuan-hsi and Network Building: A Sociological Interpretation." *Daedalus* 120, no. 2 (1991): 63-84.

Kipnis, Andrew B. *Producing Guanxi: Sentiment, Self, and Subculture in a North China Village*. Durham: Duke University Press, 1997.

———. "*Suzhi*: A Keyword Approach." *China Quarterly* 186 (2006): 295-313.

Knight, John, and Lina Song. *The Rural-Urban Divide: Economic Disparities and Inter-actions in China*. Oxford: Oxford University Press, 1999.

Koch, Pamela T., Bradley J. Koch, Kun Huang, and Wei Chen. "Beauty Is in the Eye of the QQ User: Instant Messaging in China." In *Internationalizing Internet Studies: Beyond Anglophone Paradigms*, edited by Gerard Goggin and Mark McLelland, 265-284. New York: Routledge, 2009.

Koskinen, Ilpo Kalevi. *Mobile Multimedia in Action*. New Brunswick, N.J.: Transaction, 2007.

"Laodong Baozhangbu Diaocha: Nongmingong Shouru Piandi 'Qianxin' Reng Cunzai" [Ministry of Labor and Social Security report: Migrant workers pay is on the low side, back pay still exists], February 6, 2007, http://gov.people.com.cn/GB/46737/5369775.html.

Laurier, Eric. "The Region as a Socio-Technical Accomplishment of Mobile Work-ers." In *Wireless World: Social and Interactional Aspects of the Mobile Age*, edited by Barry Brown, Eileen Green, and Richard Harper, 46-61. London: Springer-Verlag, 2002.

Law, Pui-lam, and Yinni Peng. "The Use of Mobile Phones among Migrant Workers in Southern China." In *New Technologies in Global Societies*, edited by Pui-lam Law, Leopoldina Fortunati, and Shanhua Yang, 245-258. Singapore: World Scientific Press, 2006.

Lee, Ching Kwan. *Gender and the South China Miracle: Two Worlds of Factory Women*. Berkeley: University of California Press, 1998.

Lee, Dong-Hoo. "Women's Creation of Camera Phone Cuture." *Fibreculture*, no. 6 (2005), http://six.fibreculturejournal.org/fcj-038-womens-creation-of-camera-phone-culture/.

Lee, Paul S. N. "Telecommunications and Development: An Introduction." In *Telecom-munications and Development in China*, edited by Paul S. N. Lee, 3-20. Cresskill, NJ: Hampton Press, 1997.

———. "Uneven Development of Telecommunications in China." In *Telecommunica-tions and Development in China*, edited by Paul S. N. Lee, 113-129. Cresskill, N.J.: Hampton Press, 1997.

Lei, Guang. "Bringing the City Back In: The Chinese Debate on Rural Problems." In *One Country, Two Societies: Rural-Urban Inequality in Contemporary China*, edited by Martin King Whyte, 311-324. Cambridge: Harvard University Press, 2010.

———. "Rural Taste, Urban Fashions: The Cultural Politics of Rural/Urban Difference in Contemporary China." *positions: east asia cultures critique* 11 (2003): 613-646.

Lerman, Nina, Ruth Oldenziel, and Arwen P. Mohun, eds. *Gender and Technology: A Reader*. Baltimore: Johns Hopkins University Press, 2003.

Li, Jing. "Mobiles Better Migrant Workers' Lives." *China Daily*, October 21, 2005, http://www.chinadaily.com.cn/english/doc/2005-10/21/content_486668.htm.

Li, Mingzhi, and Wang Jin. "China's Telecommunications Universal Service in a Com-petitive Environment." Paper presented at the World Institute for Development

Economics Research Spatial Inequality in Asia Conference, United Nations University, Tokyo, March 28–29, 2003.

Li, Peilin, Yi Zhang, Yandong Zhao, and Dong Liang. *Shehui Chongtu yu Jieji Yishi* [Social conflict and class consciousness]. Beijing: Social Sciences Academic Press, 2005.

Li, Qiang. *Nongminggong yu Zhongguo Shehui Fenceng* [Urban migrant workers and social stratification in China]. Beijing: Social Sciences Academic Press, 2004.

Li, Shi. "Labor Migration and Income Distribution in Rural China." In *China's Retreat from Equality: Income Distribution and Economic Transition*, edited by Carl Riskin, Renwei Zhao, and Shi Li, 303–328. Armonk, N.Y.: M. E. Sharpe, 2001.

Li, Tao. "Nongmingong Liudong Guochengzhong de Xuqiu yu Zhangai" [Demands and barriers in the flow of migrant workers]. In *Liudong he Ronghe: Nongmingong Gonggong Zhengce Gaige yu Fuwu Chuangxin Lunji* [Migration and integration: Analects on public policy reform and service innovation for migrant workers], edited by Li Zhen, 6–27. Beijing: Unity Press, 2005.

Li, Xiaojiang, Hong Zhu, and Xiuyu Dong, eds. *Pingdeng yu Fazhan: Xingbie yu Zhongguo, Di Er Ji* [Equality and development: Studies of gender and China, Vol. 2]. Beijing: Sanlian Bookstore, 1997.

Liang, Xiongjian, and Yang Xu. "Networks." In *Telecommunications in China: Development and Prospects*, edited by Lin Jingtong, Liang Xiongjian, and Wan Yan, 1–46. Huntington, N.Y.: Nova Science, 2001.

Lin, Angel, and Alvin Tong. "Mobile Cultures of Migrant Workers in Southern China: Informal Literacies in the Negotiation of (New) Social Relations of the New Working Women." *Knowledge, Technology & Policy* 21 (2008): 73–81.

Ling, L. H. M. "Sex Machine: Global Hypermasculinity and Images of the Asian Woman in Modernity." *positions: east asia cultures critique* 7 (1999): 277–306.

Ling, Rich. *The Mobile Connection: The Cell Phone's Impact on Society*. San Francisco: Morgan Kaufmann, 2004.

———. "Trust, Cohesion and Social Networks: The Case of Quasi-Illicit Photos in a Teen Peer Group." Paper presented at the Mobile Communication and the Ethics of Social Networking Conference, Budapest, Hungary, September 25–27, 2008.

Ling, Rich, and Scott W. Campbell, eds. *The Reconstruction of Space and Time: Mobile Communication Practices*. New Brunswick, N.J.: Transaction, 2009.

Ling, Rich, and Tom Julsrud. "Grounded Genres in Multimedia Messaging." In *A Sense of Place: The Global and the Local in Mobile Communication*, edited by Kristof Nyiri, 329–338. Vienna: Passagen-Verlag, 2005.

Ling, Rich, and Per E. Pedersen, eds. *Mobile Communications: Re-Negotiation of the Social Sphere*. London: Springer, 2005.

Ling, Rich, and Birgitte Yttri. "Control, Emancipation and Status: The Mobile Telephone in Teens' Parental and Peer Relationships." In *Computers, Phones, and the Internet: Domesticating Information Technology*, edited by Robert Kraut, Malcolm Brynin, and Sara Kiesler, 219–234. Oxford: Oxford University Press, 2005.

———. "Hyper-Coordination via Mobile Phones in Norway." In *Perpetual Contact: Mobile Communication, Private Talk, Public Performance*, edited by James E. Katz and Mark Aakhus, 139-169. Cambridge: Cambridge University Press, 2002.

Liu, Xin. *The Otherness of Self: A Genealogy of the Self in Contemporary China*. Ann Arbor: University of Michigan Press, 2002.

Lobet-Maris, Claire. "Mobile Phone Tribes: Youth and Social Identity." In *Mediating the Human Body: Technology, Communication, and Fashion*, edited by Leopoldina Fortunati, James E. Katz, and Raimonda Riccini, 87-92. Mahwah, N.J.: Lawrence Erlbaum, 2003.

Loo, Betty P. Y. "Telecommunications Reforms in China: Toward an Analytical Framework." *Telecommunications Policy* 28 (2004): 697-714.

Lotz, Amanda D. "Assessing Qualitative Television Audience Research: Incorporating Feminist and Anthropological Theoretical Innovation." *Communication Theory* 10, no. 4 (2000): 447-467.

Lu, Ding, and Chee Kong Wong. *China's Telecommunications Market: Entering a New Competitive Age*. Northampton, MA: Edward Elgar, 2003.

Lu, Fangwen. "Zhiye Xingbie Qishi: Yuanyin he Duice—Tan Nüdaxuesheng, Nüyanjiusheng Weihe Zhao Gongzuo Nan" [Sexual discrimination in occupations: Causes and coping measures—Why women undergraduates and postgraduates have difficulty finding work]. *Funü Yanjiu Luncong* [*Collection of women's studies*] 4 (2000): 4-9.

Lu, Hanlong. "To Be Relatively Comfortable in an Egalitarian Society." In *The Consumer Revolution in Urban China*, edited by Deborah S. Davis, 124-141. Berkeley: University of California Press, 2000.

Lu, Xueyi, ed. *Dangdai Zhongguo Shehui Jieceng Yanjiu Baogao* [Research report on social stratification in contemporary China]. Beijing: Social Sciences Academic Press, 2002.

Lukoff, Kai. "China's Top Four Social Networks: Renren, Kaixin001, Qzone, and 51.Com," April 7, 2010, http://venturebeat.com/2010/04/07/china's-top-4-social-networks-renren-kaixin001-qzone-and-51-com/.

Luo, Binbin, Zhenzhen Zheng, Rachel Connelly, and Kenneth D. Roberts. "The Migration Experience of Young Women from Four Counties in Sichuan and Anhui." In *On the Move: Women and Rural-to-Urban Migration in Contemporary China*, edited by Arianne M. Gaetano and Tamara Jacka, 207-242. New York: Columbia University Press, 2004.

Luo, Peilin, and Yinni Peng. "Guanyu Zhongguo Nanbu Nongmingong de Shehui Shenghuo yu Shouji de Yanjiu" [A study of the relationship between social life and mobile telephony among migrant workers in southern China]. In *Chenxiang Richang Shenghuo: Yizhong Shehuixue Fenxi* [Everyday life in urban and rural China: A sociological analysis], edited by Shanhua Yang, 83-101. Beijing: Social Sciences Academic Press, 2008.

Lütgens, Annelie, and Gijs van Tuyl. *The Chinese: Photography and Video from China*. Wolfsburg: Kuntsmuseum, 2006.

Lynch, Daniel C. "The Nature and Consequences of China's Unique Pattern of Tele-communications Development." In *Power, Money, and Media: Communication Patterns and Bureaucratic Control in Cultural China*, edited by Chin-Chuan Lee, 179–207. Evanston: Northwestern University Press, 2000.

Ma, Eric, and Hau Ling "Helen" Cheng. " 'Naked' Bodies: Experimenting with Intimate Relations among Migrant Workers in South China." *International Journal of Cultural Studies* 8, no. 3 (2005): 307–328.

Ma, Yunzeng, Shen Chen, Zhichuan Hu, Zhangbiao Qian, and Yongxiang Peng. *Zhongguo Sheying Shi 1840–1937* [The history of photography in China 1840–1937]. Beijing: China Photography Press, 1987.

Maira, Sunaina, and Elisabeth Soep, eds. *Youthscapes: The Popular, the National, the Global*. Philadelphia: University of Pennsylvania Press, 2005.

Mallee, Hein. "Migration, *Hukou* and Resistance in Reform China." In *Chinese Society: Change, Conflict, and Resistance*, 2nd ed., edited by Elizabeth J. Perry and Mark Selden, 136–157. London: Routledge, 2003.

Martin, Corinne. "Camera Phone and Photography among French Young Users." Paper presented at the Mobile 2.0: Beyond Voice, International Communication Association Pre-Conference, Chicago, Illinois, May 20–21, 2009.

Marvin, Carolyn. *When Old Technologies Were New: Thinking about Electric Communication in the Late Nineteenth Century*. New York: Oxford University Press, 1988.

Mazzarella, Sharon, ed. *Girl Wide Web: Girls, the Internet, and the Negotiation of Identity*. New York: Peter Lang, 2005.

McClintock, Anne. *Imperial Leather: Race, Gender and Sexuality in the Colonial Contest*. New York: Routledge, 1995.

McEwen, William J. "The People's Republic of Wireless." *Gallup Management Journal*, January 12, 2011, http://gmj.gallup.com/content/145520/article-2011.aspx.

Miller, Daniel, Peter Jackson, Nigel Thrift, Beverley Holbrook, and Michael Rowlands. *Shopping, Place and Identity*. New York: Routledge, 1998.

Mitchell, W. J. T. *Picture Theory*. Chicago: University of Chicago Press, 1994.

Mohanty, Chandra Talpade. *Feminism without Borders: Decolonizing Theory, Practicing Solidarity*. Durham: Duke University Press, 2003.

Mueller, Milton, and Zixiang Tan. *China in the Information Age: Telecommunications and the Dilemmas of Reform*. Westport, CT: Praeger, 1997.

Murphie, Arianne, and John Potts. *Culture and Technology*. New York: Palgrave Macmillan, 2003.

Murphy, Patrick D., and Marwin M. Kraidy. "International Communication, Ethnography, and the Challenge of Globalization." *Communication Theory* 13, no. 3 (2002): 304–323.

Murphy, Rachel. *How Migrant Labor Is Changing Rural China*. Cambridge: Cambridge University Press, 2002.

Nakamura, Lisa. *Cybertypes: Race, Ethnicity, and Identity on the Internet*. New York: Routledge, 2002.

——. *Digitizing Race: Visual Cultures of the Internet*. Minneapolis: University of Minnesota Press, 2008.

"New Socialist Countryside—What Does It Mean?" *Beijing Review*, October 10, 2008, http://www.bjreview.com.cn/special/third_plenum_17thcpc/txt/2008-10/10/content_156190.htm.

Ngan, Raymond, and Stephen Ma. "The Relationship of Mobile Telephony to Job Mobility in China's Pearl River Delta." *Knowledge, Technology & Policy* 21 (2008): 55-63.

Nystedt, Dan. "China Mobile Posts Strong 2007 Growth, Gains Music, Users," *Washington Post*, March 23, 2008, http://www.washingtonpost.com.

Oishi, Nana. *Women in Motion: Globalization, State Policies, and Labor Migration in Asia*. Stanford: Stanford University Press, 2005.

Okabe, Daisuke, and Mizuko Ito. "Everyday Contexts of Camera Phone Use: Steps toward Techno-Social Ethnographic Frameworks." In *Mobile Communication in Everyday Life: Ethnographic Views, Observations and Reflections*, edited by Joachim R. Hoflich and Maren Hartmann, 79-102. Berlin: Frank and Timme, 2006.

Oksman, Virpi. "MMS and Its Early Adopters in Finland." In *A Sense of Place: The Mobile Information Society. Communications in the 21st Century*, edited by Kristof Nyiri, 349-361. Vienna: Passagen Verlag, 2005.

——. "Mobile Visuality and Everyday Life in Finland: An Ethnographic Approach to Social Uses of Mobile Image." In *Mobile Communication in Everyday Life: Ethnographic Views, Observations and Reflections*, edited by Joachim R. Hoflich and Maren Hartmann, 103-119. Berlin: Frank and Timme, 2006.

Oksman, Virpi, and Pirjo Rautiainen. "Extension of the Hand: Children's and Teenagers' Relationship with the Mobile Phone in Finland." In *Mediating the Human Body: Technology, Communication, and Fashion*, edited by Leopoldina Fortunati, James E. Katz, and R. Riccini, 103-111. Mahweh, N.J.: Lawrence Erlbaum, 2003.

——. " 'Perhaps It's a Body Part:' How the Mobile Phone Became an Organic Part of the Everyday Lives of Finnish Children and Teenagers." In *Machines That Become Us: The Social Context of Personal Communication Technology*, edited by James E. Katz, 293-308. New Brunswick, N.J.: Transaction, 2003.

Ong, Aihwa. *Neoliberalism as Exception: Mutations in Citizenship and Sovereignty*. Durham: Duke University Press, 2006.

Ong, Aihwa, and Li Zhang. "Introduction: Privatizing China: Powers of the Self, Socialism from Afar." In *Privatizing China: Socialism from Afar*, edited by Li Zhang and Aihwa Ong, 1-19. Ithaca: Cornell University Press, 2008.

Overå, Ragnhild. "Mobile Traders and Mobile Phones in Ghana." In *Handbook of Mobile Communication Studies*, edited by James E. Katz, 43-54. Cambridge: MIT Press, 2008.

Palfry, John, and Uri Gassner. *Born Digital: Understanding the First Generation of Digital Natives*. New York: Basic Books, 2008.

Pan, Suiming. "Transformations in the Primary Life Cycle: The Origins and Nature of China's Sexual Revolution." In *Sex and Sexuality in China*, edited by Elaine Jeffreys, 21–42. London: Routledge, 2006.

Pan, Suiming, William Parish, Wang Aili, and Edward Laumann. *Dangdai Zhongguoren de Xing Xingwei yu Xing Guanxi* [Sexual behavior and relations in contemporary China]. Beijing: Social Sciences Academic Press, 2004.

Panagakos, Anastasia N., and Heather A. Horst. "Return to Cyberia: Technology and the Social Worlds of Transnational Migrants." *Global Networks* 6, no. 2 (2006): 109–124.

Pang, Laikwan. "Photography, Performance, and the Making of Female Images in Modern China." *Journal of Women's History* 17, no. 4 (2005): 56–85.

Parreñas, Rhacel Salazar. *The Force of Domesticity: Filipina Migrants and Globalization*. New York: NYU Press, 2008.

Peng, Yinni. "Internet Use of Migrant Workers in the Pearl River Delta." *Knowledge, Technology & Policy* 21 (2008): 47–54.

Pertierra, Raul. "Mobile Phones, Identity and Discursive Intimacy." *Human Technology* 1, no. 1 (2005): 23–44.

Pertierra, Raul, Eduardo F. Ugarte, Alicia Pingol, Joel Hernandez, and Nikos Lexis Dacanay. *Txt-ing Selves: Cellphones and Philippine Modernity*. Manila, Philippines: De La Salle University Press, 2002.

Pessar, Patricia R., and Sarah J. Mahler. "Transnational Migration: Bringing Gender In." *International Migration Review* 37, no. 3 (2003): 812–846.

Phillips, Shan. "Mobile Internet More Popular in China Than in U.S." *Nielson Wire*, August 4, 2010, http://blog.nielsen.com/nielsenwire/global/mobile-internet-more-popular-in-china-than-in-u-s/.

Plant, Sadie. "On the Mobile: The Effects of Mobile Telephones on Social and Individual Life." 2002, http://www.motorola.com/mot/doc/0/267_MotDoc.pdf.

Pollack, Barbara. "Chinese Photography: Beyond Stereotypes." *Art News New York*, 2004, http://www.artnews.com/2004/02/01/chinese-photography-beyond-stereotypes/.

Pool, Ithiel de Sola. *Technologies of Freedom*. Cambridge: Belknap Press, 1983.

Potter, Sulamith Heins, and Jack M. Potter. *China's Peasants: The Anthropology of a Revolution*. Cambridge: Cambridge University Press, 1990.

Prensky, Marc. "Digital Natives, Digital Immigrants." *On the Horizon* 9, no. 5 (2001): 1–6.

Prøitz, Lin. "Intimacy Fiction: Intimate Discourses in Mobile Telephone Communication amongst Norwegian Youth." In *A Sense of Place: The Global and the Local in Mobile Communication*, edited by Kristof Nyiri, 191–200. Vienna: Passagen Verlag, 2005.

Pun, Ngai. *Made in China: Women Factory Workers in a Global Workplace*. Durham: Duke University Press 2005.

———. "Subsumption or Consumption? The Phantom of Consumer Revolution in 'Globalizing' China." *Cultural Anthropology* 18, no. 4 (2003): 469–492.

Pun, Ngai, and Huilin Lu. "Unfinished Proletarianization: Self, Anger, and Class Action among the Second Generation of Peasant-Workers." *Modern China* 36, no. 5 (2010): 493-519.

Pun, Ngai, and Chris Smith. "Putting the Transnational Labor Process in Its Place: The Dormitory Labor Regime in Post-Socialist China." *Work, Employment and Society* 21, no. 1 (2007): 27-46.

"Qingli Shi Nongmingong Jiaofei" [Clear up fees on peasant workers], February 27, 2007, http://news.sina.com.cn/c/2007-02-27/153411299577s.shtml.

Qiu, Jack Linchuan. "The Accidental Accomplishment of Little Smart." *New Media & Society* 9, no. 6 (2007): 903-923.

———. "The Wireless Leash: Mobile Messaging Service as a Means of Control." *International Journal of Communication* 1 (2007): 74-91.

———. "Working-Class ICTs, Migrants, and Empowerment in South China." *Asian Journal of Communication* 18, no. 4 (2008): 333-347.

———. *Working-Class Network Society: Communication Technology and the Information Have-less in Urban China.* Cambridge: MIT Press, 2009.

Rabinow, Paul. "Introduction." In *The Foucault Reader*, edited by Paul Rabinow, 3-29. New York: Pantheon Books, 1984.

Research Team on Migration and Gender. "Impact of Migration on Gender Relationships and Rural Women's Status in China." UNESCO, Beijing, March 2006.

Riley, Nancy. "Gender Equality in China: Two Steps Forward, One Step Back." In *China Briefing: The Contradictions of Change*, edited by William A. Joseph, 79-108. Armonk, N.Y.: M. E. Sharpe, 1997.

———. "Interwoven Lives: Parents, Marriage, and Guanxi in China." *Journal of Marriage and the Family* 56 (1994): 791-803.

Riviére, Carol. "Mobile Camera Phones: A New Form of 'Being Together' in Daily Interpersonal Communication." In *Mobile Communications: Re-Negotiation of the Social Sphere*, edited by Rich Ling and Per E. Pedersen, 167-177. London: Springer, 2005.

Robbins, Kathleen A., and Martha A. Turner. "United States: Popular, Pragmatic and Problematic." In *Perpetual Contact: Mobile Communication, Private Talk, Public Performance*, edited by James E. Katz and Mark Aakhus, 80-93. Cambridge: Cambridge University Press, 2002.

Robinson, Jean C. "Of Women and Washing Machines: Employment, Housework, and the Reproduction of Motherhood in Socialist China." *China Quarterly* 101 (1985): 32-57.

Rodrigues, Usha M., and Belinda Smaill, eds. *Youth, Media and Culture in the Asia Pacific Region.* Newcastle, U.K.: Cambridge Scholars, 2008.

Rofel, Lisa. *Desiring China: Experiments in Neoliberalism, Sexuality, and Public Culture.* Durham: Duke University Press, 2007.

———. *Other Modernities: Gendered Yearnings in China after Socialism.* Berkeley: University of California Press, 1999.

Rose, Nikolas. "Governing the Enterprising Self." In *The Values of the Enterprise Culture: The Moral Debate*, edited by Paul Heelas and Paul Morris, 141-162. London: Routledge, 1992.

Rosen, Stanley. "Chinese Youth and State-Society Relations." In *Chinese Politics: State, Society and the Market*, edited by Peter Hays Gries and Stanley Rosen, 160-178. New York: Routledge, 2010.

———. "The State of Youth/Youth and the State in Early 21st-Century China: The Triumph of the Urban Rich?" In *State and Society in 21st-Century China: Crisis, Contention, and Legitimation*, edited by Stanley Rosen and Peter Hays Gries, 158-179. New York: RoutledgeCurzon, 2004.

Ross, Andrew. *Nice Work If You Can Get It: Life and Labor in Precarious Times*. New York: NYU Press, 2009.

Salzinger, Leslie. *Genders in Production: Making Workers in Mexico's Global Factories*. Berkeley: University of California Press, 2003.

Savat, David, and Mark Poster, eds. *Deleuze and New Technology*. Edinburgh: Edinburgh University Press, 2009.

Schein, Louisa. "Performing Modernity." *Cultural Anthropology* 14, no. 3 (1999): 361-395.

Scifo, Barbara. "The Domestication of Cameraphone and MMS Communications: The Experience of Young Italians." In *A Sense of Place. The Mobile Information Society. Mobile Communications in the 21st Century*, edited by Kristof Nyiri, 363-373. Vienna: Passagen Verlag, 2004.

Scott, Joan Wallach "Experience." In *Feminists Theorize the Political*, edited by Judith Butler and Joan Wallach Scott, 22-40. New York: Routledge, 1992.

Sekula, Allan. "The Body and the Archive." *October* 39 (1986): 3-64.

"Shandong dui 'Shiyiwu' Qijian Nongmingong Suzhi Jiaoyu Tichu Mingque Mubiao" [Shandong clarifies goals of *suzhi* education for migrant workers during the "Eleventh Five-Year Plan"]. *Worker's Daily*, November, 29, 2006, http://www.gov.cn/jrzg/2006-11/29/content_456150.htm.

Skelton, Tracey, and Gill Valentine, eds. *Cool Places: Geographies of Youth Cultures*. New York: Routledge, 1998.

Skog, Berit. "Mobiles and the Norwegian Teen: Identity, Gender and Class." In *Perpetual Contact: Mobile Communication, Private Talk, Public Performance*, edited by James E. Katz and Mark Aakhus, 255-273. Cambridge: Cambridge University Press, 2002.

Slack, Jennifer Daryl. "The Theory and Method of Articulation in Cultural Studies." In *Stuart Hall: Critical Dialogues in Cultural Studies*, edited by David Morley and Kuan-Hsing Chen, 112-127. London: Routledge, 1996.

Slack, Jennifer Daryl, and J. Macgregor Wise. *Culture + Technology: A Primer.* New York: Peter Lang, 2005.

Slater, Don. *Consumer Culture and Modernity*. Cambridge: Polity Press, 1997.

———. "Consuming Kodak." In *Family Snaps: The Meanings of Domestic Photography*, edited by Jo Spence and Patricia Holland, 49-59. London: Virago, 1991.

Smaill, Belinda. "Asia Pacific Modernities: Thinking through Youth Media Locales." In *Youth, Media and Culture in the Asia Pacific Region*, edited by Usha M. Rodrigues and Belinda Smaill, 1-15. Newcastle, U.K.: Cambridge Scholars, 2008.

Solinger, Dorothy J. *Contesting Citizenship in Urban China: Peasant Migrants, the State, and the Logic of the Market*. Berkeley: University of California Press, 1999.

Song, Lina. "The Role of Women in Labor Migration: A Case in Northern China." In *Women of China: Economic and Social Transformation*, edited by Jackie West, Minghua Zhao, Xiangqun Cheng, and Yuan Cheng, 69-89. New York: Palgrave, 1999.

Sontag, Susan. *On Photography*. New York: Picador, 1977.

Spence, Jo, and Patricia Holland, eds. *Family Snaps: The Meanings of Domestic Photography*. London: Virago, 1991.

Spielberg, Elinor. "The Myth of Nimble Fingers." In *No Sweat: Fashion, Free Trade, and the Rights of Garment Workers*, edited by Andrew Ross, 113-122. New York: Verso, 1997.

Spigel, Lynn. *Make Room for TV: Television and the Family Ideal in Postwar America*. Chicago: University of Chicago Press, 1992.

Stacey, Judith. "Can There Be a Feminist Ethnography?" *Women's Studies International Forum* 11, no. 1 (1988): 21-27.

———. *Patriarchy and Socialist Revolution in China*. Berkeley: University of California Press, 1983.

Stald, Gitte. "Mobile Identity: Youth, Identity, and Mobile Communication Media." In *Youth, Identity and Digital Media*, edited by David Buckingham, 143-164. Cambridge: MIT Press, 2008.

State Council. "Guowuyuan Pizhuan Fazhan Gaige wei Guanyu 2010 Nian Shenhua Jingji Tizhi Gaige Zhongdian Gongzuo Yijian de Tongzhi" [Notice of the State Council's approval and forwarding opinions of the State Development and Reform Commission on key work in deepening the reform of the economic system in 2010], May 31, 2010.

Sui, Helen. "Reconstituting Dowry and Brideprice in South China." In *Chinese Families in the Post-Mao Era*, edited by Deborah Davis and Stevan Harrell, 165-188. Berkeley: University of California Press, 1993.

Suleiman, Susan R., ed. *The Female Body in Western Culture: Contemporary Perspectives*. Cambridge: Harvard University Press, 1986.

Sun, Wanning. "Indoctrination, Fetishization, and Compassion: Media Constructions of the Migrant Woman." In *On the Move: Women and Rural-to-Urban Migration in Contemporary China*, edited by Arianne M. Gaetano and Tamara Jacka, 109-128. New York: Columbia University Press, 2004.

———. *Maid in China: Media, Morality, and the Cultural Politics of Boundaries*. New York: Routledge, 2009.

———. "*Suzhi* on the Move: Body, Place, and Power." *positions: east asia cultures critique* 17 (2009): 617-642.

Tagg, John. *The Burden of Representation: Essays on Photographies and Histories*. Minneapolis: University of Minnesota Press, 1988.

Tan, Shen. "Jiating Celue haishi Geren Zizhu? Nongcun Laodongli Waichu Juece Moshi de Xingbie Fenxi" [Family strategy or individual autonomy? A gender analysis of the decisions of the rural labor force to go out to work]. *Zhejiang Xuekan* 5 (2004): 210-214.

———. "Leaving Home and Coming Back: Experiences of Rural Migrant Women." In *Holding Up Half the Sky: Chinese Women Past, Present, and Future*, edited by Jie Tao, Bijun Zheng, and Shirley L. Mow, 248-258. New York: Feminist Press at the City University of New York, 2004.

———. "Nüxing Liudong yu Xingbie Pingdeng" [Female migrants and gender equality]. In *Jincheng Nongmingong: Xianzhuang, Qushi, Women Neng Zuo Xie Shenme* [Rural-to-urban migrants: Situations, trends and what we can do], 238-255. Beijing: People's University Institute for Agriculture and Rural Development, 2006.

Taylor, Alex S., and Richard Harper. "The Gift of *Gab*? A Design-Oriented Sociology of Young People's Use of Mobiles." *Computer Supported Cooperative Work* 12 (2003): 267-296.

Thompson, Eric C. "Mobile Phones, Communities and Social Networks among Foreign Workers in Singapore." *Global Networks* 9, no. 3 (2009): 359-380.

Tong, Xin. "Mainstream Discourse and the Construction of Public Understanding of Women's Employment." *Social Sciences in China* 31, no. 2 (2010): 135-149.

Turkle, Sherry. "Always On/Always-on-You: The Tethered Self." In *Handbook of Mobile Communication Studies*, edited by James E. Katz, 121-137. Cambridge: MIT Press, 2008.

Ureta, Sebastian. "Evanescent Connection: Spatial Immobility, Social Exclusion and Mobile Phone Use among Low-Income Families in Santiago, Chile." Paper presented at the Annenberg Research Network on International Communication, University of Southern California, April 2005.

———. "The Immobile Mobility: Spatial Mobility and Mobile Phone Use among Low-Income Families in Santiago, Chile." Paper presented at the 5th Wireless World Conference, University of Surrey, United Kingdom, July 15-16, 2004.

Van House, Nancy A., and Marc Davis. "The Social Life of Cameraphone Images." Paper presented at the Pervasive Image Capture and Sharing: New Social Practices and Implications for Technology Workshop at the Seventh International Conference on Ubiquitous Computing (UbiComp 2005), Tokyo, Japan, September 11-14, 2005.

Van House, Nancy A., Marc Davis, Morgan Ames, Megan Finn, and Vijay Viswanathan. "The Uses of Personal Networked Digital Imaging: An Empirical Study of Cameraphone Photos and Sharing." *CHI 2005*, Portland, Oregon, April 27, 2005.

Vincent, Jane. "Emotional Attachment and Mobile Phones." *Knowledge, Technology & Policy* 19, no. 1 (2006): 39-44.

———. "Emotion, My Mobile, My Identity." In *Electronic Emotion: The Mediation of Emotion via Information and Communication Technologies*, edited by Jane Vincent and Leopoldina Fortunati, 187-206. Oxford: Peter Lang, 2009.

———. "Living with Mobile Phones." In *Mobile Media and the Change of Everyday Life*, edited by Joachim R. Höflich, Georg F. Kircher, Christine Linke, and Isabel Schlote, 155-170. Frankfurt: Peter Lang, 2010.

Vincent, Jane, and Leopoldina Fortunati, eds. *Electronic Emotion: The Mediation of Emotion via Information and Communication Technologies*. Oxford: Peter Lang, 2009.

Visweswaran, Kamala. *Fictions of Feminist Ethnography*. Minneapolis: University of Minnesota Press, 1994.

Wajcman, Judy. *Feminism Confronts Technology*. University Park: Penn State University Press, 1991.

———. *Technofeminism*. Malden, Mass.: Wiley-Blackwell, 2004.

Wajcman, Judy, Michael Bittman, and Judith E. Brown. "Families without Borders: Mobile Phones, Connectedness and Work-Home Divisions." *Sociology* 42, no. 4 (2008): 635-652.

Wallis, Cara. "(Im)mobile Mobility: Marginal Youth and Mobile Phones in Beijing." In *Mobile Communication: Bringing Us Together and Tearing Us Apart*, edited by Rich Ling and Scott Campbell, 61-81. New Brunswick, N.J.: Transaction, 2011.

———. "Mobile Phones without Guarantees: The Promises of Technology and the Contingencies of Culture." *New Media & Society* 13, no. 3 (2011): 471-485.

———. "The Traditional Meets the Technological: Mobile Navigations of Desire and Intimacy." In *Youth, Society and Mobile Media in Asia*, edited by Stephanie Hemelryk Donald, Theresa Dirndorfer Anderson, and Damien Spry, 57-69. London: Routledge, 2010.

Wallis, Cara, and Jack Linchuan Qiu. "*Shanzhaiji* and the Transformation of the Local Mediascape in Shenzhen." In *Mapping Media in China: Region, Province, Locality*, edited by Wanning Sun and Jenny Chio, 109-125. London: Routledge, 2012.

Wang, Chunguang. "Nongmingong de 'Banchengshihua' Wenti" [The problem of peasant workers' "semi-urbanization"]. In *Liudong he Ronghe: Nongmingong Gonggong Zhengce Gaige yu Fuwu Chuangxin Lunji* [Migration and integration: Analects on public policy reform and service innovation for migrant workers], edited by Li Zhen, 41-57. Beijing: Unity Press, 2005.

Wang, Fei-Ling. *Organizing through Division and Exclusion: China's Hukou System*. Stanford: Stanford University Press, 2005.

———. "Renovating the Great Floodgate: The Reform of China's *Hukou* System." In *One Country, Two Societies: Rural-Urban Inequality in Contemporary China*, edited by Martin King Whyte, 335-364. Cambridge: Harvard University Press, 2010.

Wang, Feng. "Gendered Migration and the Migration of Genders in Contemporary China." In *Re-Drawing Boundaries: Work, Households, and Gender in China*, edited by Barbara Entwistle and Gail E. Henderson, 231-242. Berkeley: University of California Press, 2000.

Wang, Jing. *Brand New China: Advertising, Media and Commercial Culture*. Cambridge: Harvard University Press, 2008.

Wang, Min. "Quanguo Zhigong Suzhi Lantu Huijiu" [National blueprint of workers' *suzhi* laid out]. Xinhua News Agency, April 18, 2010, http://news.xinhuanet.com/politics/2010-04/18/c_1241091.htm.

Wang, Xing. "China's Wireless Service Xiaolingtong Ordered to Be Closed in 3 Years." *China Daily*, February 3, 2009, http://www.chinadaily.com.cn/bizchina/2009-02/03/content_7442803.htm.

Wang, Xingzhou. "An Investigation into Intergenerational Differences between Two Generations of Migrant Workers." *Social Sciences in China* 29, no. 3 (2010): 136-156.

Wang, Yuezhou. "Nongcun Nüxing Qingnian Lixiang Xinnian de Queshi yu Shuli" [The absence and establishment of ideals and faith among rural female youth]. *Zhongguo Qingnian Yanjiu* [China youth research] 8 (2007): 74-76.

Wang, Zheng. "'Nüxing Yizhi', 'Shehui Xingbie Yizhi' Bianyi" [On the differences between "female consciousness" and "gender consciousness"]. *Funü Yanjiu Luncong* [Collection of women's studies] 1 (1997): 14-20.

Watkins, S. Craig. *The Young and the Digital: What the Migration to Social-Network Sites, Games, and Anytime, Anywhere Media Means for Our Future*. Boston: Beacon Press, 2009.

Watney, Simon. "On the Institutions of Photography." In *Visual Culture: The Reader*, edited by Jessica Evans and Stuart Hall, 141-161. London: Sage, 1999.

Watts, Jonathan. "Workers in China Grasp the Power of the Strike." *The Observer*, July 4, 2010, http://www.guardian.co.uk/world/2010/jul/04/workers-china-power-strike-communist.

Weilenmann, Alexandra, and Catrine Larsson. "Local Use and Sharing of Mobile Phones." In *Wireless World: Social and Interactional Aspects of the Mobile Age*, edited by Barry Brown, Nicola Green, and Richard Harper, 92-107. London: Springer, 2002.

Wellman, Barry, Anabel Quan Haase, James Witte, and Keith Hampton. "Does the Internet Increase, Decrease, or Supplement Social Capital?" *American Behavioral Scientist* 45, no. 3 (2001): 436-455.

Whyte, Martin King. "Changes in Mate Choice in Chengdu." In *Chinese Society on the Eve of Tiananmen: The Impact of Reform*, edited by Deborah Davis and Ezra F. Vogel, 181-213. Cambridge: Council on East Asian Studies/Harvard University, 1990.

Wilson, Scott. "Face, Norms, and Instrumentality." In *Social Connections in China: Institutions, Culture, and the Changing Nature of Guanxi*, edited by Thomas Gold, Doug Guthrie, and David L. Wank, 163-177. Cambridge: Cambridge University Press, 2002.

Winner, Langdon. "Do Artifacts Have Politics?" In *The Whale and the Reactor: A Search for Limits in an Age of High Technology*, 19-39. Chicago: University of Chicago Press, 1986.

Winston, Brian. " 'The Camera Never Lies': The Partiality of Photographic Evidence." In *Image-Based Research*, edited by Jon Prosser, 53-60. Philadelphia: Falmer Press, 1998.

Wise, J. Macgregor. "Assemblage." In *Gilles Deleuze: Key Concepts*, edited by Charles J. Stivale, 77–87. Montreal: McGill-Queen's University Press, 2005.

Wolf, Margery. *Revolution Postponed: Women in Contemporary China*. Stanford: Stanford University Press, 1985.

Wu, Xiaoying. "From State Discourse to Market Orientation: The Composition and Evolution of Gender Discourse." *Social Sciences in China* 31, no. 2 (2010): 150–164.

Xia, Dai. "Liudong Renkou Gongzi Shouru Yinxiang Yinsuzhong de Xingbie Chayi— Yi Xiamenshi Liudong Funü Weili" [Sexual difference in factors affecting the wage earnings of the floating population—A case study of the migrant women in Xiamen City]. *Funü Yanjiu Luncong* [*Collection of women's studies*] 6, no. 68 (2005): 14–19.

Xie, Chuanjiao. "Most Migrant Workers in Cities Unhappy: Survey." *China Daily*, January 14, 2008, http://www.chinadaily.com.cn/bizchina/2008-01/14/content_6391702.htm.

Xinhua. "Backgrounder: Challenges in China's Rural Development," December 22, 2007, http://www.china.org.cn/english/China/236603.htm.

———. "Beijing's Population Exceeds 17.4 Million," December 4, 2007, http://news.xinhuanet.com/english/2007-12/04/content_7197045.htm.

Xu, Xiaohe. "The Social Origins of Historical Changes in Freedom of Mate Choice under State Socialism." In *Social Transition in China*, edited by Jie Zhang and Xiaobing Li, 35–60. Lanham, Md.: University Press of America, 1998.

Xu, Yan, and Xiongjian Liang. "Policy and Regulations." In *Telecommunications in China: Development and Prospects*, edited by Jintong Lin, Xiongjian Liang, and Yan Wan, 127–144. Huntington, N.Y.: Nova Science, 2001.

Yan, Hairong. "Neoliberal Governmentality and Neohumanism: Organizing Suzhi/Value Flow through Labor Recruitment Networks." *Cultural Anthropology* 18, no. 4 (2003): 493–523.

———. *New Masters, New Servants: Migration, Development, and Women Workers in China*. Durham: Duke University Press, 2008.

———. "Spectralization of the Rural: Reinterpreting the Labor Mobility of Rural Young Women in Post-Mao China." *American Ethnologist* 30, no. 4 (2003): 578–596.

Yan, Wan. "Sector Reform." In *Telecommunications in China: Development and Prospects*, edited by Lin Jintong, Liang Xiongjian, and Wan Yan, 145–183. Huntington, N.Y.: Nova Science, 2001.

Yan, Yunxiang. "Courtship, Love and Premarital Sex in a North China Village." *China Journal* 48 (2002): 29–53.

———. *The Flow of Gifts: Reciprocity and Social Networks in a Chinese Village*. Stanford: Stanford University Press, 1996.

———. *The Individualization of Chinese Society*. New York: Berg, 2009.

———. "McDonald's in Beijing: The Localization of Americana." In *Golden Arches East: McDonald's in East Asia*, edited by James L. Watson, 39–76. Stanford: Stanford University Press, 1997.

———. "The Politics of Consumerism in Chinese Society." In *China Briefing 2000: The Continuing Transformation*, edited by Tyrene White, 159–193. Armonk, N.Y.: M. E. Sharpe, 2000.

———. *Private Life under Socialism: Love, Intimacy, and Family Change in a Chinese Village, 1949–1999.* Stanford: Stanford University Press, 2003.

Yang, Guobin. *The Power of the Internet in China: Citizen Activism Online.* New York: Columbia University Press, 2009.

Yang, Ke. "A Preliminary Study on the Use of Mobile Phones amongst Migrant Workers in Beijing." *Knowledge, Technology & Policy* 21 (2008): 65–72.

Yang, Mayfair Mei-hui. "From Gender Erasure to Gender Difference: State Feminism, Consumer Sexuality, and Women's Public Sphere in China." In *Spaces of Their Own: Women's Public Sphere in Transnational China,* edited by Mayfair Mei-hui Yang, 35–67. Minneapolis: University of Minnesota Press, 1999.

———. *Gifts, Favors, and Banquets: The Art of Social Relationships in China.* Ithaca: Cornell University Press, 1994.

———. "Introduction." In *Spaces of Their Own: Women's Public Sphere in Transnational China,* edited by Mayfair Mei-hui Yang 1–31. Minneapolis: University of Minnesota Press, 1995.

Yang, Shanhua, and Wai-chu Chu. "Shouji: Quanqiuhua Beijingxia de 'Zhudong' Xuanze" [Mobile phone: An "active choice" against the backdrop of globalization]. In *Jincheng Nongmingong: Xianzhuang, Qushi, Women Neng Zuo Xie Shenme* [Rural-urban migrants: Situations, trends and what we can do], 301–308. Beijing: People's University Institute for Agriculture and Rural Development, 2006.

Yoon, Kyongwon. "Retraditionalizing the Mobile: Young People's Sociality and Mobile Phone Use in Seoul, Korea." *European Journal of Cultural Studies* 6, no. 33 (2003): 327–343.

Yu, Haiqing. "From Active Audience to Media Citizenship: The Case of Post-Mao China." *Social Semiotics* 16, no. 2 (2006): 303–326.

Zhang, Li. "Spatiality and Urban Citizenship in Late Socialist China." *Public Culture* 14, no. 2 (2002): 311–334.

———. *Strangers in the City: Reconfigurations of Space, Power, and Social Networks within China's Floating Population.* Stanford: Stanford University Press, 2001.

Zhang, Zhen. "Mediating Time: The 'Rice Bowl of Youth' in Fin De Siècle Urban China." *Public Culture* 12, no. 1 (2000): 93–113.

Zhao, Yaohui. "Rural-to-Urban Migration in China: The Past and the Present." In *Rural Labor Flows in China,* edited by Loraine A. West and Yaohui Zhao, 15–33. Berkeley: University of California Press, 2000.

Zhao, Yuezhi. *Communication in China: Political Economy, Power, and Conflict.* Lanham, Md.: Rowman and Littlefield, 2008.

———. " 'Universal Service' and China's Telecommunications Miracle: Discourses, Practices, and Post-WTO Accession Challenges." *Info* 9, no. 2/3 (2007): 108–121.

Zhao, Yuezhi, and Dan Schiller. "Dances with Wolves? China's Integration into Digital Capitalism." *Info* 3, no. 2 (2001): 137–151.

Zheng, Tiantian. *Red Lights: The Lives of Sex Workers in Postsocialist China.* Minneapolis: University of Minnesota Press, 2009.

Zheng, Zhenzhen. "Waichu Jingli dui Nongcun Funü Chuhun Nianling de Yingxiang" [Migration and age at first marriage of rural women]. In *Renkou Liudong yu Nongcun Funü Fazhan* [Migration and rural women's development], edited by Zhenzhen Zheng and Xie Zhenming, 195–199. Beijing: Social Sciences Academic Press, 2004.

Zhu, Hong. "Shenti Zhiben yu Dagongmei de Chengshi Shiying" [Body capital and dagongmei's urban adaptation]. *Shehui (Society)*, 2008, http://www.usc.cuhk.edu.hk/wk_wzdetails.asp?id=6932.

# ABOUT THE AUTHOR

Cara Wallis is an assistant professor of communication in the Department of Communication at Texas A&M University. She studies new media technologies and issues of power, difference, subjectivity, and social change in China.

CPSIA information can be obtained
at www.ICGtesting.com
Printed in the USA
LVOW11s2305041217
558590LV00006B/1529/P